For Love and for Prussia

A Novel Based on the Life of Philipp Wilhelm Sack

Gertha von Dieckmann
Stephen A. Engelking

For Love and for Prussia
A Novel based on the Life of Philipp Wilhelm Sack
by Gertha von Dieckmann
Translated and interpreted by
© 2020 Stephen A. Engelking
Texianer Verlag
www.texianer.com

ISBN: 978-3-949197-65-9

Title Illustration: Portrait of Philipp Wilhelm Sack in possession of the Simon Heinrich Sack Family Foundation

Table of Contents

Introduction..7

Preface (1930)...11

Questenberg..15

From Golden Meadow to Nordhausen.....................67

Halberstadt..123

Wolfenbüttel...147

Minden—Porta Westfalica...................................157

Kleve..167

Journey to Düsseldorf...183

Kleve..203

Rothenhof...269

The Rothenhof Legacy...333

Notes..355

Philipp Wilhelm Sack

Introduction

In 1929 Gertha von Dieckmann announced a family novel based on the life of the Rothenhof Privy Councillor Philipp Wilhelm Sack, entitled "Fifty Years from a German Bourgeois Saga. Breslau-Glogau-Kleve-Rothenhof-Hausberge. 1763-1813". She wanted to have the novel published linen-bound in the spring of 1930.

Her previous book (which has recently appeared under the title of "The Making of Prussia" in English by this house) had just been published at her own cost and work was nearing completion on the historical novel about her own direct ancestor.

It remains a mystery why the novel was not actually published. Maybe she had run out of funds or perhaps the political situation in Germany at the time may have led to a conflict with the contents of the book. In fact her sense of honor and tolerance for other religions comes over strongly in the book and that could have been a problem in the arising culture.

The manuscript came to light again a few years ago and Ines Stollwerck, assisted by several helpers, was able to transcribe the old German handwriting into modern text. Unfortunately, a number of pages are missing from the manuscript and the book seems not to have been quite completed or a section has been lost. Some of the text was unintelligible and it was a real challenge to transcribe the book.

Others worthy of mention who also put in a considerable amount of effort in this project are Olaf Beer, Mechthild Hauck, Uwe Scherpe and Albrecht Fischer v.

Mollard. Needless to say, my wife Sandy is always an indispensable help when proof-reading and brain-picking are required.

What I have attempted here is a reconstruction and reinterpretation of the text into English. The last chapter about the fate of Philipp Wilhelm's children has been constructed from another text that was written in 1900. I think it is fair to say that Gertha would have included material from this research into the book so the hope is that the reader will also find it an appropriate finale to the book.

The novel contains a lot of history, culture and geography surrounding the actors and much will be undoubtedly new to the current reader of English. I have therefore included notes at the end of the book as further explanation. Some information could be gleaned from Wikipedia and some had to be translated from German and other language encyclopedia sources. Some other sources of information could be found and these have been appropriately cited when they differ from the above.

Gertha's style reflects the rather exuberant prose of the time and, whilst attempting to maintain its historical character, I have done my best to make it readable for today's readers.

The descendants of Philipp Wilhelm Sack have spread across the world, especially into Texas. They have kept records of their offspring as they are all members of the Simon Heinrich Sack Family Foundation that was established by Philipp's brother of that name. They number in the thousands, have tales and achievements to tell that would go far beyond the scope of this book. They meet regularly, help each other according to the example they find in their progenitor and continue to supply society with new impulses guided by strong principles.

I hope you will get engrossed in this life drama and that you will become fascinated by Philipp's world, as he unknowingly becomes the father of many generations.
Stephen A. Engelking.

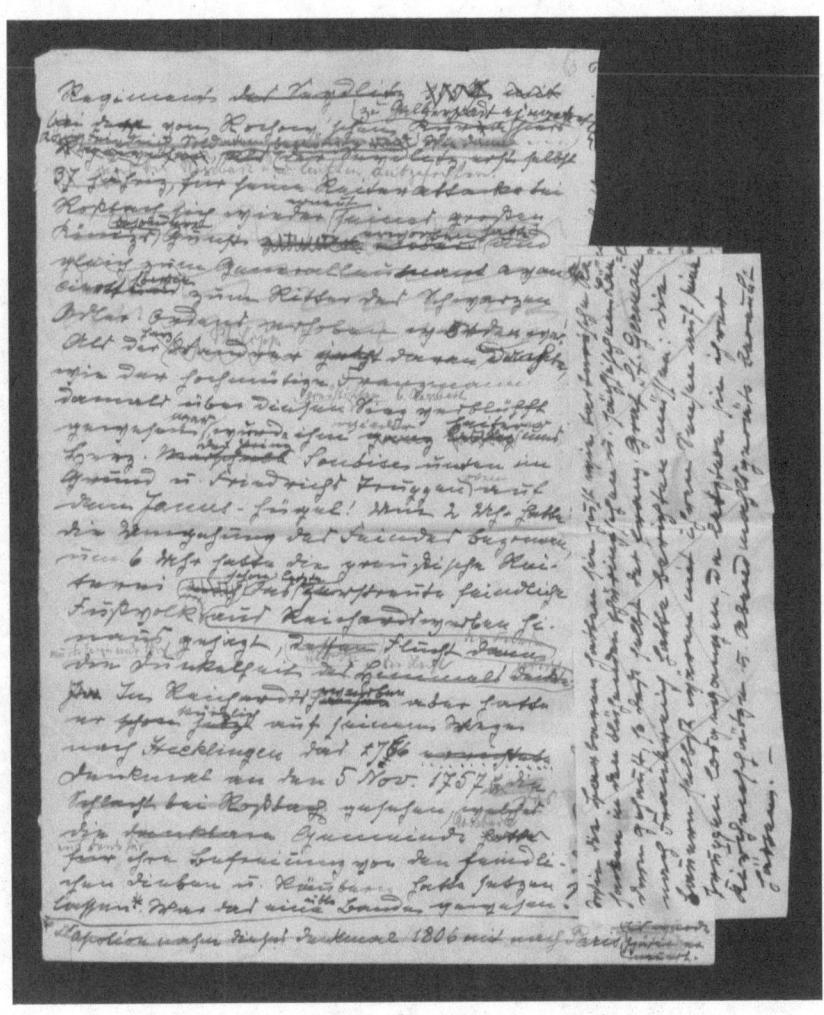

A Typical Page from the Manuscript

Preface (1930)

The following life story is an excerpt from the work of an eighty year long and busy life, *For Love and for Prussia – A Novel based on the Life of Philipp Wilhelm Sack*[1] is intended more for the family of the founder of 1500 descendants during a single century than for the general public[2]. With the help of historical sources, which are to be verified in the intended book edition, the story attempts to show my great-grandparents on the background of patriotic conditions in the period 1774-1824, as they were obtained from the handwritten notes of the hero before my eyes.

Philipp, the protagonist of the story is the brother of Simon Heinrich Sack, the former resident of the Hindenburg House, Mohrenstrasse 29 who has been brought before our readers several times in recent years. Simon Heinrich was a contemporary of Frederick the Great and was Privy and Justice Commission Councilor. He lived there in the 18th century and has been known and revered in our family as "the founder" for 140 years.

I therefore believe that the story will also meet with some interest among the readers of the *Clevischer Volksfreund*, since Philipp Sack himself spent fifteen years in the house of his elder brother, who had lived in Kleve in the Stechbahn Street in the mid-18th century.

Philipp Sack himself spent fifteen years in the house of his elder brother, Criminal Councilor Carl August Sack,

---

1 Original title in English would have been: *Philipp Wilhelm Sack: Fifty Years from the History of a German Bourgeoisie.*
2 Things have changed a lot since 1930. In the meantime there are thousands of descendants and the book is also likely to find general interest among the public of today.

who had been resident in Kleve on the Stechbahn in the middle of the 18th century, until he himself founded his own home in Rindern, in order to pursue his profession in the local government—so that here too the words of Goethe apply:

The place which a good man entered is blessed.

The author G.v. D. née Sack

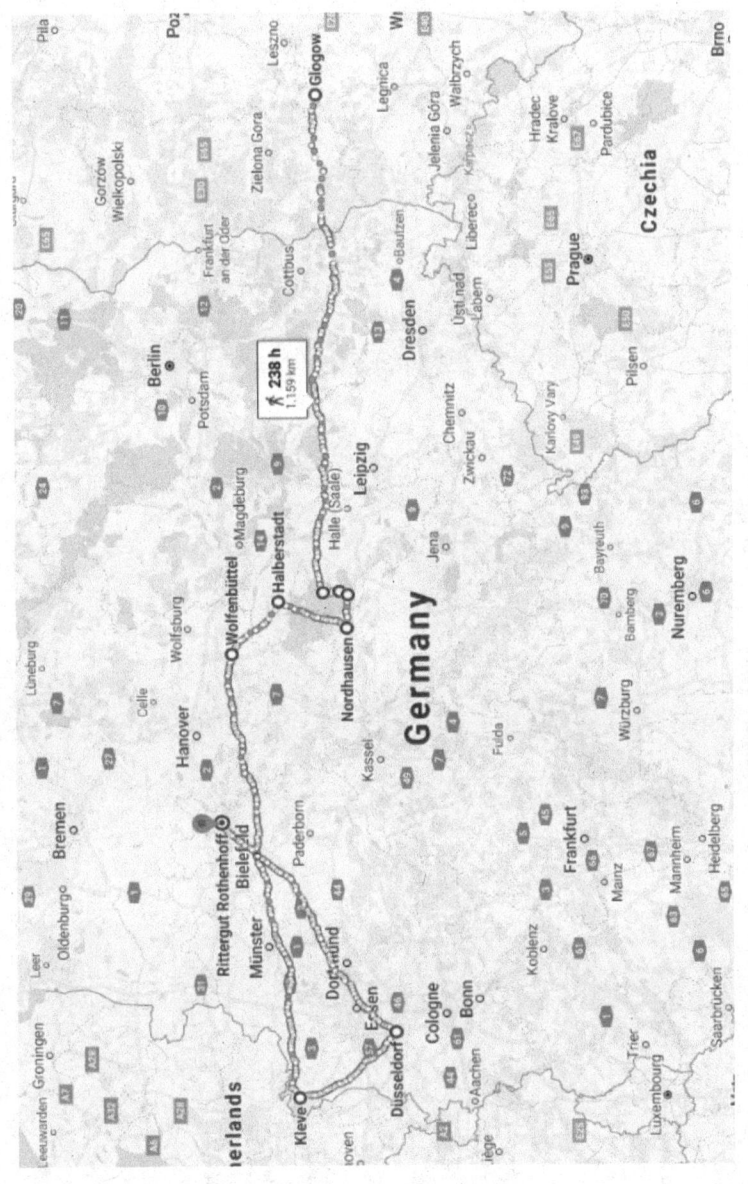

Philipp's Journey on a Map of Germany Today

I

Questenberg

It was Whitsun 1774, and rarely had so much light and delicate spring tapestry as in that year poured over the lush meadows and sprouting valleys as it did over the fresh deciduous and coniferous forests of the southern Harz Mountains.

Day after day, the sun shone in pleasant warmth and the stars sparkled down from the cloudless firmament to the earth. After a cool and rainy May, nature had now put on its highest festive garment. The flower-rich corridor, like those in the gardens with their blooming bushes and fragrant shrubs, the chirping of birds and even the singing of nightingales, was the most lovely greeting for the annual festival.

Even the lonely wanderer who descended fresh and joyful from the heights of the Upper Harz Mountains on his way could rejoice in the beauty of his surroundings. Because even though he was walking in military constancy through undulating places, he often stood still and let his eyes drink in the glory around him.

The golden river meadow was the set destination of his hike for today. It should soon reveal itself now, for his path, although interrupted again and again by small climbs, now fell noticeably to the valley. Since he had left the mountain town of Harzgerode in the still cool early morning after having had a short break for lunch, the sun was already sinking to the horizon and dazzled him more often than he would have liked. Over and over again a new chain of hills pushed themselves forward and now even steeper mountain walls were rising up on his road, denying him any possibility to see clearly.

In Rotha they had said that there was a straight road via Wickerode and Bennungen to Rossla from where the golden meadow stretched westwards almost to Nordhausen. He asked himself whether he could have gone astray. The way was further than he thought and a weather change seemed to be imminent. His old wounds suddenly began to hurt and made walking difficult for him, so he had to take a short break at the edge of the forest.

Thus the reader is now obliged to listen to the wanderer in his thoughts because then he will immediately become familiar with who the wanderer is, where he comes from and where he is going. This is of some importance for the order of the whole story, whose hero he is destined to be.

It had already struck him how this central part of Germany, which he now traversed and which actually represented his homeland, had become more or less alien to him in the long years he had already spent in the East in the Royal Prussian Service.

Only a few days ago, in Hecklingen in the Principality of Anhalt, where fifty years ago his father had been preacher for the beautiful collegiate church and its Protestant congregation, standing at the graves of his parents, he had felt urged to make a brief visit to the sites of his youthful memories before he was to move from the eastern border of the Kingdom to the far west for his subsequent career. After all, he was the youngest of the dozen sons and daughters that his excellent mother had given as a daughter of the well-known Lucanus family[1] in Halberstadt to his elderly father in his second marriage, and who had already reached the age of forty. Yes, that mother!

The father was descended from an old mayor and preacher family, which had already condemned the heresies of the Roman church at the end of the 15th century before Luther's bold intervention. His mother's family had originally moved from Upper Hesse to Halberstadt, where they had long since acquired a respected patrician rank. The family was intertwined with the outstanding families who carried their heads as high as the lords of nobility. His own brothers had already before him chosen the province of Silesia, newly won by the King of Prussia, as their home because his mother's brother Johann Heinrich had at the same time acquired the beautiful estate Schrien near Glogau. A lawyer by profession, as president of the chamber at the Glogau Royal Administration he offered them considerable support.

Over the years, his own brother Simon Heinrich, the youngest lawyer, had become the King's Commissioner of Justice and since the province enjoyed peace, he had devoted himself to the amicable settlement between Austrian and Prussian estates. As a bachelor, however, he also carried out family research and family welfare and, like no other, insisted that the siblings support their offspring and by means of good education, for which he donated many a secret assistance, educate them to grace their fatherland. It was this brother, to whom he owed so much since his father's death, who had given him a home there in recent years.

How long had it been now since he had flittingly left the university as a student and entered the service of the

King as a soldier in the cavalry regiment of Rochov zu Halberstadt and under Seydlitz as a lieutenant in Rossbach and Leuthen, standing his man with the wounds that were reminding him today. Yet thinking of how the haughty Frenchman was amazed at the Rossbach victory of the Prussian king, he started to become quite cheerful.

The war of Soubise—marching forward down to the bottom—and Frederick's troops keeping pace with him up on Janus Hill! At 2 o'clock the surrounding of the enemy had begun and at 6 o'clock the Prussian cavalry had already chased the last foreign foot soldiers out of Reichardtswerben and the enemy's flight was only possible due to the darkness of the night. Only recently he had proudly stood at the memorial that in 1766 the municipality of Rossbach had placed at Reichardtswerben in gratitude for their liberation from those enemy thieves and robbers—truly an evil mob.

December 5, the only beautiful, even memorable day at Leuthen, suddenly stood vividly before him again. How the devious battle order of the immortal Frederick had proved itself so brilliantly there. Unforgettable were the sublime hours when, after victories facing the thousands of corpses, the chorale rang out from 25,000 hero's throats in the dark night, "Now Thank We All Our God" all over the battlefield! Yes, how he would have wished to remain in the army of the great King.

However, when the war was over, the King had to save money again and only kept the officers of the nobility as his bodyguard in pay and position. As a very rare privilege, however, that young cousin August, the Royal Court Preacher[2] of Berlin, had remained a son in service. At the age of 16, he was called into the army and now spent his life as a perpetual First Lieutenant. Actually, he himself had had it much better then that.

As a trained farmer on the estates of his brother Heinrich, he had already saved himself a considerable sum of money and wrote to his eldest brother from the Lower Rhine saying that the prospects in agriculture were the best there. Also he could expect a faster advancement at the Military and Domain Chamber in Kleve, because there no one would dispute his rank, indeed the King would like to see such officials located in the border province.

And so it came about that the wanderer, now rested under all these thoughts, rose to continue his way to the Rhine. From Harzgerode, the siblings Ernst, who now held the position of pastor from his father and the only remaining unmarried sister Friederike, who was in charge of his household, had accompanied him for a long way in the morning. Now that the day was drawing to a close, a melancholic feeling of being alone came over him. Every parting is a little piece of death, he banished the thought. Be gone! It was time for him to move on towards a new future!

At the next bend in the road, a building caught his eye, surrounded by black spruce trees, then a hilltop emerged on the right and he even thought he saw a castle on top as dusk fell. The road led around the castle hill, and suddenly he noticed at its foot a very picturesque little town. Oh! What a pleasant sight! Yes, he had grown weary of the unusual day's walk and welcomed a soon to be night-time lodging. The old men who were smoking gathered on the benches in front of their front doors were already preparing to retreat and when he saw the overhanging sign "Zur Sonne" on the right hand side of the main road, he decided that he would stop here.

"Do you have quarters for me?" he addressed the innkeeper, who was eagerly running back and forth in his inn serving the guests. Oh, someone from the military he thought, bowing before him, "But most certainly Your Grace will find a nice parlor on the upper floor and step this way, if Your Grace will follow me," the Sonne Landlord reassured him friendly, silently measuring the martial figure of the former Seydlitz cuirassier anxiously with his eyes.

He was wondering how this giant could fit into the narrow bed. The imposing guest, well used to such things, immediately noticed the wide and longer horsehair canapé in the chamber when they reached the top and settled down on it without further ado in one of the elevated corners.

"If you also have some food and a drinkable drop, please bring it here to the chamber. I am very tired and above all I want to have a rest here."

"At once, but at once!" replied the innkeeper, relieved.

"But where can I find Your Grace's baggage?"

"My baggage, my friend, has already left ahead by mail for Nordhausen because I wanted to walk through the golden meadow tomorrow. For one night our sort can make do as a former soldier. Just provide me with plenty of water and soap and don't be stingy with the towels. Do you by any chance have some slippers at hand so that I can get rid of the heavy boots? Also perhaps a village barber will be in your establishment tomorrow to powder my hair? You can have him come to me at nine o'clock. One more thing, What is the name of this place and how far is Rossla from here?"

"Oh, Your Grace, our town is called Questenberg, has its own jurisdiction and office with an officially installed mayor, attested by the statue of Roland[3]. But do you want to continue your journey and not stay for our beautiful festivities?"

"What festivities and when? However, for the time being, please speak to me reasonably, I am not a Grace, do you understand? I am a lieutenant, moreover discharged by the Great King but at present a Senior Official Clerk on a journey. I am on my way to the Rhine but my homeland should now blow through my hair once more and soon hopefully allow its sun to shine upon my face. Now, above all, let's have some wine. I'm dying of thirst. Oh, the day was hot! Here the air is oppressive and sultry. Please open the window and door of the alleyway to allow a passage through the lower chamber. Is there anybody else sleeping in the hallway?" However, the host had already disappeared into the lower rooms.

His watch—could it be?—showed the 10th hour when the well-slept wanderer rose on stockings to breathe in the fresh evening air. On the table he found wine, bread and cheese prepared for him but for the moment his thirst seemed to have vanished with the invigorating mountain air. What he found outside captivated him more. The moon had risen almost full over the heights to his left and was casting its silver glow over the whole town, which, squeezed together in a narrow basin, could be seen from up here. He thought he could make out some sort of formal human tangle under his windows and wondered what it could mean. He considered why it was so mysteriously silent and not a sound was coming up to him. As he looked longer, more and more figures streamed towards the country road on the square in front of the Sonne Inn.

It was a puzzle to him what the nocturnal enterprise was gathering here for. Not only men but also women, boys and girls mingled amongst the crowd—but everything was transpiring quietly and ceremoniously and the meaning was unclear to him. A sound behind him made him draw his attention to the landlord who had probably already come back to clear the table.

"Stop! I haven't eaten yet! Tell me frankly, what does the crowd at your door mean? Why are all these people assembling at night like a masquerade?"

"Yes, guest sir, it's the third day of Pentecost and we're celebrating the Quest Festival[4]—it starts shortly before midnight—then we all go up to the Quest for the Solstice Night Feast. This year it will be particularly fine up there, as the day falls in the middle of June, which is not always the case—but sire forgive me, I must go downstairs, for the men from Rossla are already there and the priest will be coming soon. I will send my daughter up to explain it to you."

With that the busy landlord had disappeared again and while the guest was enjoying the evening snack, the maid stepped into the door, visibly trying to overcome her shyness.

"I am to inform sir about the feast that is about to begin. We will then all go up the mountain where the Quest is. The boys have already taken down the old ring and stripped the brushwood from the iron wheel. Also the men from Rossla have already brought the bread and cheese to the priest the night before and after his sermon the supper will be distributed. However, it is best if sir also comes up there, then he will see and experience everything." Before the youthful apparition could be thanked for the report, she too had disappeared into the darkness of the corridor.

"Of course I'm in on it," shouted the guest and Philipp Wilhelm, our hero of Rossbach[5] und Leuthen[6], not paying any attention to his pain, squeezed himself back into his dusty boots, quickly washed his face and hands and within minutes was downstairs in the dining room. However, this room was already empty and the crowd in front of the house had already left. The only thing he could distinguish was the procession, which was winding its way uphill like a black snake between the high trunks of the oak trees. Storming after them was the task for the next few minutes. What luck. As the last of the people, the innkeeper's little daughter, who had just departed so quickly earlier, walked with a companion and he now asked politely whether he could now accompany the two maidens. This was granted to him by the maid Lotte, who now felt safe and secure and who, as she moved forward in her haste, tried to catch up on her delay, probably joining her father at the front of the procession.

Then Philipp went up with the young maidens, who were climbing like two chamois and, not denying his chivalry, he was able to offer a helping hand to an elderly mother in the bumpy and steep places, cheering her joyously on. The two maidens however, seemed to quietly enjoy the company of the distinguished stranger. Silently and solemnly like all the others, they had finally reached the summit of the mountain peak, which Philipp's practiced expert eyes saw as belonging to a gypsum mountain range.

Up here, an undulating plateau offered enough space for the impressive crowd of people. During the first ten minutes the peaceful silence of the crowd persisted and Philipp used this to scrutinize the whole crowd. He noticed a particular landmark, rising darkly against the moonlit sky, facing the town in the depths—a high trunk with a crossbar on which a large circular hoop of at least twelve feet in diameter was attached at a short distance above, below and to the side. Meanwhile, in a sheltered indentation in the forest, a taller heap of brushwood had been set alight, its flames held within limits by young boys, blazing brightly towards the sky and appearing as if it was a thanksgiving or sacrificial fire, especially since it was accompanied by the loud echo of trombones sounding from the mountains.

For the first time he saw the figures and facial features of his young companions in the glittering, dancing glow of the fire and he noticed with artistically educated eyes that the face of the companion of the innkeeper's daughter surpassed her with a finer and more delicate, almost madonna-like expression. The charming appearance of the maiden, doused with the warm glow of the fire, captivated him for quite a while until she looked up and noticed him and turned away to escape his gaze. The whole thing had only been the mute play of a few seconds or minutes but it had cast its spell upon the man. This night apparition remained impressively and unforgettably engrained in his mind.

What happened next was that while the fire was blazing, the people arranged themselves in a circle to settle down and he realized that he had to find a resting place for his companions as well. Lotte, who was familiar with the place, had already preceded him and had spotted a hilly ledge where both girls were about to settle down. Their knight therefore remained hidden in the background, from where he could watch them unseen.

He had quickly recognized one of them who was proudly wearing a crown of blonde braids around her head. As she now glanced around, she thought she was unobserved and quickly seized the moment to reattach the crown of her hair with her broad-brimmed bonnet neatly hanging on her arm. Philipp wondered who she might be. Certainly not a girl of this people — thought Philipp, who never lost sight of her for a moment.

In the meantime, the voices of the clergymen could be heard circling around them and, distracted by this, all eyes and ears now turned their attention to the beginning of the solemn act. The speaker did indeed compare the flames rising to heaven with a sacrifice of thanksgiving offered to the Creator for all the blessings of the departing solar year that had come upon the valley. He praised the star-studded firmament as a cathedral dome over the devout congregation that had gathered here for another sign of thanksgiving and in memory of the corporal blessings to receive the bread from his hand together.

They pushed themselves forward while the first signs of the new rising day became visible on the horizon in the east, facing the erected ring cross. Finally, all were united around the cross, its annual decorations blazing up in the pyre, as Philipp later learned. As some men with musical instruments stepped out of the bushes to sing a choral-like song, the crowd cheered as the new solar year began. The whole eastern sky was flooded with sparkling light and the fading disc of the moon slowly sank behind the forest in the west. Philipp, who was a stranger to the chorale, tried to understand some words from those closest to him and thought he could clearly hear words like "Tree of life in the space of time green, guiding light—wreath of victory pure within—cross of light surround us with your radiance."

While the sweet innkeeper's daughter had sung the song, which was so unfamiliar to him, her companion, like Philipp himself, had remained a silent listener but he thought he could clearly see how the hour was captured in this way until the sun itself, as Queen of Heaven, appeared in all its power and fullness on the horizon. The descent into the valley now took place with the advance of the pastor and the music but now the people who had come were animated and talkative. The innkeeper's daughter also told her companion that the main celebration would only take place after church on the mountain and in the afternoon they would go to the town fair, where she was looking forward to the great wheel of fortune. Young Lotte now revealed that her companion Maria was her cousin, who had come from the Lower Rhine, and had been visiting them for three weeks.

She did not participate in the other conversations, and Lotte even seemed to want to excuse the fact that the cousin spoke a completely different German dialect and that it was often difficult to communicate with her. Philipp, who was embarrassed to talk about her in the presence of this silent second companion, said goodbye with relief when Lotte met some acquaintances on the way who approached her.

As fast as the difficult undulations of the hill allowed it, feeling very tired again, he used every possible shortcut to enable himself to stretch out his aching limbs on a bed. Arriving at the inn, upstairs in his chamber, he tore the bedding out of the narrow drawer, threw off his constricting clothing and flung himself onto the bed that he had arranged on the floor.

The sun, which he had seen rising so festively on the mountain—or had he dreamed all this in his strange surroundings here—was already in the sky when he woke up with a jerk wondering where he actually was. Someone knocked at the door and he puzzled who it could be and what he should do. A submissive voice outside the door could be heard. "Your grace, I am the barber who was ordered at 9 o'clock and it is going to soon be noon, the mountain festival is about to start and I have to be there. Should I rather come back later?"

With one sentence the sleeper stood at the door again and let Figaro enter. While he was doing his toilet and the barber was combing out his hair and powdering it, he learned all about the strange customs regarding the Questenfest, the most important event of the day, from this talkative man without having to ask him.

The strong oak trunk, the most important of the Quest, was renewed every year, and preparations for it had already begun since Ascension Day. With ropes and axes the young boys went out to hew the trunk in the princely Stolberg forest. The men from Rossla, who at the presentation of their consecration gift would say the words, "We are the men from Rossla, and we bring the cheese with the bread," would be punctually at the pastor's at 2 a.m., would be served, handed a receipt that was kept on file and would have to be on their way home before sunrise. But if the Rosslas should ever fail to meet their obligation to deliver, the Questenbergers would be entitled to fetch the best head of steer from the pasture. However, to the dismay of the Questenbergers, this had never yet happened.

"What a pity that the gentleman must already be on his way today," the talkative man concluded, after he also collected his fee for shaving with a deep bow. Meanwhile our guest seemed to have changed his mind, for shortly afterwards he announced in the kitchen that he would like to stay there that day but not have breakfast anymore and rather take lunch later.

When asked about the young companions from yesterday, the innkeeper raised his arm affirmatively, "They are already up there, helping the old men with the winch. Sir will certainly find them again".

The first time Philipp got together with the festive girls on this day, he was struck by the numerous fairground stalls lining the road. Lotte's longed-for wheel of fortune was also advertised in large letters. Then the thought shot through his mind to correct Fortuna a little in favor of the two maidens, since they would surely try their luck there in the afternoon.

So he decided not to follow the forest roads but first turned to the lower parts of the town and soon found some nice gifts there, taking them into his possession and making a special arrangement with the owner of the wheel of fortune. Afterwards he walked towards the uphill path with great agility.

Halfway up, he suddenly stopped as if spellbound. He wondered where his eyes had been yesterday, that this beautiful picture had not aroused his admiration before. For sure, he had come up yesterday in the dark. He saw a wildly romantic ruin on the nearby opposite mountain and recognized the archway and keep from days long gone by. Perhaps the Quest celebration was not related to this castle and was originally started by a local inhabitant.

Yet as quickly as this thought had risen in his mind, he rejected it again. The statue of the knight Roland, which he had just seen down below in front of Questenberg's town hall meant the sword of jurisdiction of a town in earlier centuries. It was inseparable from medieval narrow and strict thinking. On the contrary, perhaps the cultic meaning of the Questenfest could be united with medieval narrowness and severity as it was obviously expressed in the symbol of the ring or wreath circle and the whole tradition of the celebration of light in the free nature of God. No, its origin was that celebration of power, which he had attended and which must have been much more profoundly rooted in primeval times.

After all, the landlord of the Sonne had told him that apparently his daughter could tell him what the Quest and the Quest Festival was all about. The prospect of finding the two maidens up there seemed to spur his final ascent.

Looking down into the depths of the valley, he saw Maid Maria standing lonely on the edge of the mountain but could not see Maid Lotte and wondered where she was. Meanwhile strong men had already climbed up to the top of the trunk to help by tugging on a rope and pulling it up. Whoever had pulled the bells up in the belfry of the collegiate church back home in Hecklingen, must certainly have enjoyed such a sight, he contemplated.

When finally, after some critical moments, the heavy wreath was attached to the big iron wheel and tested as weatherproof, Philipp felt quite relieved and delighted. He politely waved in agreement with the cheerful Lotte, who applauded the lads with a clap of her hands.

As the general rejoicing began, the lonely dreamer from the edge of the mountain had also been lured back into the crowd and suddenly Philipp saw her close at his side. As if she was seeking his protection in a strange environment, her silent closeness touched him and he involuntarily offered her his hand in greeting. Since she was timid, but seemingly grateful to have put her hand inside his, he held on to it and tried to find an alley for the two of them through the crowd of people who were gathering closer and closer together, towards the quiet edge of the forest. This succeeded quickly and soon he also discovered the small elevation in the terrain where he could invite his companion to sit down, since she probably needed rest after standing for so long. She did this with pleasure and then looked up to him questioningly.

"Does the maiden Maria know the meaning of this feast?" were the first words of address that the knight spoke as he stood, bowing down before her. He wondered if she had understood him as she obviously pondered for a while, then shook her head in the negative and shrugging her shoulders, as if apologizing, answered with a somewhat foreign sound, but very clearly, "No, sir, I am a Mennonite and a stranger here."

How strange to him here on the quiet mountain heights —far from the hustle and bustle and the understandings of the people, her simple confession touched him! The tender modesty appearing on her face, causing her to look gently beyond the castle as if into the farthest distance, did not escape his notice.

"Does the maiden Maria like it here?" Philipp asked further.

The answer came immediately, "Oh, no!"

Her gaze returned from the distance and remained kindly attached to the festive crowd, which had meanwhile divided into two halves to allow archers sufficient distance. He continued his research, "Is it more beautiful on the Rhine, the maiden's home, than here?"

"Yes, oh yes, much, much more beautiful, sir!" it now came almost tempestuously from her lips and her gaze lifted up to his, beaming with joy. Her blue eyes sank into his for a moment, as if drunk with delight in the thought of this homeland.

"Does the maiden have parents there and brothers and sisters?"

Then she bowed her head and looking down said sadly, "My parents are dead, I have no brothers or sisters, only my uncle and the cousin Lotte."

It seemed to him that he suddenly knew the whole story of this delicate creature and at the same time felt an obligation to be a knight and protector, because Lotte seemed to have forgotten her cousin completely.

In the meantime shooting through the wreath had commenced up front and arrows were flying incessantly through the green wreath into the distance as a symbol of joy. A cheerfully animated picture! Beside the hoop, however, large tufts of leaves hung like tassels from the crossbeam and a particularly strong tuft crowned the top of the oak trunk, which Philipp now observed there for the first time! He had probably not paid attention to this when they were avoiding the crowd of people earlier.

The picture of the complete Quest structure only now had become completely clear. When the last arrow of joy was shot off, a wide alley was formed. Boys and girls arranged themselves right and left of the wreath circle to dance. Lotte was one of the first to be seen spinning in circles together with a handsome boy. The girl seemed intoxicated by the mood of the festival.

When the maiden Maria rose, he gently slid her arm under his own and to the sound of the merrily blaring trumpets, as well as the more delicate flutes, the two strangers flew just as lightly in circles around the Quest Cross as the other couples. However this part of the celebration did not last much longer. As it seemed, it was just the joyful final accent to the successful erection of the Sacrifice of Thanksgiving to the Majesty of the Sun and as this Queen of Heaven poured her rays onto the back of the wreath, the music gave the signal for departure.

In a few minutes, the mountain peak with its new green symbols lay silent and deserted. Philipp and Maria were the last ones to decide to join the procession of the guests going down into the valley. As if by appointment and yet only by chance, they both looked back at the enigmatic structure whose meaning and significance had remained alien to them, while a particularly warm ray of sunshine had crept into both hearts here on this day of the summer solstice.

Philipp was now determined to stay in Questenberg. After they had first eaten a hearty meal at a country table that the landlord of the Sonne had arranged to be set up in the free space in front of his house under the arcades. Lotte and her Aunt Gote helped the landlord with serving, while Maria was one of the guests and had joined the wives and daughters at the lower end. The young people had gone down to the fair stalls and Philipp indulged in a rest for some time in his room upstairs.

Sleep eluded him. His thoughts were far too aroused. He wondered if he had drunk the restlessness into his blood from the wine down there. Nonsense! He had not even emptied a bottle because a young boy sitting next to him had helped him. So Maria was a Mennonite[7], and stood alone in the world. Alone, just like him.

Menno[8], as he still knew from his father, had established his main community in Holland but had also found many followers in Germany, mainly because of the depravity and immorality. During the Thirty Years' War, the Mennonites had multiplied considerably, for their teaching was characterized above all by a great strictness of morals. They also rejected infant baptism and only baptized after receiving religious instruction and from the age of fourteen at the earliest, before assembled congregation. Just as he recalled, they also rejected the oath and military service.

Nevertheless, the Prussian King and also Frederick II had protected their peculiarities and gladly let them settle in Prussia. Wherever they, who also called themselves simply "baptizers", were at home, they lived as quiet, industrious subjects. They were probably the closest to the Reformed in their beliefs but they kept to themselves as a separate church.

He mused on the impression that the half Christian, half pagan cult on the Questenberg must have left on this young Mennonite woman, "How did she even get here? Lotte had probably once hinted to him that the cousin actually spoke Dutch but she herself had shaken her head vigorously. It was certainly only here that she understood the Thuringian or Saxon or Anhalt—so one could ask where the Questenberg actually belonged. She didn't speak the dialect but she always understood High German correctly although she herself was unskilled in it. I suspect that she speaks a border area mixture, like the Kleve nephews and nieces who once parried the almost Dutch-sounding Platt of the Lower Rhine in Glogau, to the delight of all of us.

"Well, what he had heard today under the bower from the youth of Questenberg, he, the born Anhaltiner, had understood only half of it. The confusion of languages of the tower builders of Babel still existed among the people in their own country. It occurred to him how the great Nordhausen ancestor Siegfried[9], in which his name and the designation in all identical languages of the earth had remained the same, had already composed an ode. This Siegfriedus must have handled his language magnificently. With no little emotion he himself had recently marvelled at the large crossbeam that had been placed between the nave and the body of the church in remembrance of his ancestor's first Protestant sermon in the previously Catholic house of God – also a cultic monument!"

And from that wooden beam in Magdeburg, Philipp's thoughts returned to the Quest Cross he had danced around today, dancing around with Maria, the Mennonite, without having discovered the actual meaning of these cult symbols until now. Considering whether the two maidens had still not returned home from their happy day, he decided to go down and investigate, perhaps he would meet Lotte, who still owed him the explanation of the Quest.

It was all deserted downstairs. There were only two bad-tempered maids still working in the kitchen doing the last washup of the crockery used at the feast. The maids told him that Gote was in the garden but the others were still downstairs at the fair. In the garden he found the friendly little maid he already knew from the table as a waitress. She was sitting in the arbor, hands folded in her lap and enjoying the peace and quiet after work. She rose as he approached but he told her to stay seated, he did not want to disturb her, if only she would allow him to sit with her in the arbor.

She seemed to like that, and soon a conversation about the Questenfest was underway. "Yes", Gote had said, but actually Lotte had better tell him what the Quest was all about. Nevertheless incidentally she would love to tell him too. Children learned the old sagas at school, but there would always be something new that the old ones did not know or perhaps had never heard before.

"And how did Maria come to be here from her homeland," asked Philipp.

"A Mennonite pastor had brought her," said Gote, "He will pick her up again soon, because Maria would rather go back to her fellow believers. She is fading away here from homesickness and longing, in spite of Lotte's cheerfulness."

"She is a very sweet and modest child but seems as delicate as her prematurely deceased mother and feels depressed by the mountains. On the Rhine, where there is no obstruction, the land is flat and the view unlimited. That's what Lotte's mother had always said to her and she hasn't been happy here in the mountains throughout her life. And she died because of it. Lotte's just like her father. She's a healthy, funny thing. The pastor of the Lower Rhine probably believed that he could place Maria here, with the only relative she has left—her parents both died in a shipping accident and the Mennonite congregation raised the child—because the congregation is preparing to emigrate. But this is probably still undetermined, so the clergyman travelled further to the river Volga in Russia, to get to know the country that Empress Catherine had offered them. However, Maria immediately told him that she would return with him to the Rhine and, if need be, go to Russia with all of them. The landlord of the Sonne would rather see it than that she, like his wife, became ill here and it is, after all, so difficult with the language."

But before she could finish her sentence, Lotte suddenly stormed through the garden gate, straight towards the arbor where she suspected Gote to be alone.

"Gote! Gote!, look what I won on the wheel of fortune! It was only there one time as a prize and was the most beautiful thing that had ever been there, the showman from the wheel of fortune said, that I, of all people, have to win it!" In her first expression of joy, she had not expected the guest in the arbor, hardly noticing him, because she was constantly grasping and admiring a small coral chain with a heart of the same kind attached to it. Meanwhile, the silent observer in the corner had his bright satisfaction at how well he had succeeded in his little joke.

"Show me too, maiden Lotte, what the bringer of luck has just won for you," and when she found an opportunity to let her treasure be admired, her expressions of joy took on even warmer tones.

"Now we must also see how the red chain matches your dark hair." And with that, Philipp rose and himself wound the lucky winning around Lotte's radiant face.

"Behold, there you have a spare heart on top of the one you've got when you lose your own." teased Philipp and, despite the dawning light in the bower, he could see the adorned maiden blushing and embarrassedly caressing the little heart.

"It suits her well, does it not, honorable sir," said Gote, "but what the soothsayer has told you, you have not yet revealed," said the elder woman, who must have noticed the embarrassed expression.

"I'd rather tell you that up in the chamber," said Lotte with a characteristic side-glance at the stranger and wanted to leap up and get away.

"Stop! Stop," shouted Gote after her, who was now also getting up to go into the house, "the gentleman here would like to hear the legend of the Quest from you. Tell him that you will tell him here after supper in the bower. Now we are all hungry and father and Maria are waiting — where did you leave them?"

"Maria has also won something beautiful," Lotte continued to chat in her joy, "but she went home earlier because she had a headache, she wanted to lie down a bit. I want to look after her now and bring her down for dinner," the little one jumped away but not before calling back, "and I'll tell the master about the Quest later!"

So Philipp separated from Gote at the porch entrance and tried to find a quiet corner in the guest room, where he stayed completely alone during his evening meal. The whole party bustle had apparently moved to the lower town, which the innkeeper confirmed to him with the philanthropic remark, "You have to treat the pub owner down there to his share, too. We share the business here honestly. That man with six children needs it more than I do with just the one who still gets her maternal inheritance."

The pale Maria, too, had gathered in the arbor after the meal, together with Gote and with the polite request, "If I may?" a young man had also approached and then sat down at Lotte's side, while Gote came to sit on his right. Opposite them sat Philipp and Maria. There was no table in the arbor. A plate filled with cake for everyone had found its place on the bench between Lotte and Philipp.

The little innkeeper's daughter, among other things, told the saga, without embellishment, fresh and joyful.

"Every year here and in our region—seven villages, I think—there's a folk festival. The boys in our village are allowed to choose the largest oak tree they can find in the surrounding forest. They cut it down and bring it up the high mountain among a crowd of cheering spectators, accompanied by horns and trumpets. They have to roll or pull the enormous tree themselves up the mountain with their hands, according to an old tradition. On top of the peak it is erected and a large wreath of green branches is attached to a crossbeam.

"The oak that is sold after the new one is felled carries the cost of the feast. Each oak will remain standing for a year. The wreath of beech branches with two tassels of branches at the top is called the Quaeste or Queste. Thus our village is called Questenberg and the old castle remains on the opposite hill are called the Questenburg.

"One of the old castle lords had an only child, a daughter. When the child was four years old, she got lost in the heath. In the evening, a charcoal maker found her while he was busy braiding a wreath. The child only knew his first name.

"The charcoal maker took the child to his hut. The father had all his squires and servants look for her. Only after several days did they find her with the charcoal maker and brought her back to her father with the wreath. The happy lord of the castle then ordered the celebration of this festival and from then on called his castle the Questenburg.

"The meadow where the child was found is called the 'Maiden's Meadow' and was donated to the village of Rossla. In return, the men from Rossla have to deliver bread and cheese to Questenberg every year for the festival. Why they have to do this at night and bring it to the priest, I can't remember."

With that Lotte finished her simple story and mischievously added, "Now we will have to eat the Quest Cake" with that she grabbed the plate at her side to let her young neighbor take it first. But Gote did not refrain from gently poking him in the ribs.

"Please, first to the gentleman."

He thanked her kindly and passed the plate on to Maria, who rose to give the first piece to Gote, then handing the cake back to the young man. However, he gave the plate to Lotte, who in turn resolutely put the largest piece on his knees and put one in her mouth.

"There are still some legends handed down here in the area," the younger man now raised his hand to pick up the thread of the story that Lotte had so quickly broken off. "Similar tales are told of Count Stolberg's son, and that when the son was found again, the father had given the Seven Villages, whose inhabitants had the count's son, the forest, which is still called the Forest of the Seven, from that time. And many such old explanations for entitlements to traditional fiefdom or for legal claims to gifts have, over time, become legends.

"But recently a professor from the high school in Erfurt was here again, who said that our quest had a completely different, even much older meaning. It comes from the oldest pagan Germans, before Christ's birth, who still adhered to the belief in light and prayed to a single God, the God of light. Therefore the old custom, e.g. the nocturnal procession up the mountain and the offering of thanksgiving songs to the sun at the time of the summer solstice, must have been preserved. What this professor told me seems to me to be much more likely than the origin of the festival from the lost child in the castle."

"And so do I," the stranger affirmed from his corner, "that seems to me a worthwhile task for the historians to trace this certainly cultic origin of the celebration of the Quest. What they told about the legends was correct—I know the one of the lost Count's child from my homeland in Anhalt, with all kinds of echoes. Indeed, our German fairy tales of Sleeping Beauty, Snow White, Little Red Riding Hood, Cinderella and whatever they are all called, are basically just about ancient nature themes repeating themselves everywhere. With time, they have been fantastically expanded and made more and more mysterious, until now they are really only believable for children.

"All the superstitious and ghostly creatures also belong to this chapter of fantastic enlargement. This jubilation—the solstice fire and thanksgiving for the supreme unfolding of all the crops of the field—the power of the sun may be necessary for the prosperity of the human race. However, for me a simple and pure expression of recognition of the caring power of God in the universe in enough."

The convincing way in which Philipp had presented his high opinion of their very own Queste culture seemed to have made a deep impression on the small company in the arbor. Even Lotte, who almost had the courage to interrupt his speech at the mention of the ghost spook and ask him for a ghost story, was quite moved by the turn his speech had taken and only nodded to the young lad, who had found in it the confirmation of his own thoughts.

"There is actually something beautiful about this hymn of praise to the blessing power of nature, which is sung at the top of the mountain. This festival is almost even more beautiful than the harvest festival in the church." said the young man, pleased that his mention of an ancient Germanic cult had found the applause of the guest.

"Yes, on the mountains and in the groves under God's heavenly canopy the Teutons performed their prayers and hymns of praise and had no need of the Irminsul[10] made of stone," Philipp replied meaningfully.

"But how could they have celebrated their weddings and christenings in the open air — and that with snow and ice in winter? The poor newborn babies, did they also carry them to the Quest?" asked Lotte, who had suddenly become courageous on this occasion.

Philipp had to smile when he gave the answer to the harmless question. "My dear maiden, the Germanic women did not carry their little children to baptism on the Questenberg, for they were not baptized at all! Baptism only became known much later through John the Baptist, and since Christ, our Saviour, was also baptized by him, it was first established by the Christians in their holy religious practices. And as far as the marriage of our Germanic forefathers was concerned, it was considered binding and holy when a loving couple was given together by their relatives, receiving blessings on their common path of life. And no marriage was probably purer and more faithful than such a family contract, without priestly ordainments, introduced by the Roman Church centuries afterwards and even raising it to the status of a sacrament."

"Don't you want us to hear a little more about our earliest ancestors, who are said to have had their homes here," asked the younger guest, and gratefully supported this request from the maid Lotte, who saw this as a small extension of the evening get-together with her admirer in the arbor.

Once more the cups were filled and the Quest Cake was handed round and the stranger, who was completely absorbed in his Germanic material, continued, "It did not harm the intimacy of Germanic marriage that it had been a family contract since time immemorial, concluded in the interest of both sexes. Unfortunately, no hand has ever recorded how the Germanic people thought and spoke in the happy hours of their lives in the peace of their homes, enjoying a modest life of wellbeing united with their wives and children, but we suspect that a rich stream of joy, of intimate feeling and joyful comfort flowed through their days. For above all, man and woman were always joint farmers of their land. The thoughts and feelings of their working day, even in their faith, flowed through them. The oldest Teutons were most highly attached to a monotheistic veneration of the light. Since, depending on nature, this was only possible through sowing and harvesting and by grazing their livestock, it was only natural that they should regard the sun, which was beyond their reach, as the great divine omnipotence and giver of all good things, and that they should venerate and pay homage to it.

"It was only in the later centuries, when the Romans, who invaded their lands and huts that the Germanic tribes in their nomadic existence came to know the Roman encroachments and their philosophical culture. Their monotheistic belief became adapted to the belief in the gods of their conquerors and masters of their habitat. Odin or Wotan now became their Zeus and the Aesir in Valhalla corresponded to the protectors of the battle, which they now called upon for conquest or defense. Just as in the farm and the fields the woman was their companion, so in war with the enemy she became the defender of the wagon fortress.

"Even the wives of the Teutons fought when the men were captured or fell and countless were the women who killed themselves and their children so as not to fall into the hands of the Romans. Up to the year 113 A.D. the Romans were strangers to the peoples who were to become their heirs. Probably half a million Teutons had been exterminated in the first twelve-year war of the Romans against the Cimbri[11], but the Romans were to realize that only a small part of the people unknown to them up to that time was here.

"Caesar already saw with concern that the colonization of the Cimbri had not been the first and only colonization of the Franks, the great central tribe of the Teutons[12] — the Suebi[13] had already sent their colonist campaigns across the Rhine to the neighborhood of the Roman province. In Germania itself, there was a continuous suppression of the various Teutonic tribes, so that he had to fear that the Celtic Helvetians[14], too, would be infected by the same passion for migration, would find their own borders between the Jura and the Alps unbearable and would start to pick up woman and child and invade Gaul.

"Only Emperor Augustus[15], the great statesman of the Romans, succeeded in containing these Germanic invasions for some time. After him, the Roman Empire exerted its strongest military force over the centuries to hold the Rhine and Danube against the Germanic tribes until finally, when the Roman Empire first divided and then disintegrated, it conquered both river basins.

"The Franks and Saxons, who were at home in these meadows and mountains of the Harz Mountains and beyond the Kyffhaeuser[16] Hills, did not remember that their forefathers should ever have had inhabited anywhere else, even at the time of the first clashes of the Germanic border tribes with the Romans. They considered themselves to be the natives. The 'Charudes' or 'Harudes'[17] were the people and they spoke their own language. They acknowledged each other as tribal comrades, although the other tribes spoke many different dialects.

"There were large groups of people who were connected by their cultic sites, customs and living environment in the fight against foreigners and although they were often at odds with each other because of arable land borders, inheritance claims and the like, they felt themselves to be one people who had had their home between the Oder and the Rhine since time immemorial because of the old family lines and the marriages of their princes".

It was Gote who found it good to bring this all too scientific discussion to a close. She said that it had suddenly become noticeably chilly and that one must now end this beautiful day with a bedtime farewell. Everyone rose unanimously to obey her beckoning. When Philipp went to Gote as hostess to make sure that he would not be a disturbance if he were to leave early to continue his journey and had bowed chivalrously, thanking everyone for such beautiful and instructive hours in Questenberg and here at the Sonne Inn, he was the first to walk through the garden towards the house. The others followed after a long delay, still cleaning up in the summerhouse.

In the tavern he still found the landlord of the Sonne, who was busy with preparations for the end of the celebration. Philipp arranged with him that he would continue his walk over the Questenberg down to the Golden Meadow early in the morning, without morning refreshment. He also settled the bill that the innkeeper had already drawn up in response to his wish expressed at the evening meal. After a warm thank you for the pleasant lodging in his house and the pleasurable hours in Questenberg, Philipp climbed the steep stairs to his chamber.

So he was really leaving in the morning. It suddenly seemed very strange to him that he should leave this house, in which he had really been given warmth and sunshine above all expectation, in the usual way like a paid guesthouse. And he was astonished at himself particularly that he was to leave that so lovely creature, Maria, without saying goodbye. She had last been sitting in the circle of the bower.

It was hard on his heart that he, spurred on from his young teacher who was always eager to know more and more, had devoted himself so completely to his favorite dream, world history, and had forgotten all about the women in the darkness of the bower.

Tomorrow he was to leave without having even squeezed her hand to say goodbye. At the top of the stairs this question kept him busy and it seemed rude not to have said goodbye to her. The question was what she must think of him. He decided to go down again, to ask for her, to at least leave a farewell greeting for a reunion on the Rhine. To do this he had to allow a few minutes to pass before Lotte and her admirer, the dancer from the Quest and the young teacher he had met today in the summerhouse in order not to be disturbed at their farewell down the hall.

He now opened the door of his room, wondering if the air was now free below, when he heard a slight step on the stairs and recognized the figure of Maria in the light that came out of his open room. "Do not be frightened, maiden Maria, I had wanted to look for you once more, for I want to say farewell to you," he said.

"You know that I have stayed longer than I intended to but tomorrow I must continue my travels. I learned from your relatives that you live on the Rhine. Would it please you if I came to visit you there one day?" With that he had stepped upon the stairs, so as not to let her escape. "And I'd like to know what you won today on the wheel of fortune. Your Lotte told me it was something really pretty."

"Yes, something very pretty," Maria kindly assured him. I'll show you," and with that she slipped past him in gazelle-like fashion into the chamber next door. Then she brought him the small chain, which was not unfamiliar to him, and went into his room as if to admire it in the light.

"Oh, a golden chain with a little cross on it," and because she had followed him, he searched her face to see if the prize had brought her joy. When he then wanted to put the little chain around her neck, as he had done with Lotte earlier, she fought back, frightened and pleading, "Sir! Please, no, we Mennonite women do not wear jewelery".

Unfavorably affected by the answer, he put it back in the box and said regretfully, "Oh, then this gain has no value for you, maiden Maria?"

"Oh, yes, very much," she said simply, "this necklace will be a souvenir of this festival," and her voice trembled with emotion. As she tried to leave with her treasure she suddenly sensed that she was at the end of her strength.

"But Maria! Will you say farewell?" Then she looked at him again with an unspeakably sad look on her face and he stood there offering her both hands. She closed her eyes and staggered. He caught her and held her in his strong arms. Gently he carried her over to her chamber as Lotte appeared at the same moment. Both tried to rub her temples with eau de vie and bring her back to consciousness.

"Ask Gote for some cognac and pour it down her throat."

"Oh, she won't take it," said Lotte quietly but when Philipp then noticed that Maria was slowly opening her eyes, he quietly and unnoticeably moved away, soon hearing the motherly voice of Gote from nearby. When it became quiet in the chamber after half an hour, he could assume that sleep had settled compassionately upon the exhausted child and that Maria had found the necessary rest after those strenuous days.

What a pity that he chose a gold chain for this maid and that she, as a Mennonite, did not wear any jewelery. He wondered how he could turn her sad look into a happy smile. Perhaps if he stayed tomorrow and told her that he had stayed only because of her and that he would certainly visit her in her home on the Rhine, she would then look cheerfully and joyfully into the future, hopefully overcoming her homesickness. These and similar thoughts went through his mind. At the same time he still searched in his memory whenever and wherever in his life two eyes had looked at him with such a melancholy gaze.

Finally he had it. It was the dear eyes of his mother. How proudly and with fighting spirit as a Halberstadt cuirassier had he bid farewell to his parents and how his mother had accompanied him to the gate—He, who was so happy and confident of victory—she with a motherly smile at his joy but with such a melancholy expression in her eyes. And never had his mother's eyes ever been able to rejoice again. Now they were closed forever in the cemetery of the Hecklingen monastery church, where he had recently taken leave by her grave. No! No! Never again would eyes, grieving eyes haunt and fill him with melancholy.

Instead of getting ready for an early departure, he still sat there brooding as he thought that he could make out the sun shining again beyond through the Quest Wreath. Truly, the young day was already there! So he quietly unpacked all his things from the narrow drawer and prepared his camp on the floor again. He locked the door, got rid of his clothes and determined to sleep until late in the morning and allow himself some further rest.

It was not just one day, but four more days, on which he had to use the Questenberg barber every morning to redress his hair. Soon he was concerned about the fact that he had sent his bags to Nordhausen in advance and could only appear before his young girlfriend in the same set of clothes. The next morning—it was already noon before he had even finished his toilet—he had not only succeeded in conjuring a happy smile on Maria's madonna-like face but he himself felt at that moment that those eyes had become precious to him. He silently wondered whether they would not be the best guide through his new life, helping him to regain and maintain the balance of his already tested mind for the new change he was about to undergo.

The young teacher had promised to pick up maid Lotte for a walk on the castle hill for the afternoon of the next day and after a long afternoon rest in the heat which the sun's star now sent down on the earthlings, he had recommended that everyone should catch up on the sleep they had missed during the previous nights. Only between five and six o'clock did Philipp and Maria join the younger couple in visiting the nearby castle hill.

At first it had remained unknown to Philipp that the young teacher had asked the Sonne landlord in the morning for the hand of his young Lotte. Already this evening he had announced their engagement, offering all his friends and relatives to join him in the betrothal toast. The innkeeper had also announced the news to him at the midday meal and invited him to stay for the family celebration. So a happy bridal couple walked up to the castle hill in the late afternoon and while the other two followed with a good stretch between them, father and Gote in the

"Sonne" were again busy preparing for the engagement celebration in the evening.

These were then the last days of June. When the later couple slowly arrived at the castle hill, god Cupid was already eagerly fluttering around the two of them but did not have much trouble to make the flapping of his wings audible and to wound them with his arrows. A tender cord that was already entwining around their hearts united the two young people.

It was Maria's soul that opened up surprisingly freely for her companion by confessing to him that what he had told her yesterday about the Germanic tribes seemed quite familiar to her as a Mennonite, for in their case, too, baptism was not a sacrament as with other Christians but only a confession of Menno's teaching and confirmation of the now sixteen to seventeen year old person to follow the faith of her teacher out of her own conviction before the assembled congregation.

They are probably the closest to the Reformed faith. Marriage is also a family contract, which the pastor may bless, but in special cases it is valid without his blessing. The Mennonites also did not recognize the Christian oath, or even the oath itself, nor the duty of partaking in military warfare. A promise made was considered a binding word and in all other respects the same Germanic simplicity of life governed their way of life, except that strict regulations concerning clothing, hairstyle, unadornedness, and the like prevailed with them. Nevertheless, a married couple would have the Germanic love of agriculture. Their strict customs were the fear of God, out of their own conscience and will—all this she told him plainly and simply, courageously stepping out of her previous restraint.

This turned his soul towards his parents who had been brought up in the Reformed faith under the influence of the brothers in Silesia and now strongly adhered to the beliefs of his great King, who let everyone become blessed according to their own vision. This involuntarily directed him towards her pure, modest and yet ever more understanding confession. He believed in his inner being that he had never met such a genuinely feminine person, tender and yet strong in faith, as this tranquil human child.

Indeed, Maria was growing in his esteem and veneration with each of her utterances, which now revealed her thoughts and feelings quite unselfconsciously. He regarded it as God's will that, at the ancient celebration of the Teutonic Cross, he had been able to approach her unexpectedly through the purity and greatness of the monotheism of the oldest Teutonic ancestors and had found in her that consecrated power of a like-minded, highly tuned and rare female pearl.

She was almost the only narrator here on the castle hill path and he was only the silent and deeply touched eavesdropper. He became aware of this, however, when the tender inclination to be together was interrupted and they arrived at the height of the castle hill, where the other couple were already impatiently waiting for them. He had no idea that the young teacher was already eager to surprise him with his thanks for the lecture he had enjoyed in the arbor the previous evening.

"It is a very special honor for me," said the latter enthusiastically when they met, "to be allowed to show you the ruins of the Questenburg up here and the Jutta legend of which my fiancée told me last night. Additionally I would like to point out that up here there was originally a Cherusci wall and the seat of Armin the Cherusci prince[18], because here in its keep the castle holds a treasure that nobody will be able to raise but everyone has to look at. Look at this figurative and symbolic sign, which reminds of runes and it is still clearly visible in the embedded rock. Nobody can say whether they might not give an explanation for the cult signs of the Quest. It is said that the Germanic tribes, who had driven the Celts out of northern Thuringia as early as 500 BC, i.e. half a century before Armin, chose this valley as their cultic and spiritual centre.

"Isn't this a highly significant discovery up here? Doesn't the sign here, for example, resemble the six-spoked wheel, which is interpreted in the upper half as the highest sun position, i.e. representing the solstice day in summer and in the lower half of the sign the setting into the sea of the world, the winter solstice or the shortest day".

Philipp now looked closely at the strange figures and signs, following them with keen interest. Keeping firmly by his side, Maria had turned her eyes to the opposite mountain of Questenberg, where the sinking sun now surrounded the wreath on the cross with a golden halo. "Oh, please, turn your eyes over to the wonderful image of the sun," she then said softly to her neighbor, and turning his gaze to the miracle of the sun from across the dark rock, he too was deeply moved by the sublime spectacle that Questenberg was offering at that moment.

Simultaneously, watching that the other couple had entered behind the archway ruins of the castle, he passionately took Maria's hand and bent down to kiss it in the most polite manner.

"Please accept my heartfelt thanks, demoiselle Maria, for this auspicious moment. In this way, we have experienced it together, seeing the beautiful cult sign of our ancestors, like the first ray of sunshine, even now on the longest day of the year, the day of St. John, a sunset.

Both walked in silence to the arch of the castle ruins, always looking at the image of the sun opposite, as if bidding farewell, until the other couple reminded them to return home. They let them go ahead again, following them as if uphill, at a measured distance.

"I now owe you an account of my own religious upbringing, demoiselle Maria," he broke the silence, "but I would rather put that off until tomorrow. After the celebrations of your relatives this evening, which I had not anticipated, I must sleep in again tomorrow morning. In the afternoon I would perhaps like to walk with you to the Maiden's Meadow. We should also visit the Castle Hill today and get to know the place where the damsel Jutta was discovered during the winding of the wreath.

He was sure he saw the tender red that flitted across his companion's cheeks, or perhaps it was a reflection of the sky that was already glowing all around in the wonderful evening light. It was now Maria who only silently affirmed his proposal. In a few minutes they had arrived back home.

The engagement celebration—the so-called *Polterabend*[19], in which again the whole town seemed to take part, lasted until the early morning but Maria had sneaked into her chamber early to avoid the increasing drinking, since she was not at all interested in such loud celebrations.

Philipp had fled immediately after she went, continuing to pursue his thoughts for a long time in the lonely, dark bower. The louder the voices sounded from the arbors, the more wistfully he wished for the quiet, meaningful orphan at his side, never to let her go from his protective arm again. The deeper the night sank, the more hopeless this wish seemed to him. As he faced an uncertain future in a completely foreign part of the West, he could not take his loved one under his wing. No! First he must have a home for her, in order to give the right position to her from the outset as befits a companion of his own. He must set this in relation to his brother with his succession of growing sons, who was so much older and in a higher position, in whose government he never would have been appointed without his intercession,.

"Why struggle with fate for that?", he thought, "No! Soon Maria would be picked up by her Mennonite pastor, and would come to the Lower Rhine anyway. There he would find her and know how to put her under some other kind of protection until he could take her to their own home. Yes, reason commanded him to only make firm and feasible decisions and to grow to male maturity, far from Maria."

But he had no idea how difficult the following day would be for him. On the walk to the Maiden's Meadow, for the first time just alone with Maria, there was a soft, overcast sky under which he soon led the beloved girl in his arms on lonely paths, meandering or climbing steeply between flower-filled meadows and enchantingly beautiful woods. His whole strong will had been necessary to survive the terrible battle and to make the path that he had recognized as the only right one comprehensible to his beloved.

In the morning she had learned that he was formally asking for her hand and that her uncle and only relative, had given him the warmest of blessings. He said that he had first had to make arrangements to consult with Gote and his daughter and afterwards they had joyfully given their consent. Now, in the middle of the Maiden's Meadow, where they had both rested in the grass, the loving man had told her that he had chosen her to be his companion and whether she was willing to become a faithful and loving wife to him? Then she had sunk wordlessly into his heart and received his passionate kisses just as hot and glowing as she returned them in raptures. Then he knew that this heart would give him everything it was able to give and that she would be his for life.

All the words and feelings he had learned to know and sympathize with in his favorite poems now seemed pathetic compared with the depth and force of his feelings when he knew that pure and fine girl's soul was his own.

Maria, under the exchange of their caresses, from the white marguerite flowers with which the Maiden's Meadow seemed to be almost flooded, had wound a wreath, as much to her liking as once to the castle child Jutta. Her Philipp knew how to steal this with a bold grasp, putting it on her magnificent blond hair, around the plaited crown.

"It's your wedding crown," he said, as she was just going to take it off. She looked too lovely in the jewelery of this white floral thread and he now took her broad-brimmed straw hat in a second gesture to hang it on her arm and put the wreath out of danger of being exchanged with the hat.

As the sun broke through the delicate veil of cloud and stung equally sensitively, he suggested stepping into the shelter of the small bark hut he had spotted behind them at the edge of the forest. The little hut was probably the same one that Lotte reported as having been renovated by subsequent generations since the time of the nobleman of the castle, who had ordered the erection of a shelter on the spot where his daughter was found. Yes, the Harz folk adore their legends and carefully maintain them.

How long the two of them had been chatting and enjoying themselves under the cooler shelter, where seats running along the walls gave them a more comfortable rest than the meadow floor. Here in the sunny and flowery solitude they had not been disturbed by any human presence and finally it was only the chirping of the birds, already resembling a goodnight message, which reminded them to go home.

Enraptured and deeply happy, they walked gently, she resting securely and carefree in his strong arm, which he had now placed around her hips. Only here, when they were no longer under the confining care of her relatives, had she, full of joyful astonishment at her inwardly admiring Philipp, uninhibited and free, revealed to her Questenberg relatives her outstanding intellectual development. He also learned that in the evening, in the arbor, she had followed his historical explanations with great understanding and lively interest until the end.

When he then asked her curiously where she got her knowledge and her interest in the historical events of the past, she at first admitted to being much more mature than the anxious shyness and her girlish natural character would have led him to believe. From her initially faltering but then, always fluid accounts of her childhood and subsequent life in response to his stormy questions, it was clear that her father had been an unusually well-travelled, classically educated and wealthy merchant's son and a capable economic politician in the Dutch borderlands and by no means a pious sectarian. Rather, he was a philosophically freethinking follower of the modern age yet inwardly of a deeply religious nature.

Her mother, on the other hand, had been a serious, extremely simple and strict Mennonite. In her clear, cheerful piety, however, she had been able to influence her father in his sense of greatness and breadth. He had therefore liked it that she had been faithfully absorbed into her religious community and had also taught the daughter to find her quiet satisfaction in the unpretentious way of life with certain state restrictions on Mennonite religious customs, as well as in purposeful seclusion. But Maria knew almost more about Spinoza's pantheism and even about Kant's "Critique of Pure Reason" than he himself, even if her knowledge of it was in somewhat blurred terms.

It was apparent that the reflections emanating from her father's study had stuck in the receptive young girl's mind just as much as her knowledge of the Bible sayings, which she owed to the pious devotional exercises with her mother. He had to admit to himself that these Mennonites led a completely self-contained existence. To penetrate this existence more closely seemed to him to be one more attraction for his future on the Rhine in the happiness of his new possession.

When he asked her about her Rhine homeland connections, she said that her father had often said that his own family Jacobs and that of the often mentioned Johann Georg[20] and Fritz Jacobi[21] from Düsseldorf belonged to one and the same clan, for the Düsseldorf brothers were also said to be more Dutch than German and had also called themselves Jacobs. She had been affected by the severe accident that had befallen her parents on their return from Dutch India through the collision of their ship in the fog with a vessel that had just left its homeport. She had found it only natural and right in the midst of her mother's fellow believers, to whom she was entrusted even during the absence of her parents.

She was always at home with her fellow believers. The fatherly property that had fallen to her had been in the administration of the Mennonite congregation, because she had been only 19 years old 4 years ago. She received from the pastor of the congregation the necessary amount of money for her living expenses and minor special requests. However, only the pastor could give information about the extent of her wealth.

Even if Philipp was quite touched by the unadulterated trustworthiness of these Mennonite believers, he was nonetheless surprised to hear the sober prose of their material living conditions woven as if it were as a matter of course into the serene prose of the graceful creature at his side in the most delicate poetry. In fact, if he had not spent most of his youth in the eastern border province of Silesia and had already become acquainted with a little more of the folk style of the West, he would have felt the impact of the Dutch father in this mixture of opposites and would not have been at all surprised.

There was another feeling aroused in him by the open explanation of their financial circumstances and this feeling was of an embarrassing nature for him and hit him in a sore spot. He asked himself what did he himself have to offer this girl, who was obviously completely independent and how he could he have dared—and what about his own honor as a man—to reach out his hand to a Maria Jacobs. He—the discharged lieutenant without a position, without a home, without a secure income, in possession of only a small parental inheritance and his own savings that he had painstakingly acquired through hard self-expression. He thought he could still be able to bring his elevated position in life to bear this very morning, when he saw in Maria only the poor orphan, of simple origin. Now, in contrast, he who was the one yet to be trained for his social position, still regarding it as a task, albeit a delightful one that still lay ahead of him.

Now he felt deeply ashamed by the knowledge of her intellectual background and her financially secure conditions of existence granted to her by an unusual couple of parents. His conscience, constantly at work in the deepest depths of his soul, imposing on him the imperative of an accelerated separation as the first commandment of courtship, was literally increased to agony by this new, almost embarrassing insight.

She chatted with him, unbiased, about the changes and actions in her community, which had already noticeably dwindled as a result of the many emigrations abroad in recent years. The community was now on the verge of embarking on its journey to the richer regions of the Russian Volga with a longing, albeit wistful expectation.

He scarcely listened any more, so powerful was he under the, for him now doubly more serious, commandment to speak to her today of the future separation necessary for both of them. Now he had to immediately create conditions in which he could offer his future young wife a truly permanent and solid home, which would probably meet the demands she would have from her birth and family. His honor as a man would suffer it no other way!

The old building that he had already noticed on his first hike to the unknown little town of Questenberg appeared on his right. The fact that they were approaching the Sonne Inn just around the corner, up the busier street, was a cause for concern. He suddenly found the strength to tell her that, now that he was sure of her love, he thought it was the right thing to leave first thing tomorrow, to prepare a nest for her on the Rhine, in which he could take her as his own and make her his wife.

She stood motionless, as if rooted to his words. "Already tomorrow?" she said, shaking her head.

"Tomorrow... I can't do it yet."

"No, not you, but I my dear, and when you follow me later with your companion, the pastor, then I hope I will have everything ready for you, that we will then remain together forever and ever."

Since she remained silent, as if lacking comprehension, he continued more emphatically, "Now you are still better protected with your own than with a journeyman on the road, who does not even know the place where he wants to build his hut and for the time being has no home for his beloved on this earth."

Then she looked at him with eyes full of devoted love. "But it's nothing," she said simply. "Where you go, I go. Your house is my house," quoting the biblical words of Ruth, "As it is written in the Scriptures, 'I go with you now as your wife and we will build our house together'. I can be ready in three days, but if I have to, maybe the day after tomorrow. Can't my lord and master be patient for two days?"

There was silence in him and as she anxiously looked for his averted eyes. While they both remained motionless in their excitement, his voice sounded strange and dull from the inner conflict when he, with all the strength at his disposal, replied mildly but firmly, "It is you, my dear love, who must be patient! You must let me go my way alone for a while longer to our new home, you will see later that I am doing the right thing and that this separation is only a test of our love imposed on us by heaven. It will only grow in longing. You know the saying, 'If suffering never came through love, then love never came through suffering.'[22] We shall now have the opportunity to prove our loyalty to each other and soon we will celebrate a blessed reunion on the Rhine, only to be united forever."

"On the Rhine," she repeated sonorously. Then she was the first to walk on and in silence they both continued their way to the Sonne Inn. Oh, how bitterly painful was her heart! As she prepared to go to her chamber on the stairs, he took her hand. Pushing it up the banister, he pulled the dear figure towards him, deeply moved, his lips still pressing fervently on her mouth as she took leave.

"Trust me, my dear. God save you and bring you to me soon."

"No! Take me with you!" she sobbed painfully, burying her face in both hands.

"It cannot be yet—but soon you will follow me! Be patient and trust in God! We'll meet again in Emmerich." He was also at the end of his strength and he turned towards the dining room, in order to no longer require his unbearable painful inner being to suffer the torment of farewell.

After a long wait, the landlord of the Sonne appeared, which helped him regain his composure to some extent. He then commended the host to take care of his future bride and in the morning the two men had already agreed that Maria should travel back to the Lower Rhine with the pastor to be handed over to Philipp as a bride to be wedded to him. Philipp then gave the innkeeper his brother's address in Kleve, so that he could send him regular news about Maria.

The first news of how she was surviving the separation was to be sent to the post office in Nordhausen to where he had ordered his luggage from Harzgerode and news from Glogau of his brother Heinrich. The men parted warmly and heartily and in order that Maria might find complete peace and that her mind might come to terms with the separation more quickly, it was agreed with the good Gote that Philipp should be given a lad to accompany him on his way over the Quest early in the morning in order to reach Rossla more quickly, either on horseback or on foot.

After the hearty blessings of the two old folks he crept into his chamber for a short last night's rest. He was literally expecting the first ray of sunlight, after having spent the night hours trying to explain to Maria the deeper reasons for his farewell in writing. She was not allowed to blame him, as a man, but had to sympathize with him. He had to feel that the sweet woman, whom he wanted to introduce as his wife into his family and his future circle, could in all decency and respectability first be called his own after a wedding ceremony in his church.

Under the unusual circumstances that she would probably lose her present home before winter — as her uncle, the Sonne landlord had revealed to him — due to the emigration of her religious community. He would only receive an income in his new position from October, the wedding feast was probably best held at the beginning of October, likewise at the same time. The fact was that on the Rhine it would be Michaelmas, it was the next possible date to be able to move into a suitable apartment for them as a married couple. By the time they could buy a property near Kleve, which would be his dream for the future, she would have long been united with him under his strong wings.

However, the three-month transition period was difficult for both of them. Whereas in Questenberg he would know that she was still under the safe protection of Uncle and Gote for the time being, he would still have to familiarize himself with a foreign city, with a foreign authority, with the strange environment and duties connected with his position at his more mature age when such a complete change of circumstances was no longer so easy.

"I know my nature too well not to expose a delicate flower like this to all those initial battles and struggles. I have too much to do with myself in my hard-headedness. I could often be a frightening and roaring lion from whom his beloved would soon run away. Now that you have given the whole of yourself to me, grant me only a short time to gain love for your homeland, so that I can also stand before you. Find strength and power for the short separation in the thanks to God and our Lord Jesus Christ, so that your precious Rhine, in which your noble parents have found their resting place, may now be preserved as your home through our covenant of hearts. So that both of us may find our happiness there, I commend you to the grace of the Most High, now and forever. May he grant us a blessed and peaceful reunion. Always and forever, your Philipp Wilhelm."

II

From Golden Meadow to Nordhausen

How he had looked forward to the walk to Rossla along the Golden Meadow[23] when he said goodbye to his brother and sister in Hecklingen! Now he was already on top of the last ridges of hills and had the wide plain in front of him with the stately hem of the Kyffhausen mountains on the horizon. It was truly a magnificent panorama, after the view of the narrowing forest and mountain area of the Harz roads he had first walked through.

The morning air also brushed freshly up from the valley, the larks swarming merrily up from the fields into the ether, the sun greeting him from beyond the Questenberg in his back as if rejoicing. Yet he could not join in the glory of the young day. Now, when the view was so clear and the destination for today was below him, the princely town of Rossla became more and more recognizable to the eye as it came closer and closer. Soon he would be there. Indeed, he had thought about the visit to the young parish candidate recently. Eight days ago he had already determined and purposefully fixed the daily program of his visit but now it did not even occur to him.

He would find the castle anyway and be able to ask for the Princely Court Preacher and his current assistant Candidate of Theology but imagine how the poor dear girl in Questenberg might feel now. If he already felt depressed up here on the high Harz Mountains, which otherwise always liberated him—who knows how she would overcome the hour of farewell down there in the narrow valley.

"Oh take me with you! Take me with you!" Her plea, so sadly voiced at the end, remained ringing in his ears. Her urgent, pleading tone was still tearing at his heart. If his poor mother had still been alive, he would have chosen the way back to Hecklingen and entrusted the poor homeless child to her care. How she would have loved to take the tender thing to her heart until he took her to his new home on the Rhine. Yet she was dead, her brother was a bachelor and her sister had never been married and now reigned in Hecklingen's parsonage.

In Silesia, too, he had broken off all bridges in order to reach the area completely new to him. There was a much older brother, whom he knew only from letters to the Glogau brothers and a sister in law completely unknown to him, where he first had to secure himself a new position under their hospitable roof. But first he had to build himself a new bridge.

For quite some time now the way had been leading downhill — only a few hundred steps and he would reach his destination. Before anything else he would have to visit the barber again, because without a remedy for his outward appearance he could not possibly present himself to his future nephew. Both paths he had been able to complete relatively quickly. The helpful Figaro himself had led him to the postmaster. In the postmaster's office he also found a clean and comfortable room, whereupon the girth of the friendly postmistress promised that no one would starve in her house.

He had no appetite for food though. At the most, if they could get him a cup of the popular Glogau drink, the royal Prussian coffee, he would acknowledge it with thanks. He knew that the eager landlady would not succeed so quickly and after the hike he was at first glad to freshen up and rest in his chamber. Just around the corner, the barber had told him, there was the church and rectory and the old gentleman Court Preacher was also at home—he knew that, as he had just come from him. A splendid old man and so popular in the congregation! And the young gentleman Candidate also showed a kind heart and it seemed as if the two of them would get on well with each other.

"I wonder if that boy will be your new preacher?"

Philipp could not give an answer to this, for he only knew from his sister Einecke in Mansfeld that the young theologian had come from there and was an old playmate of her children.

"Our mother likes him so much and since he has always been her special friend and protector from an early age, he is known and familiar with all our experiences and hopes like a child of our house. You must get to know him. Dearest brother, please write to me openly whether you like him," she had said in her last letter. Philipp had promised not to pass by Rossla without having visited the Candidate.

Ah, yes! The Royal Prussian coffee! He wondered if they already had princely café depots here in Rossla. It got there faster than he thought. And how it smelled and tasted! Philipp enjoyed the invigorating effect in energizing draughts and it did not take long before he was confronted with his sister's high-flying but already quite stately protégé.

"Salutations, esteemed Uncle!", was soon resounding across the church path from a sonorous chest to the visitor, when he inquired at the gate about the presence of the gentleman Candidate of Theology Noth.

"Uncle? Shall I also say nephew? Warm greetings to you there," he replied to the gracious address.

"Your damoiselle niece and I are long since promised to be bride and groom—even when we could barely walk, we agreed upon this," was the response and a particularly firm handshake made Philipp immediately recognize a cordial natural disposition, which warmed his heart.

Before long, the two relatives in the making sat each in a corner of the old-fashioned sofa in the candidate's room and drank a welcome German greeting to each other as uncle and nephew, "So you came here from Questenberg, uncle, having celebrated Pentecost there. My superior here was also there with his brother-in-law and attended services on the third holiday."

"And how did he like it all," asked Philipp pleasantly.

"I think he was very satisfied and even seemed to be quite excited about the nocturnal celebration at sunrise."

This was followed by discourse and counter discourse in a lively flow and Philipp heard many more new things from the young clergyman, which had remained unknown to him even in Questenberg. The Court Preacher and the Questenberg clergyman were also in complete agreement that the Questenberg festival was a pre-Christian cult ritual that had become Christian in the course of time—just as Christmas and the Germanic festival of light were of one and the same origin. The God of creation, who gives rise to nature, can even be recognized in the Christian Easter feast. And so almost all our church celebrations are based on the cultic traditions of our forefathers.

Philipp realized immediately that he had a sincere and lucid theologian for a nephew and not one who started his career with an empty literalist belief.

"And now, esteemed sir uncle, are you intending to found a new home on the Rhine and have decided to leave your excellent brother in Glogau?"

"I can honestly assure you that this has not been easy for me. On the contrary, I must say that it has been extremely difficult," the interviewee confessed.

"I look up with the deepest veneration to this very brother Heinrich, a noble and truly well-meaning man and the best of all brothers. I have a great deal to thank him for. Since I left our blessed father twelve years ago, this very brother has taken the most fatherly care of me. Even before that, when our venerable father was still alive, when after the Battle of Leuthen[24] I had fallen into the unfortunate captivity of the bestial Cossacks who had taken me to Poland, he did not hesitate, nor did he rest, until he got me out of it and freed me. He succeeded only after the exchange of the first prisoners. After the Peace of Hubertusburg, after I had to quit our great King's army, like other middle-class officers, I went to my brother in Breslau.

"Then on his estates that he administered and which my brother Heinrich owned in part himself, I tried my best to restore agriculture, after the Cossacks had destroyed the castles and manor houses. I was also able to receive training as a government secretary in the administration and thus was able to find the means to make a good living.

"However, ever since my brother bought the house in the Topfgasse in Glogau[25], he has not been to his estate himself, which the Cossacks had devastated terribly. He is now trying to restore it with considerable sums of money in order to sell the property soon. This excellent, far-sighted man now has the opinion that, because the Lower Rhine lands are considered to be established property of the House of Brandenburg and very much favored by it, there are prospects there, not only for a farmer, but also for a judicial officer.

"It would be easier for him to advance there and to acquire some fortune for his own establishment, which he himself is intent on. And so, full of fatherly kindness, he recommended me to his brother August in Kleve, where my niece from Pasewalk, who is also a little delicate, has gone and is very happy there."

"And is this brother, who was appointed a Prussian civil servant there some time ago, also of such a good opinion of the Rhineland?"

"In any case, this our eldest brother, has a fine position and provision as a Judicial Councillor at the Military and Domain Chamber. He got married there too and has grown up with small children, his own house and many friends in Kleve, so that he has never regretted having moved there. He agrees with his brother in Glogau on this, so it's all the more reason for me to leave and try my chances on the Rhine.

"As you have certainly heard from my dear sister, our eldest brother Friedrich died in Pasewalk last year. His parsonage had not had a housewife for a long time and so his three children were left as homeless orphans. My brother Heinrich invited these three children to Glogau, taking the two sons into his house for a while. In any case, he now looks after them like a real father. The daughter from Pasewalk has gone to my brother in Kleve because my brother Heinrich still has a foster daughter himself who is now old enough to be introduced to the social world. Having two marriage-loving demoiselles in the house is definitely not for a bachelor.

"As for myself, I'm also not suited for the protection of the young nieces in Glogau. There is probably already a suitor for his own daughter, who is very concerned to be at his service—de facto for me it was time to go and say farewell to Silesia."

"I wish with all my heart that all your hopes will be fulfilled on the Rhine. A full glass to that, my dear Uncle!"

Although their drinking mood seemed full of merriment, one could read in the eyes of the men that in front of them lay a struggle and striving for a home of their own in a yet undetermined future. They drank a toast to the young candidate's bride and their imminent marital bliss before arranging a hike together in the beautiful forest of Kyffhausen for the afternoon.

"I still would very much like to hear from sir uncle about the battalions under the great King, of which the father of my bride has extolled so much praise about their battles under General Seydlitz," the young nephew implored as they parted. The former cuirassier lieutenant gladly promised to tell him as much as he wanted to hear.

Philipp decided it was time to try out the postwoman's culinary skills on his own because the charming nephew-to-be believed he would be obliged to dine with his court preacher, as was the rule. He seemed uplifted by his young friend's open talk and fresh, cheerful nature and did not regret having got together with him but not spoken freely about his depressed and thoughtful heart.

The meal was simple but invigorating. He thoroughly appreciated the Thuringian grilled sausages, reminiscent of old wartime experiences and the meal was quickly consumed. Soon afterwards, he allowed himself a siesta from which he woke up dreamless and refreshed with renewed strength and a heightened will to live.

A few minutes later the young candidate was already standing in his doorway to pick him up for the hike across the golden valley over to the Kyffhausen Mountains. Soon they walked down further, past the cemetery, across the footbridge and past the last houses of Rossla. They crossed the plain to the broad Kyffhausen massif, which geologically is still a foothill of the Harz Mountains but has been part of the Thuringian Forest Mountains since the victory of the Thuringians, who conquered the old Staufen Castle of Barbarossa.

"Shall we climb the Kyffhausen Mountain with its old imperial castle remains via the former imperial palace of Tilleda or shall we choose the shady forest path to Rothenburg on the right, passing the expansive keep?" the young hiker was now asking his older comrade, who was visibly bathed in sweat from walking along the country road without shade.

"If you wouldn't mind, I would appreciate a cool, wooded atmosphere," replied his companion, who stood still, wiping the pearls of sweat from his forehead with his silk scarf.

Delighted to be able to please his amiable uncle, the young clergyman soon led him onto the next path to the protection of the deciduous forest on the otherwise bare and stony mountain range. On its elongated ridge, which is split in the east by a deep valley that runs lengthwise through it, the ruins of Rothenburg rise above Kelbra at the very end, while the legendary Kyffhausen Castle stretches its extensive debris on the eastern corner abutment. The massive square torso of the keep in particular dominates the entire mountain range and can be seen from afar.

Of course the old Kyffhausen Saga[26] became the subject of their conversation, as the two hikers had reached its perimeter and were now on the cool forest paths to Rothenburg Castle. The young Noth presented the common form of the saga, that Emperor Barbarossa had had his residence here and when he had died and been buried in Kyffhausen and was waiting there until the ravens would wake him up and a new German Empire would be born. Philipp was able to tell him that the Emperor Barbarossa had drowned in a river while taking a bath on a crusade against the Saracens[27]. The legend was of much older origin and had probably evolved earlier on and referred to a long forgotten, great ruler of prehistoric times. The same is sitting asleep in the mountains. In the Kaiserpfalz, near Kaiserslautern, the coffin in question is displayed with the long beard growing through the table. Every now and then he had to get up and ask whether the ravens were still flying and the defoliated tree was not green once again.

First the slumbering Lord of the Wind had been an old pagan god, then he became Charlemagne, then Emperor Frederick. Since then the reign of the German emperors has been, right up to our days, the dream and refuge of our nation. It will live on insatiably until a great German emperor becomes the leader of Europe again.

"And you do not believe that our Frederick of today is called to become such a leader?" Noth asked, moved by the historical truth which had just been revealed to him and which had previously been unknown to him.

"Our great Frederick would probably have had what it takes, but the Margrave of Brandenburg, who had to assert himself against almost all of Europe, had no desire to be and remain more than King of Prussia. I do not wish to deny that his empire, which is now building up its interior since he has fortified its borders, will one day not acquire the strength to become the bearer of the culture and will dominate not only Europe, but the whole civilized world.

"Whether such a cultural carrier would therefore also have to own the land of the earth and rule it as an emperor is not what is meant by this. History shows us already with the great Alexander, with Emperor Augustus and our Hohenstaufens[28] that, on the contrary, it always meant the decline of the empire when its ruler, in addition to his cultural longing to please his people with education, indulged in the ambition of constant territorial expansion. I, for my part, am in any case satisfied that our great King has known how to keep peace for his Prussia for more than ten years now, and is content with his previous fame as a general."

"You also promised to tell me about the battalions under the great Frederick," recalled the twenty-four-year-old candidate, admiring and eager to learn. He had been a thirteen-year-old pupil at Schulpforta[29] when the Hubertusburg Peace Treaty[30] was concluded. As in almost all schools, he had been taught more about the battles of the ancient Greeks, Persians and Romans than he would have heard about the wrestling of his own generals that took place around him. The boy at the time had no idea of the school of patience through which the King of Prussia had gone in the Seven Years' War[31], which he himself had called protracted, cruel and even barbaric.

But the Prussian officer striding beside him—albeit twenty years younger than his warlord—had ultimately spent the long campaign in the captivity of the enemy, living through it with similar feelings as his King.

"If you won't hold it against me, I'd rather tell you about it tonight over a glass of wine, in the very pleasant Post House Inn, to which I hereby invite you. It is better to ride against the enemy in one's own memory, if one feels something fiery about it, even if it's only a drop of Grüneberger Wine[32], which revives and lifts the bones."

The candidate accepted with thanks the invitation to the hours after the evening meal that had been reserved for him. He felt indescribably happy in the presence of his companion. How cheerfully the two of them wandered together! Their thoughts were so completely different and how instructive and stimulating was the exchange with a like-minded soul who was just as enthusiastic about God's wonderful nature, on this wonderful forest path to Rothenburg.

It was now that they reached the famous lookout point at the end of the ridge. The young preacher candidate was somewhat disappointed that his companion had shown so little warmth for the relatively pretty castle remains. He also seemed to have little taste for mythology. He had already taken away his belief in the beautiful Kyffhausen Saga earlier on.

Yet he was apparently a skeptic, like his king. As they descended to the viewing platform, he now dared to do more than before, expressing the thought that it was a pity that the great Frederick showed so little feeling and so little sympathy for all the beautiful German traditions which the people had passed on and that, in order to preserve them, poetry and literature should be cultivated.

"Why is it that the King only likes that French stuff? And how sad it is that this so caring sovereign, who does so much for the development and freedom of the Reformed faith and the absolute parity of the Christian doctrines, is himself such an outspoken free spirit, even an atheist, who eliminates religion from his life."

His mute companion did not reply to this, only a slight shake of his head indicated to the young, eager theologian that his uncle did not quite agree with him.

"Let's sit down here on the stone bench for a little while," Philipp then suggested in a friendly manner, and took a wallet out of his tunic pocket, from which he removed a somewhat worn and written paper.

"Do you know these verses by any chance?" he asked his future nephew who shook his head.

"No? Please read it."

"I have copied them down and I carry them with me always, like a talisman, because they are so worthy of the great King."

"Are they verses by his friend Voltaire?" the candidate asked, "I see they're written in French."

"No," replied Philipp, "not by Voltaire, the vain poet, who would never have been able to write this. But read first, and I will explain the poem at the end."

Noth seemed severely embarrassed, "I do not know the French language so well that I could easily grasp written verses. I can understand the language better when I hear it. Would it be possible for Uncle to read me the verses?"

Meanwhile, Philipp had already cast a glance over the landscape that was presented to the beholder from the bench. "I am happy to do so," said Philipp, raising himself, "but let us first admire the wonderful landscape here, which spreads out before us in a quite unexpected way."

They both stepped forward now, to the edge of the vantage point where they were and were equally overwhelmed by the view that this place up here offered across the German countryside.

"That's the village of Tilleda. Down there," Noth explained, "the old imperial palace belonged to the Staufen family. And there to the northwest, are the towers of the old imperial and royal city of Nordhausen."

"Where I intend to stay tomorrow," his companion interrupted him, his eyes shining into the distance.

"And here in the south there is the Thuringia region, Frankenhausen, Sondershausen, in the west up to Weissenfels and Naumburg in the east. If you can' t exactly see the cities themselves, you can see the heights and mountain ranges where they are down by the River Saale."

"Could you also show me the Janus Hill from up here?" the older one mischievously asked the younger one for these local explanations.

"Janus Hill, no, I don't know that one." The latter replied somewhat embarrassed.

"If it lies near the Wartburg, it would be found approximately over there," and thus he pointed almost exactly to the south.

"No, my most esteemed one, Janus Hill is not located there, it is an old friend of mine, between the River Saale and Weissenfels, I will tell you about it tonight—but you asked me to read you the poem."

Philipp looked around for the first suitable seat, observing a fallen tree trunk, which, illuminated by the already sinking sun, seemed to him better for resting than the cool stone bench now lying in the shade. Thus they both sat, in view of the almost edifying landscape. Philipp read the simple poetry with deeply felt warmth, clearly, with good emphasis, without any pathos. It was an epistle to Alembert from April 1773 and read in the translation that the reader later sent to the listener at his request:

> No, a tyrant is not the god,
> Before which my heart prostrates;
> Mine demands no sacrifice of reason!
> By earth revealed and sky that praises,
> A purpose in **all** that speaks for Him.
> Digestion has been given me;
> Nourishment refreshes my body
> And prolongs my life.
> The eye God created for me to see,
> The ear so I can hear;
> The foot to carry me,
> His arm protecteth me,
> And if I now have spirit,
> It must be in the hand
> Of him that gave it me,

In more abundance than any mortal,
Who gives me what he doth not have himself?
— That's why I worship a profound force.
Copernicus and great Newton you;
You wise men of Gaul and Albion, you have guessed
The law by which the universe moves,
And stars move in never changing course!
Can it be of mere chance?
Full of change and fickleness,
Shield this eternal law,
That so many worlds at once
Keep afloat and hasten on!
So let us confess then:
A wise being drives the wheel,
That makes this drama full of power;
A duty that my heart doth honor
And does not try to fathom out.

Philipp had finished and quietly put the paper back into his wallet. While the theologian, still moved by what he had heard, waited to get to know the author of these verses, Philipp had risen and looked up to the sun, now saying goodbye to it in its glorious gold and purple mantle, and turning to it, repeated the last verse once more raising his voice:

A wise being drives the wheel,
That makes this drama full of power;
A duty that my heart doth honor
And does not try to fathom out.

And then he turned to the man still sitting and called out to him quite enthusiastically, "Is this the confession of an atheist? My King wrote this to his friend d'Alembert last year, and so it is in the soul of the philosopher who strives for the highest virtue and who, in spite of it all, abandons theology."

Noth was silent, only pointing to a nearby flattened rock ledge inviting to descend. Here one enjoyed the most beautiful view of the Thuringian countryside, which had become more and more a golden meadow due to the restless work of the people of Flanders. On the other side lay the entire Harz mountains stretched out before them, from the Brocken to the right the view swept across to the Rabenkopf, the Auerberg, the Ramberg and as far as the Mansfeld highlands in the east, while in the west the hills and heights of the Weser mountains shimmered blue. The farthest view, however, was to the south, over the Hainleite and Schmücke to the multi-towered city of Erfurt and beyond to the former Loiba. The Ramsteig is the forest of the Thuringians on whose back the Ramsteig stretches, with the Ingelsberg clearly visible. The panoramic view here was so powerful and charming that it was easy to understand why the old Emperor Barbarossa chose this site for his favorite castle.

The young theologian climbed around on the ruins of the former lower castle and down to a new ledge, which had been connected to the castle by a ring wall. He was able to explain that the castle chapel had once stood here with its small cemetery. The memory of the past, however, was now even more powerful than the beauty of the landscape, and it was here that the memory of the past entered the soul of the romantically inclined young bridegroom.

When even a few ravens croaking from the rocks below ascended to the heights, his receptive mind sank back into prehistoric times, when Hugin and Munin (Odin's ravens) were still the messengers of the pagan god Wotan. Here on the mountain, the ancient Germanic peoples no longer worshipped their sun cult but, influenced by the Romans, offered their sacrifices to the almighty Odin. So many transformations in the history of the German people and their imaginary world had passed through the centre of the German-speaking countries and still exist today. Over there in Morungen, in the proud knightly days of Minnesang[33] and the accolade, the singer Heinrich von Morungen[34] had sung of spring joy and winter mourning — of Minnelust and Minneleid — and together with the other Saxon knights Eschenbach, Ofterdingen and Frauenlob had fought with lute and song for the victor's palm of the festival.

What a miracle that the young minister, barely needing to shave, also remembered his queen of hearts, pulled a little book out of his pocket and quickly threw in a few verses of love, for he too was a deeply poetic soul. Philipp looked at him favorably. Then Noth continued, "Here the people of Kyffhausen themselves were probably less inclined in this respect but their knighthood and the old Morungen estate also played a direct part in the history of the Questenberg castle hill. In later years, the 'Castle Damsel of the Maiden's Meadow'" — Philipp listened with interest — "became the bride of her young musician, that famous minstrel, Heinrich von Morungen, who took part in the Minstrel Contest on the nearby Wartburg, there behind those mountain heights.

"The Morungen was a jolly knight who desired to bring art to the Frankish courts of Normandy and Picardy and the young Questenberg girl allowed him his rest. Meanwhile, groups of singers of lesser standing, who came to the large markets of Nordhausen and Sondershausen and found shelter in the eastern part of the landscape, soon knew how to tell of the relaxed life with the ladies of King Karl, in which he himself had set the example with Agnes Sorel.

"Young Heinrich von Morungen was one of the most skilful leaders in his shepherd plays, but he also knew how to get his reward from the beautiful shepherdesses. The Questenberg lady, to whom the direct emissaries of her Heinrich found the way less and less often, mourned her years of youth for the unfaithful one. When he finally found his way back home, like his companion Tannhäuser, full of weariness and remorse, he found his abandoned bride faithfully at the side of her Questenburg mother, meanwhile living as a widow. But in spite of all her applicant's efforts she showed only friendship for him and took the veil in the monastery of Lellungen after her mother's death.

"However, we really should be going. We still have a long way to go and you don't bear me a grudge, Mr. Parish Candidate," Philipp gave in politely and offered the young clergyman his right hand, as if for reconciliation.

"I may have become a little too brusque earlier with my slander of theology".

Nonetheless, Noth took the hand he had been offered and openly confessed, "Such effusions of our monarch were foreign to me until now. May I ask to be allowed to copy it down?"

"I will be happy to do that for you and I even think I have a German translation which is quite good and which will make you even more excited to read it in our mother tongue".

This promise was gratefully accepted and then the time had been fully blessed. Neither one nor the other returned to the royal creed. Noth knew a short way down into the valley and after a brisk pace on the good paths in the plain, their way back home in the long summer twilight was most satisfying. As the separation of the two men who had been brought together after today's common enjoyment of nature proved to be more difficult than they had anticipated in the morning, Philipp had persuaded his very likeable nephew without much effort to ask his Court Preacher for a whole day off and to join him on tomorrow's exploratory trip to Nordhausen. "After all, it is the ancestral fathers of your dear bride and one day it will be those of your children who we will try to track down tomorrow." The helpful candidate was particularly happy to agree to this.

"In any case, I already know how to decipher old church books, and my habit will also be useful for the brothers in office, thus sparing you, dear uncle, many a complicated introduction."

Since Philipp wanted to occupy two places when he got back, Noth was supposed to inform him at the post house before the evening only if his vacation was denied. At first they parted at the rectory gate and Philipp walked in a satisfied mood to his nearby quarters. How beautiful the day had been! He had had to think up there, at Joseph's height on the Kyffhausen mountain range in view of the tremendous spectacle of the parting sun, of the similar experience of its decline on the castle hill. Suddenly, it was as if Maria's delicate, madonna-like features were standing beside him and he could feel her soft hand in his.

When he had later ordered two mail seats for the morning mail coach to Nordhausen and then stood at the window of his chamber for a while, looking at the golden meadow and the dark mountains on the horizon and thinking it all over, a wonderful peace came over him. Nothing in the world would have moved him to speak of his acquaintance with Maria with the young friend. The pain and restlessness had gone from him and he now remembered the lovely girlish figure like a sweet secret that belonged only to him and her and that he kept in the depths of his soul.

It was not until around nine o'clock that Noth entered the lounge downstairs.

"It's a deal," he shouted cheerfully, "the reverend even granted me two days, in case the return trip was not convenient or in case there were difficulties with our research."

After the two new friends had uncorked the bottle of wine in front of them and had drunk a quick toast, Philipp began his account of the events of the war, which he had promised in the afternoon, without further ado.

"Let me tell you about my first battle, the battle of Prague. I must be brief, about how and when I came to the military profession in the first place, my brother-in-law Einecke can tell you about the details later. In the winter of 1756 to 57, the King had to increase his army forces against his will because of the increased number of nations aligning themselves with Austria after the imperial failure at

Lobositz to strengthen Austria and had to increase his army by 20,000 men over his initial target. My regiment von Rochov was admitted to the Zieten[35] Corps and our first action was the invasion of Bohemia on April 18. 'Everything is going wonderfully, my dear Marshal,' wrote Frederick to Schwerin at the time. 'Our secret is well kept and the enemy will be taken by surprise.'

"On the 30th we crossed the Eger and stood on the other side of the Moldau almost on a par with the troops of von Schwerin[36] with twenty-five battalions and thirty-five squadrons, in order to crush the House of Austria by a joint attack. He did not take his entire forces across the Vltava but left 30,000 men on the riverbank under Keith's leadership. The King's detachment was united under the eyes of the Austrians, 25,000 men with those of von Schwerin and von Winterfeldt[37]. Together we were 63,000 men.

"The cavalry of the attacking wing was led for the first and last time on that day by the hereditary prince of Schöneich-Carolath. Three times Schwerin sent him the order to attack and finally rode to the cavalry himself to get them on their toes. However, the enemy hussars won the flank from the attackers. A second attack was not successful against the superior numbers. It was only the intervention of our reserve under Zieten that deprived the enemy of his advantage. The defeated Austrian regiments rushed forward and dispersed like sparrows and it was impossible to think of stopping or even holding together.

"Winterfeld, who had led the preceding grenadier brigade, had been no less in a hurry than Schwerin. He had succeeded in reaching the Sterbohol outpost and now he believed that he would be able to seize and overthrow the enemy in an instant by a rapid advance. They approached the enemy at two hundred paces under Austrian cartridge fire. Winterfeld already noticed that the enemy's wings were receding when he himself, hit by a bullet in the neck, sank unconscious from the saddle.

"When it became clear that their own troops had been overtaxed by the ban on firing when their leader fell, those who had just been advancing stopped and fled back. Then Schwerin came, bursting at the seams. He overlooked that the enemy was in exactly the same disorder—he had been leading his regiment for thirty four years—he loved it, trained as a model troop as it was and as the victor of Mollwitz, Chotusitz and Hohenfriedberg with true tenderness. Now he saw it fleeing from the defeated enemy.

"A staff officer had seized a flag to bring the fleeing men to a halt, when Schwerin himself took the flag from his arm, ordered the crew to follow him with a strong shout and carried the standard in front of them. A moment later he was lying in his blood, hit by five cartridges, covered by the flag.

"The 72-year-old field marshal had been granted a heroic death, as he had always wished for but with the renewed advance of the Prussian regiments the battle was not yet averted. The Austrians had seen their advantage and their grenadiers advanced as far as Sterbohol, until our batteries, which had been raised in the meantime, gave us support.

"But the Prussian battalions were also put to the test. Only the two princes of Brunswick, Franz and Ferdinand, came with their troops just in time to help with the decisive action. The grenadier regiments began to storm.

Prince Franz wanted to leave the fight behind already. However, all orders didn't help and he had to follow them, for better or worse. The Prince was carried on the shoulders of his musketeers through the terrible mud to the village of Werschowitz. At the Taborberg the fight came to a halt once again.

"The bloodstained battles were only resolved by Prince Ferdinand, who began to threaten the enemy's rear. The latter's cavalry from the Ziska Mountain saved the fugitives from total annihilation. They advanced so suddenly that for a moment the King was in serious danger.

"Once the decision had been made, the King rode with the Jung-Braunschweig Regiment[38] right through the Austrian camp, to the greatest concern of his companions, amidst enemy projectiles everywhere. It was about four o'clock in the afternoon and the sun was still high in the sky. At 8 o'clock in the evening the King sent his adjutant to the front of the fortress to ask those who were trapped to surrender. However, he received the reply that it was hoped to gain the respect of the King of Prussia through putting up a good defense. 'After the painful losses we have suffered, we are left with nothing but the consolation of making prisoners of the people who are in Prague,' the King wrote to Keith. 'And then I believe the war will be over.'

"When the news of the defeat reached Vienna, it had an astounding effect."

"A toast to the co-victor of Prague!" shouted the young candidate enthusiastically in between. "How old were you, my uncle, when you went into your first battle?"

"Just 23 years old as you are now, dear nephew, but not yet as broad and sturdy as I am now, if however, still strong enough to carry the cuirass and swing the saber firmly with my arm. As you can imagine, the Empress and the whole of Vienna was shaken by the news of the defeat. What was most feared in Vienna at first was that the King of Prussia, instead of keeping Prague surrounded, would now attack the empress's last army. Frederick and his generals had not forgotten Marshal Daun's[39] army during the deliberations on the subsequent campaign but the task of keeping Daun away from Prague seemed to him to be solvable even without a battle.

"The King recommended to General Bevern[40], who was already worried about the weakness of his pack and an attack by Daun, that he should methodically turn the enemy army away, i.e. to gradually snatch his magazines from him, for which purpose he increased it to twenty battalions and ninety squadrons. In this way he managed to capture three magazines at once and on June 5 he managed to make the Hungarians flee, seizing their supplies. Frederick was very satisfied with Bevern's success but at the same time he convinced himself that Daun was stronger than he thought.

"On the other hand, Prague was not to be starved before July. On June 5 we were told for the first time that the king would probably send Daun to battle. A reconnaissance trip by Zieten in mid-July clarified the situation. Friedrich immediately sent orders to the hereditary prince Moritz of Dessau[41] to send six more battalions and 10 squadrons to reinforce him.

"Disturbed by the Prussians' march, Daun pushed his army to the right to the height of the ridge near Kolin—at the west of the ridge two streams with ponds and swampy meadows covered the flank of his army excellently. Around 2 o'clock in the afternoon the attack began. Daun was able to observe every movement of the enemy and to parry every threatening blow carefully and wisely. From Zieten's corps the King had called for the Brigade Krossig and the two cuirassier regiments Prince of Prussia and mine of Rochov, and the Norman Dragoons under their incomparable leader Colonel Seydlitz the black dragoons flew through the alley with their bayonets felled and infantrymen broke into the front line of the enemy. The infantrymen were as resolute as the dragoons, and when formed into a semicircle, victoriously repelled three regiments of enemy cavalry.

"One could already believe, at this critical moment of the whole battle, that the Austrian battalions were being pressed more and more at the front, with the whole regiment cursing behind them and ranting that the retreat had been ordered. Then two squadrons broke upon a bunch of Prussian cuirassiers with the shout 'This is for Striegau!'[42] and Saxon squadrons followed them with load upon load until there were eighty enemy squadrons.

"The Prussian battalions, already exhausted to death and widely dispersed in the advance, succumbed to such an onslaught. Under Prince Moritz of Dessau, the cuirassiers of the Prince of Prussia had made a new attack on the wavering infantry of the enemy but were repelled by canister shots while riding over their own troops of Dessau. Just as this storm had blown over them, the Musketeers were surrounded and almost completely annihilated by the enemy cavalry.

"The regiments of the Princes of Prussia and Munchov did not fare much better. The King saw the decisive turning point of the battle in this shattering of entire regiments. Four fresh battalions, he thought, and it would have been won. Unfortunately, with no reserves of any kind, the gap could no longer be closed. At about the same time as the defeat of the left Prussian wing and the vanguard, the resistance of our troops was also broken in the centre. Of the approximately three thousand troops who had intervened in the battle at Chotzenitz[43], von Manstein[44] wounded himself, led only about twelve hundred back from the burning village.

"With the crushing of his infantry, the king had repeatedly sent messengers to the right wing and finally he himself rode to his own, 'but, gentlemen generals, shall we not attack? In the devil's name attack! Can't you see how the enemy is hitting our infantry? *Allons!* All cavalry, march, march, let's move out! The King leads the way,' but when they reached the village of Bristivi, they were met by a rain of cannonballs and after several failed attacks, the reluctant flock could not be kept together. Save yourself if you can!

"The King gathered about 40 men around the glorious flags of the Anhalt Regiment, the main troop of the Old Dessauers. He caused the game to stir, blasting ahead, hoping to turn the general flight around by his example. But the crowd behind him also began to thin out, only his adjutants followed. Then Major Grant calls out to him. "But Sire, do you want to take the battery all by yourself?'

Then the King stops his horse, looks through his glass at the enemy position and then rides slowly back to the Duke of Bevern to order the retreat. While Zieten had thrown back the Hungarian leader Nadasdy a third time on the other side of the battlefield, the exhaustion of his own troops led to the decision to refrain from pursuing the enemy and to abandon the battle.

"Zieten was carried wounded from the battlefield during the third attack. Krosik had fallen and Norman declared that he would only leave the field at the King's command. The King had left the battlefield immediately after the dissolution of the left wing to hurry to his second army. He sent Major Grant[45] ahead, telling him to try to penetrate the Austrians and get ahead of them. He had to deliver a message to his generals outside Prague that the city was lost and that they should prepare everything to give up the siege at the next command.

"During the night darkness the king rode taking a long detour, crossing the Elbe at Nimburg, riding through the Iser by way of a ford and crossed the Elbe a second time at Braunbeil, taking with him the Gardes du Corps and a troop of Hussars. His brother Heinrich is said to have proclaimed 'For pity's sake!' when he received the news after midnight from Major Grant, who had taken Prince Ferdinand of Brunswick with him. Then leaving the camp immediately in the early morning with all his generals, these were: the King's brother, his brother-in-law, the Princes of Brunswick, Marshal Keith, Generals Schmettau, Winterfeldt, Goltz, Retzow and Schoeneich, he gathered them together. The generals kept the news of the lost battle top secret. Some rumors ran through their army but nobody took them for real, because their King was considered to be insurmountable.

"In the afternoon, after having been in the saddle for 36 hours, he himself came into the camp, his eyes lowered, barely standing upright from fatigue. In front of the vicarage of Michle, his old quarters, three brothers were waiting for him. Prince Heinrich, whom he called in, found him exhausted in body and soul, lying on a straw sack, deeply sad and longing for death. He entrusted his brother Heinrich, now incapable of doing anything himself, with the care of the march of the occupying army. He approved his plan to march off with the troops at three o'clock in the morning. The lifting of the siege and the continuation of the operation took place without any major disruption. Later, when he entered Leipa's camp, Prince Wilhelm failed to protect the just two-mile-long connecting route with his other generals, and so the enemy could march on Silesia undisturbed. The King and his guards reached the camp of Bautzen, where Prince Heinrich had retreated to after the loss of Galch. 'If I don't hurry, I won't see my brother again, I think they're going to flee to Berlin,' the King is reported to have said on his departure.

"In Bautzen, the generals were afraid to appear before their King. Prince Wilhelm, asked the brother to relieve him of the supreme command of his unit. A broken man, the Prince went to Dresden. But the king was determined to make amends for the brother's mistake. The Austrians were still in their camp near Zittau and were gradually withdrawing their advanced posts to the main army, except for the occupation of Görlitz.

"On August 14th—time must have seemed like an eternity to the King in his camp in Weissenburg—the Prussian army was finally provided with nine days of bread provisions again and marched towards the enemy. The King took his quarters in Dittelsdorf and his own mood was very depressed. He planned to engage the enemy the next day but during a reconnaissance ride that he made in the morning with all his generals, he found that the enemy had made great changes overnight and that the King was prevented from advancing by a marshy lowland stream that separated him from the enemy.

"So he ordered the retreat to Ostriz, 'Daun will not fight with me!', he is reported to have given as his reason. However, he was able to gain a small advantage by his advance. Görlitz was won back. The connection with Silesia was restored. But this positive result did not last long. General Winterfeld, who he had left behind to defend this connection, had been attacked by his old opponent Nadasdy on September 7. After several hours of hot fighting, the Prussians were defeated after severe injury of their leader Winterfeldt who succumbed to his wounds the next day.

"The king, who was in a camp near Erfurt, could not hold back his tears when the news came. Winterfeldt was for him the most indispensable man in the whole army of the Duke of Brunswick-Bevern, upon whom he had probably counted most for the defence of Silesia. 'Never will I ever find another Winterfeldt!', he is said to have exclaimed painfully over and over again. Overall, this autumn was a time of dark experience and bitterness for the King.

"The appeasement for peace, which he had been advised to follow up with the French, did not lead to any particular response and the mood in Paris was also reflected in the decline of the allied, so-called Reich troops. The commander-in-chief Prince Josef von Sachsen-Hildburghausen, long since decrepit, who had been brought back to light by Empress Maria Theresa, complained that the constant encouraging of the advance that was taking place from Vienna made it seem as if there were doubts about their genuineness.

"Hildburghausen's plan was now to reach out a hand to the Austrian corps for the liberation of Silesia at the Elbe and attack the King of Prussia there. Suddenly, the Prussians had arrived and it was time to get serious."

Philipp looked at the clock, "But it has become late, dear young friend, one always becomes more detailed than one intended, let us still share this small remainder in the bottle and then indulge in our rest. In Nordhausen there will also be an opportunity to tell you about new heroic deeds of our King, with which I was privileged to be present. As far as I'm concerned, I don't want to part with the defeat at Kolin."

Noth, who could have listened to his admirable uncle all night in his fervent and youthful love of the fatherland, said goodbye obediently without argument, promising that he would be at the post house in time for the journey.

"Onto the Rhine! Onto the Rhine!", he would finally see her again and from tomorrow on he would be closer to his goal again. To Nordhausen, then straight to Kleve-Emmerich. With this, Philipp soon fell into a healthy sleep in blissful recollections of the Questenberg events and his former wartime experiences.

Fresh—cheerful—free the world lay before them as the two friends from yesterday were driving along their postal route, the postilion up front singing a cheerful morning song to his heart's content. In the evening Noth had received a short letter from his bride and had been given the best possible recommendations from her parents to her uncle, if the same would happen to pass through Rossla, once he had first completed his mission. This made Philipp think that he still owed his sister a letter about his future nephew, thus prompting him to make up his mind to write this report immediately after leaving Nordhausen.

While on the road in Kelbra, some guests boarded the stagecoach and turned out to be Pentecost visitors, among them an elderly couple that had relatives in Stolberg and who were now driving home again. They came from Corvey, the old abbey town on the Weser, and although they had much to say about the romance of their homeland, their sense for everything ancient and historical was awakened by the fresh impressions of the princely residence town of Stolberg and the beauty of the castle and the surrounding area. A third person was apparently only a friend from Stolberg who they were taking with them.

"Yes, I should have shown you this pearl of the southern Harz mountains but uncle is in such a hurry," he excused himself and after the plaudits of the fellow travellers of the candidate, he had eagerly agreed with them, because of his own recently acquired experiences.

"Anything more? Our castle is well worth seeing and the little town itself is so picturesquely built around the castle hill—and all these old half-timbered houses with their Gothic gables are they not beautiful?" said the couple's companion and obviously the most talkative.

"And then the treasures inside the castle. My husband is the count's librarian and has all the Rossla books and writings—thousands of volumes under his belt. He's busy all day just looking through and filing the things that arrive. The older, more valuable things, remain untouched from year to year and should have been checked and filed by now."

"That's how it is," said the master of the archives, "I would so much like to have made some excerpts from the oldest eulogies—the prince is said to have several thousand of them—but there is no way of getting at them and there is no directory yet to be able to pick out a volume."

"Do we not have such eulogies in Corvey?" asked his wife rather timidly, "Are ours so precious too?"

"They are even more precious, I can tell you," her husband replied, "because in our abbey they are mostly old monastic charters, the German emperor's, which have the church treasure newly certified with every change of government. The abbey also has the eulogy on the death of each friar though everything here refers exclusively to Corvey. In Stolberg, on the other hand, the prince has rich collections of such sermons from all the famous people in the empire—there whole treasure troves lie fallow and inaccessible to the explorer".

Since he had attentive listeners, the speaker continued, "Yes, and in nearby Nordhausen it is not supposed to be any better at the moment, there is a great public library, for example, which can be seldom and sparsely staffed, making it difficult for researchers to get help."

"One should found associations, so that such sources for the past centuries are more accessible to the circles of interested people," the elderly woman interfered again in the conversation.

"We are also on the research trail at the moment and would like to pursue research on our former ancestors in Nordhausen, at the moment in particular," Philipp interjected.

"Oh, I can at least name the gentlemen who can help you. As you will have guessed, I am one of their colleagues and I am in charge of the collections at Corvey Monastery. Today, it is mostly the teachers in the small towns of our empire who are responsible for preserving the values of our traditions, as it was with the monks in the monasteries in the grey Middle Ages."

"Nordhausen even has an emeritus principal teacher Meyer, who is the head of its excellent public library. Make sure you contact him — he is the absolute authority. He will help you as much as he can. If it were in Corvey, I would be happy to serve the gentlemen myself and show and explain the treasures of our abbey to them. In Nordhausen, even if Meyer should not be there, the theologians are very ready to serve. For example, there is the pastor from the St Nicholas Church — what's his name now?"

Then something promptly occurred to the wife from the other side, "and don't forget the gentleman — I can't remember his name — because the pastor won't want to look for anything in the Catholic cathedral!"

The latter had already been busy writing down all the people he discovered in his notebook. Now he politely affirmed that no, the information he was looking for could certainly not be expected among the pastors of the cathedral church. Thanks were also given for the information that the Nikolai Church was located behind the guest house, whereas the Blasiikirche was located in the northern part of the city.

As soon as there was a small break in the flow of speech, the companion, who had apparently only waited for this, returned to her special advantages in Stolberg and asked them if they had already seen the beautiful cave of Old Stolberg, the Heimkehle near Rottleberode[46], or if they wanted to visit it from Nordhausen. When those asked said no, she could not help praising the enormous halls, the magnificent underground lakes and the huge masses of rocks and shell limestone that fell from the ceiling.

Under such instructive and stimulating conversations, the hours in the mail coach flew by very quickly and the postilion was already blowing his horn outside to loudly announce the arrival of his heavy vehicle in the mail yard of the former capital of northern Thuringia and imperial palace of Nordhausen. The two travellers who had arrived at their destination dismounted, then their three companions left with repeated assurances of gratitude and good wishes for a pleasant continuation of the journey.

They strolled off, bracing their limbs and now stretching delightfully, through the post house gate straight ahead towards the beautiful ancient town hall. It had caught the young pastor's eye right away and already he could see the majestic Roland under his canopy on the south side, while Philipp followed slowly, his thoughts flying back to the Roland down in Questenberg, remembering the fact that he had bribed the man on the stand, despite the threat of the sword of justice, to direct his wheel of fortune pointer to very special prizes, if the little innkeeper's daughter would come out of the Sonne Inn and his pretty cousin would try her luck with him.

He wondered what Maria was going to do with her little chain, while his companion was thinking he could claim that this was not a medieval Roland but at most he had been doing his guard duty here since the beginning of the century, the town hall itself being several hundred years older than the guard. Philipp was pleased with the candidate's excellent judgement but nevertheless he suggested to ask for the way to the library or to the apartment of Mr. Meyer, the head teacher, now without delay, since it was after usual business hours when one could perhaps still meet him, while it might also be possible to visit the church gentlemen later in the afternoon.

"But the Church of St. Nicholas, our most important point, is right in front of us. This must be it, according to the description of our stagecoach companion—without towers, close behind the town hall—shouldn't we perhaps first visit the interior of this church," the theologian modestly suggested.

"If we can get in easily, we certainly will," answered Phillip, whereupon Noth hurried ahead to scout out the sexton.

He found him in the nearby dwelling and got him to unlock the main entrance. A well-proportioned, astonishingly well-kept interior with a beautiful baroque organ on the gallery, opposite the altar, received him and, moved, he looked up at the pulpit, opposite which his ancestor Thomas Sack, once the Lord Mayor of the free imperial city, was supposed to have found his resting place. At that time, here in Nordhausen, Thomas had appointed and introduced Luther's friend and cellmate, Lorenz Füsse, to be the first preacher of the Protestant doctrine, at the risk of his own life, together with the mayor Branderodt, and had registered himself as the first member of the Lutheran congregation.

Seventy years earlier, Thomas' father Heinrich, also the head of the Nordhausen community, had already publicly declared that it was impossible for the monks' teachings to be correct and a considerable number of families from the circle of the nobility had agreed with his opinion. Even if they did unite, it was done without causing an official apostasy from the Church of Rome.

His father had often told him about these brave old ancestors and now he stood in the church and next to it was the town hall. It was here where these forerunners, and finally defenders of Luther's teachings, had worked against the all-powerful Rome and fought for their faith.

"Is it possible to see the tomb under the church?" he asked the guide, "There's one of my ancestors lying in it."

"Alas, Lord, the many fires that have ravaged this very church must have devastated the crypt, because the floor collapsed and burned, and the coffins — the remains — had to be removed. At the town hall outside there are still some gravestones from the former cemetery, which bordered the church, all crosses were also destroyed and they let the cemetery deteriorate."

While Philipp was still searching for but did not find a possible wall epitaph in the nave, the front part of which could also still be counted as part of the room "against the pulpit above", as it was called in an old document, Noth had found nothing behind the gravestones mentioned above outside at the back of the town hall.

"Are the church records still preserved?" Philipp then asked the sexton. "When the church was still Catholic, there were none and although much has been preserved from the earliest Protestant times, the plague left a lot of gaps in the records." The sexton was not able to indicate where they were kept now but he advised them to enquire at the municipal library. "Let us hurry to the library," Philipp urged and, after a last farewell glance at the historical church, the two researchers began their search for the more remote municipal library. To find their way to it, they had to cross the most ancient part of Nordhausen, a town that owed its foundation to Henry I. But their efforts were richly rewarded.

There was a lot of uphill and downhill climbing and accordingly a lot of picturesque nooks and crannies were revealed for which Philipp had a receptive eye. Nordhausen appeared to him to be a town similar to Glogau, which he had grown particularly fond of over the years. He felt like his great King, who had taken Glogau to his heart before all the other Silesian towns. He had been the first to fight for this fortress and had had to battle stubbornly for this property. The exchange and trade of Nordhausen could probably not be compared of course with Glogau and its beautiful Oder River, which formed a major traffic route for the East through its lively shipping traffic. He wondered what the small river Zorge offered that washed around the southern edge of the town. Yet the churches and squares, the fountains and flights of stairs, the wider streets, the very narrowly built, cramped corners of houses, the entire inner city, evoked memories of his dear Glogau.

His companion now was knocking triumphantly at an elongated low building. After the late guests had been directed up a dark hallway, at the end of which a steep staircase led to the upper floor. They found themselves upstairs in front of the door, behind which, according to its inscription, they might have guessed the city's publications and writings were located. A friendly old gentleman worked there, who, at Philipp's mentioning his own name and introducing his young companion, immediately turned out to be the longed-for head teacher Meyer. He was immediately ready to give all the assistance he could.

Once Philipp had explained his search for older town histories as the reason for their visit, he was able to obtain the extensive work of Kindervater, who had dealt with the town chronicle in an excellent manner on the basis of an in-depth study of the sources. Soon the foreign guests were sitting comfortably between the shelves with the opened folios and absorbed eagerly in the history of the time when Nordhausen was subjected to the Evangelion. While searching, Philipp found confirmation that it was precisely during this intervening period that the ancestors of his grandfather in the Harz Mountains or Harzgeroder had lived here in Nordhausen and how they had extended their benevolence as elected councillors and governing mayors for over a century.

Philipp, adept at summarizing significant details, was able to dictate to his young companion all the notes that the young theologian wrote down with eager attention. In between, the busy family researchers and the friendly authority of the library engaged in an animated question and answer session. Finally, the material to be collected resulted in such an abundance that the two inquisitive minds had to limit themselves to only noting the titles of the books and volumes in which the names and deeds of their forefathers were mentioned or described in more detail.

A beautiful reminder of that unforgettable great heyday of Nordhausen's spiritual life, of which the cathedral preacher Dr. Siegfriedus in Magdeburg wrote the testimony that Nordhausen was one of the first cities to accept the only sanctifying gospel.

"The gentlemen will find it in the Church of St. Blasii. There you will also see two larger paintings: An Ecce-Homo by Lucas Kranach the Elder and a poignant resurrection of Lazarus by Lucas Cranach the Younger. Above the latter of the two contemporary creations are portraits of all the reformers, Luther, Melanchthon, Jonas, Erasmus of Rotterdam, Bugenhagen, and whatever their names are. Nordhausen can be proud of the treasure of a family portrait of the famous mayor Michael Meyenburg[47], a friend and contemporary of your famous ancestor, also of Cranach, which is also kept in the Church of St. Blasii. However, I would like to caution against the handwritten record of a certain Ratzeburger about Luther and his time, which, for example, turns the events of the interim years literally upside down".

Extremely satisfied and grateful for all the excellent advice and the rich information, Philipp and the extremely enthusiastic Noth soon found themselves on the way to the Church of St. Blasii and from there, quite taken with Cranach's masterpieces, they returned to their inn.

"Thanks to the recommendation of our polite travel companion we have already reached our objective quite quickly today, so that you, my uncle, can even use tomorrow's mail coach to Nordheim and Hannover to meet the main post route through Westphalia to Kleve."

"We certainly have had exceptional good fortune here," said Philipp, "and my brother Heinrich will certainly be happy in Glogau when I can tell him about the forefathers of Nordhausen, who have secured an indelible memory for themselves in the old town history. I would gladly have used tomorrow to write to him and my sister in Mansfeld, but perhaps my nephew might be in the habit of having me recommended to the mother of your demoiselle bride for the time being, until I can give her my account from Kleve. I could thus report many things to her about the impressions from my journey."

A bulbous bottle was sitting in front of the two of them during the conversation and they slowly settled down in the garden in a cosy vine arbor after the evening meal. What was in front of them was real Nordhausen grain spirit, which they did honor to here in its homeland. After all, they could hardly have refused it from the landlord earlier on.

"It won't take too long today, just a few glasses of this fiery drink will do," consoled Philipp at the Nordhausen innkeeper's request, which had appeared somewhat dubious from the nephew, to indulge in such an evening drink.

"We also have to have checked the age of this bottle at its source, as we did my lineage's today," Philipp said cheerfully, pouring a good sample into the fearfully defensive candidate's glass.

"Don't be afraid, dear friend, we have often had to use the grain and the chewing tobacco, in order to satisfy our hunger in the field." Philipp also pulled out a packet of such a tobacco product, which he had secretly purchased earlier, encouraging the young theologian to take a sample of it as well.

"By the way, Martin Luther also chewed and spit and if you want to be a real Martin, you have to emulate him in everything."

"All right! But now, beloved Uncle, you must also keep your promise not to leave it at Kolin's defeat but to tell me about your other war experiences."

"Hail to the Great King!"

And with that the brave Martin Noth emptied his glass, drinking to his uncle's toast and promptly began the chewing procedure.

"Cheers! Then I don't want to be in your debt either — but where was I?" mused Philipp and secretly enjoyed the well-behaved nephews manner.

"We had just got as far as the march on Silesia," he eagerly assisted him, falling into it without hesitation.

"Yes, now the Prussians were suddenly there and if the King had not granted his army a day's rest and had left Leipzig the day before, he could have seized and crushed the weak and miserable imperial army on this side of the

Saale. However, it had its good points. If he had defeated Hildburghausen the previous day, he would never have had the cautious Soubise under his blade. Several days passed until the bridges at Weißenfels, Merseburg, Halle, destroyed by the allies, were rebuilt. The enemy had not attempted to make the Prussians' transition more difficult or to prevent it. Soubise, too, strengthened by twenty squadrons and just as many battalions from Richelieu's camp, believed that in view of the small Prussian army he could not be left behind now on account of his honor. On November fourth at four o'clock in the morning our troops marched off to the left to embrace the enemy on his right flank, the parties were only two hours apart.

"The enemy was estimated at sixty thousand men. The same had exchanged the unfavorable position scouted out by the King himself the previous night and was now in a camp that was sufficiently secured against a frontal attack by the forest on the right. Our King therefore went back via Schortau at nine o'clock in the morning and moved into his new camp between Rossbach and Bedra, opposite the enemy.

"There was loud rejoicing in the army of the allies and the battle roused in all units, the guns thundering after us as if it were Victoria who had to be shot. 'We only have the German lethargy to oppose the French fanfare,' said Frederick. The Reich troops had been without bread and forage for several days. In the high spirits of the moment, the Reich Field Marshal received approval for the offensive from the French general for the next day. It was decided to march right to Merseburg to jeopardize the Prussian line of retreat. His telescope in front of his eye, King Frederick watched the movements of his enemies from the first morning hour from the balcony of the Rossbach manor house (the manor house is today owned by the owner of the manor together with historical lookout of the King — the manor house has remained like this for a century and a half). He had roof tiles and shingles, as well as bricks removed to enlarge the opening.

"The squire provided information on the localities because scouts brought contradictory news. At last, he left his observation post and sat down to eat. Then at 2 o'clock Captain Gaudig brought him the news, at first received with complete disbelief, that the enemy was indeed advancing.

"Hurrying back to the roof, the King saw for himself how the marching columns instead of taking the road to Naumburg, were turning towards Lauchstädt, where the morass masking the Prussian camp at the front came to an end. Departure was ordered immediately. The horses were saddled in no time and within minutes the tents disappeared like a table decoration, to the astonishment of the enemy. We had about twenty-five battalions, thirty eight squadrons and a little over twenty thousand men at our disposal for the battle.

"The left wing intended for the attack was led by Prince Heinrich, the right wing, which was to hold back and seek cover behind Leihabach, by Prince Ferdinand of Brunswick. At half past two they marched off in the direction of the ridge that stretched towards Janus Hill. The Prince of Brunswick was assigned only the field guards, who were to be set up in a single thin line to give the appearance of cover.

"We, i.e. the entire remaining cavalry under the command of the youngest major general, 36-year-old Seydlitz, set off at a trot to the head of the infantry. The latter marched at the foot of the ridge, through the high ground, out of sight of the enemy. The cavalry of the allies at the head of the first and further marching columns still continued their march in two long parallels, unsuspectingly, when from Janus Hill the projectiles of a tremendously raised battery rushed towards them and at the same time man and steed appeared above the height behind Reichhardt's recruits on a long splendid front, 15 squadrons, dragoons, and the Life Cuirassiers in two branches.

"With our sabres in our clenched hands, we chased like lightning down the slope. The attached marching columns, one, as we learned later, seventy-six, the other seventeen squadrons deep, were taken completely by surprise by the sudden attack, enveloped and overthrown. Only the imperial cuirassier regiments, the dragoons of the Electoral Palatinate, the Ansbach and Württemberg had time to gather and now, under the leadership of the Reich Field Marshal, the attackers fell upon us. Head to head, the horses held against each other, the riders hit each other in the face and the imperials broke through. But already eighteen squadrons from the second Prussian lines are on the spot, led by Seydlitz himself. The retreating squadrons join up again and so everything, cuirassier, dragoon, hussar, went at the enemy like the Furies[48].

"At this point the horsemen of the Imperial Army have already become invisible. Broglie is now intervening in the battle with fourteen squadrons of infantry and the Raugraf is apparently blasting from the other side with eight squadrons — in vain! Everything has to clear the battlefield and leave the infantry to its fate. It had not been taken by surprise like the cavalry, because the Prussian battalions, left behind in the battle, only emerged when the cavalry fight was already raging.

"They push the battalions of the left wing diagonally towards the enemy in a well-arranged squadron. The King leads the regiment 'Old Brunswick', twenty paces ahead of the front. A wide ditch does not deter those who are hurrying forward. The most agile climb the slope and pulling their comrades by the arm, quickly reposition, continuing to storm the line. 'Father out of the way, so we can shoot!' the Musketeers shout to the King, 'The French infantry, whose fire you received, has already disappeared.'

"Now a ravine cuts across the regiment and forces it to split. At this moment the cavalry comes blasting in and the King vehemently orders the cavalry to close the gap. When this doesn't work, he shouts to the musketeers to get their act together pronto. A well-prepared volley drives the enemy riders up into flight — their leader falls. The victory was ours.

"All in all, only seven of our battalions came to fire, the infantry firefight lasted only ¼ hour and all order among the enemy was broken in a flash. The second rally had fled first, either because it feared coming under the blade of Seydlitz or without any reason.

"The French battle reports could only relate that it was incomprehensible how things had happened. No sooner had Soubise had a battalion together again than a bit of bullet would go flying between them and everyone would scatter like sheep again. The Prussian cavalry, which was preparing to follow, encountered obstacles due to the rapidly incoming force in the intersected terrain. While trying to take a ditch, behind which a thin infantry still remained, Seydlitz, like Prince Heinrich before him, was wounded. I, too, received a bullet in my left arm while digging the trench, but I was still able to hold the reins and swing my sabre with my right hand.

"At the height of Obschuetz, the King made us all stop. We camped under the open sky — the cold was biting. The soldiers gathered the enemy's rifles, piled them up and lit the shafts to make watch fires. All around, from each regiment, the solemn chorales rose up to the night sky.

"The consecration of the hour made a deep impression on all of us and the pious devotion of the rough Prince Moritz particularly moved the audience. The King took his night's lodgings in the Hall at Burgwerben. The lady of the castle had to give up her linen to make bandages for the wounded French. From here he dispatched an adjutant who had to bring the message of victory to his wife in Magdeburg. Not until the next day did the full extent of the success become apparent.

"There was a little verse on everyone's lips in our camp:
Here comes the great Frederick and slaps his pants,
And the whole Imperial Army,
Pandurs and Frenchmen run like ants."

"That was wonderful, Herr Lieutenant," cried the candidate Martin enthusiastically and filled the narrator's glass without hesitation. "Hurray for Seydlitz and all his cuirassiers!" "You don't have to grease them when you go all the way." Isn't that what it says in some soldier's rhyme?"

"Perhaps," replied Philipp with a smile, "but the main thing is yet to come." And without bringing the fiery water to his mouth, he continued, "So this was our much-praised Battle of Rossbach and one must always admire the genius of our King for having instigated this coup. Now it was time for us all to leave there as quickly as possible — on to Silesia!

"The concentric advance was immediately directed at Leuthen, the attack being carried out by the outer right wing of the Prussians as advance troops. The King chose his location in the grove of Radaxdorf, where he was able to get a view of, not only the fire on Austrian troops but also his own batteries. The battle for Leuthen lasted about an hour. Behind the village new resistance was waiting for us. In the end all Prussian battalions were caught in the line of fire, a precarious turn of events that did not correspond at all to the intentions of our commanders. But the Prussian cavalry is in a very different position today than on June 18 at Kolin. A huge cavalry encounter begins, the enemy is thrown everywhere, seized in front, flank and back, what escapes the broadsword of the Prussians, flees in all directions.

"During this battle I received two sabre blows in the leg and had to be carried from the battlefield, weakened by blood loss. However, bandaged up, I was soon back in the saddle. The King had hurried with us Seydlitz cuirassiers and some cannons to Lissa. From time to time cannon shots were fired to keep the fleeing ones from getting the chance to catch their breath.

"Shortly before Lissa, we were greeted with fire by a large bunch of stragglers as well as from the windows of the little town. The King, however, had our cannons fired at the exit of the bridge, thus securing the town and the river crossing for the next day.

"Then he did something astonishing — it happened at the castle of Baron von Mudrach — the Austrian officers who had been cut off when he said, 'Good evening, Gentlemen, I dare say you did not expect me here. Can one get a night's lodging along with you?'". The King took a meagre supper and slept on a litter, just as his opponent Charles is said to have slept in his bed the night before under the same roof as his opponent.

"While the King then prepared for the siege of Wroclaw, Zieten followed the defeated army with fifty-five squadrons and eleven battalions. On December 20, Field Marshal Sprecher von Bernegg capitulated with the fortress of Breslau and almost 18,000 men. Liegnitz handed over Colonel von Bülow in exchange for free withdrawal of the occupational forces. The siege or recapture of Schweidnitz was suspended until spring, as severe frost had set in.

"A 'Now thank we all our God' went everywhere through the churches of the German countryside, as was already intoned after the battle of Leuthen. When the King and his troops were finally allowed to rest around New Year's Day, I came to Breslau to see my liberated brother Wilhelm, in order to recuperate during the winter. In spring I went to my brother Heinrich's estate, as my leg wounds were festering constantly and I was visibly losing my strength.

"How I got into the captivity of the Cossacks there, who took me out of bed, tied me between their horses and dragged me through the Oder River is a sad chapter that I prefer to ignore. For the rest of the war I sat in Poland in their and the Russians' captivity until I was finally among the first prisoners to be exchanged through brother Heinrich's constant pleas. I have already mentioned this once. But I am proud of the scars on my arm and leg and hope to be able to serve my King as an official for a long time to come. Hail our great Frederick!"

Finally, the narrator got up with a final, sturdy movement, asking his young listener to take a little tour with him through the city that had now fallen silent. "My mail coach will arrive here at noon tomorrow — we can sleep in, especially since you, dear nephew, also want to stay here in Nordhausen tomorrow and your mail coach will not leave until the day after tomorrow."

How the ancient imperial city lay there, so quiet and carefree, with its walls and towers, over which the consequences of the Seven Years' War were still a rich blessing. Nordhausen grain spirit, Nordhausen chewing tobacco and Nordhausen lard, the three coveted trade articles during the war years had brought the city near the Golden Meadow a significant prosperity and the economic boom had also favored a cultural advancement. Only the politics of the free imperial city had remained a fatal monster. Through eternal tariff squabbles, around which petty quarrels were fought with the neighboring Prussia, the great King, disgusted, had pushed the Nordhausen lawyers aside with a dismissive hand movement, replying that the trials were full of loathsome chicanery. Thus a great time and in it a great spirit simply walked over a decrepit and senile structure of idiosyncrasy, as Nordhausen now portrays, as if it were a matter of course.

Only very recently it had already lost its beautiful cannon, the so-called 'Lindworm', and had thus forfeited its most precious piece of German craftsmanship next to the magnificently carved choir stalls of its old cathedral, which had remained Catholic. Once before, an attempt had been made to incorporate the free imperial city into a principality but now all omens seemed to indicate that the Kingdom of Prussia would not tolerate the neighboring small-scale economy and special position of a narrow-minded city for long.

"I, for my part, can only hope that my ancestral city will soon be incorporated into our Prussian Kingdom," Philipp concluded the conversation about the political situation to which the nocturnal walk through the mountainous streets and alleys had provided the inspiration.

"What a rich and exquisite day it has been," the young theologian said to himself, as he was used to letting the utilization of his time and the course of the day flow past him before his evening prayer of thanksgiving. "What a whole man he was, his future uncle. How worldly-wise and warlike, how well-versed in history and politics. Why had he never married? Surely the female sex has not scorned this tall equestrian officer — how many hearts must not have set his glowing eyes on fire. And how those eyes sparkled and shone when he spoke of his King and the days of his own participation in the battles had been erased from his memory yet in every detail had come to life again. All of this experience had been etched in his memory with a pen of iron and yet it was a pity that such an enthusiastic soldier should have been simply discharged into ordinary life, having to lay aside his unusual powers in his prime.

"What glorious discipline the great king nurtured among his soldiers. What a contrast between such training of the mind in contrast to the rampant pietism that now spread among the educated classes. No, this exuberant sentimentality, which today everywhere, through the literature of poets and writers, has been gushing out into the heroically inclined soul of the Germanic tribe, was something contrary to nature."

Yet the reflecting young scholar of God stuck to his position. This veneration of French and thus effeminate Romanism, to which the Great King, so highly esteemed by his uncle, and his indifference to the sounds of the German language, was in his opinion the main reason why today a book like "The Sorrows of Young Werther" could incomprehensibly cause a sensation and even find life-weary imitators! Ah! How much more he would like to know about the judgement of this uncle, who is so profoundly endowed with such composure. Tomorrow their paths should part and he himself would return to the small provincial town of Rossla with its moderate forms and customs of a time that was dying away. How his own heart longed for experience and upliftment. Already the early red glow was shining into his small sleeping chamber. Finally he found his accustomed equilibrium again after a short morning slumber.

Neither had his room neighbor and yesterday's companion Philipp found much sleep, despite the nocturnal stroll, from which he hoped a reflection of his all too vivid images of the past. When he returned home, the servant who shone a light into his room had already told him that an express letter had been delivered for him at a late hour, which had been placed on his table in his room upstairs.

"From Maria," had been his first thought but in the light of the now ignited lamp he recognized the handwriting and seal of his brother Heinrich in Glogau and wondered what he had to tell him here in Nordhausen in such a hurry. Then he read immediately the accompanying words to an insert in the letter, "That you make it possible to assist our cousin in this marriage and represent our family is not only the request of cousin Johann Heinrich Lucanus[49] but also my own urgent wish. We owe it to the memory of our blessed mother to maintain every connection with Halberstadt and its relatives. It is you in particular, who received so much kindness and help from the President, Uncle Johann Heinrich, before his death. You know how much I and we Silesian brothers all owe him and you will do your utmost to arrive in Halberstadt on time.

"According to cousin Henriette Charlotte, Uncle Wilhelm's eldest daughter, who has been married to local councillor Heyer in Halberstadt for two years, her brother Johann Heinrich, who is also the godchild of the late Mr. Uncle Wilhelm, the President, is also linked to our family through his bride. You will remember that our deceased wife sister-in-law Pasewalk, Margaret, née Doering, was also from Harzgerode. Our oldest brother met her when he was a young student visiting his grandparents in their house. The bride who now intends to bring Johann Heinrich home, Susanna Doering, is a godchild of our deceased sister-in-law. As I was told here by the latter son Friedrich Leberecht, who stayed with me for eight days on his onward journey to brother Wilhelm in Breslau, she was born in the same year to brother Doering in Güsten, just like his parents in Berg before our brother came to Pasewalk.

"You will surely know how to find the relatives in Halberstadt. Our uncle Wilhelm, the bridegroom's father, who still keeps the famous library in his father's house in Westendorff, has been thinking about this. Friedrich Johann Lucanus wants to acquire three estates in the district of Glogau: Malschwitz, Herrenlauersitz and Irrsingen in addition to the Setria Estate inherited from his father. Moving the book collection from Halberstadt to Malschwitz, where Friedrich Johann wants to add a special room for it is now necessary. Uncle Wilhelm doesn't want to provide space for it anymore, since it is now supposed to amount to about four to five thousand volumes. You will find this valuable and to be in the spirit of the family and scholarly passion of your maternal grandfather and his four equal sons in Halberstadt. In the not too distant future I will probably meet them here in Silesia.

"We saw the beginnings of this when we were children in grandfather Simon Heinrich's study. You won't remember it as well as I do — you were still small when he died, whereas I was already 14 years old. How I would like to refresh all the memories of my childhood in the old house in Westendorff. Give my best regards to the elder two brothers of our beloved dear mother and all the relatives and friends present there. Don't miss greeting Uncle Friedrich, whom I often see here in Guaritz. He should be in Halberstadt for the festival. And don't miss having the deed of the president's fief title shown to you in the library. It shall be a second *documento familiae*.

"We Silesian brothers send a piece of the finest Silesian linen as the bride's wedding present, which your cousin Johann Heinrich should announce immediately. Our dear mother would certainly have gone to the marriage of her youngest brother's daughter, if she were still alive. I hope that this letter will reach you, since you wanted to surprise the Eineckes with your visit in Erdenborn. Since you have probably spent a few days with her, and since I suspect that you must rent a riding horse in Nordhausen for the bride and since such a horse is not cheap, I will send you two Friedrichs d'or[50] to the Lucanus' in Halberstadt.

"Apart from you, no one from our Hecklingen family, except brother Christian in Lübeck, could accept the invitation, because our brother Friedrich Ernst does not like celebrations and Carl in Kleve expects new additions to the family and, as he writes, has to save for his young wife's childbirth. Write soon and more about how you and all those you have already seen again are doing.

"You are still expected in Kleve in September. If possible, arrange your onward journey so that you don't arrive at the house before the baptism of your sister-in-law's youngest. Even better—if you arrive earlier find another lodging. Louise sends her regards. Mr. Cramer asks to be allowed to recommend himself to you.

"Your faithful and sincere brother Heinrich, Glogau, the 8th Julius 1774"

The reader now slowly unfolded the insert of the letter that contained an invitation in the ornate style of fashion, richly framed with cupids and elegantly engraved inscription, to the wedding of the demoiselle Dorothea Doering with Mr. Johann Heinrich Lucanus to the very honorable Uncle Heinrich and Philipp zu Glogau in Silesia on the 20th Julius 1774. For a while the recipient of the message stood dazed in front of the two sheets, then he moved his chair to the light and read the letter of his brother Heinrich a second time. As suddenly as this unexpected change in his entire travel program had come upon him at the last hour, so firm was his decision now as an unalterable obligation of duty in his mind.

To deny his brother Heinrich, who had always been as kind as a father from the time he joined the army until today, a wish that he even called urgent—no! That simply could not be! Then, in memory of his mother, so dearly beloved, the task of standing in for her among her own was also considered an equally great duty of love.

Now he thought flittingly about the travel changes to be made the next morning. There was no possibility of postponement. The wedding ceremony took place in three days, scarcely could he manage the ride across the Harz Mountains in the time remaining in between. In Kleve they did not expect him yet! Yes, his commencement of service first required him there on October 1.

No one could have guessed that the Rhine had recently gained a completely different attraction—Maria! When he thought of his beloved creature, every brief interruption increased in intensity and an obstacle to be pushed aside until he was able to introduce her into the home he had created for her there. The longing to be allowed to work and create something for her now was silent, however and when he spoke of sober reality and reason, he had to say to himself, "It may still take weeks, months, until her pastor picks her up from her relatives in Questenberg, alas! And it will be just as long until I have first worked my way into the ministry and the probationary period has become a permanent position." Deep down, he was already considering the idea — following the example of his brother in Glogau, in addition to his work in the government — of looking for a nearby country estate and buying it as their married home.

He had lived all his years since his return from war captivity like a hermit — already 10 years — and only saved and saved and saved to suddenly sit as a free man on his own patch. In the meantime, land ownership had become unaffordable in Silesia but on the Rhine it was supposed to be cheap to have your own little estate. Indeed, his heart was drawn there but reason told him to wait and see. Autumn is a good time for land acquisition — be patient! — be patient until then. Until then is still the free summer time, until then are the days of roses. How he had intended to make use of and enjoy this free time of unbound, wonderful wandering through the dear German land. And now what?

> *O love, how are you so lovely?*
> *Oh love, that came over me mighty.*
> *Oh love that took all my will away.*
> *Silence of lips and silence of gaze.*
> *I flee to thee lost and crazed,*
> *O love to thee, my bliss always!*

He wrote these lines in his notebook and then first went to his resting place in the early hours of the morning.

III

Halberstadt

The next morning, he had already discussed with the landlord in the inn the purchase of a horse accustomed to the mountains and had now inspected a strong, inexpensive animal. He mounted it for a short test ride on the nearby footpath along the rushing River Zorge and met the rather surprised candidate there, who he assumed would have still been having sweet dreams. The latter had felt the desire to offer his uncle a modest gift of remembrance as a farewell gift and to substantiate his extraordinary morning walk, he pulled out a delicate little booklet which he handed to his uncle on horseback, somewhat awkwardly.

"I believed it to be suitable, for example, the verses that the uncle had written so loosely on loose sheets of paper, just as the great King carried the unforgettable verses with him at Kyffhausen, in order to keep them better protected. I hope that at our next reunion some exquisite verses will already be hidden in the unimposing cover."

Visibly pleased and grateful, the rider accepted the very dearest notebook bound in finest leather and reserved the right to contribute a useful poem as a wedding gift in honor of the fiancée of the giver.

A short time later, Philipp was already familiar with his Rocinante, an amazingly well broken in mare, along the banks of the Zorge now following the road into the mountains. He left the famous and popular preserve, the park of Nordhausen, at the top of the hill and soon was drawing in the strong forest air of the Harz hills, unbound, fresh and free. He was quite lonely here, far from the noise and traffic of the city. The only amusements up here were his own thoughts. How right it had been for him to leave Maria in the care of her relatives and not to take her away from Questenberg with him, as she had so implored. The question was, how could he have taken her with him to his formally and morally strict Protestant relatives in Halberstadt, if she had already gone through the world with him before she was his wife. Certainly not before his brother and his numerous relatives, who were so much older and had always opposed him pedagogically.

It was the only sensible and right thing he had decided to do, even though it might have seemed so difficult in Maria's presence and so cold and harsh to her pure trusting mind. But honor demanded it so! Such was life. An idyll like the one they had enjoyed together in Questenberg, there was no time in his rough existence where he had ever found and experienced anything like it. In such a calm mood, after he had left the towers of the imperial city and the home of his family that had become so familiar to him, far behind him, he realized that he had already reached the foot of the Netzberg along the course of the Baehre, a tributary of the Zorge.

As the horse seemed to be a magnificent climber, he should be able to reach Hasselfelde by the evening and spend the night in Blankenburg tomorrow evening. From then on, the Harz mountains with their ups and downs were vanquished and its roads would soon lead him on the third morning over the Regenstein to his destination Halberstadt. It was almost too delightful riding through the forest again — and what a forest! He would never have dreamed that on this journey, on which he had chosen the ultimate pleasure of hiking along the eastern edge of the Harz Mountains from Harzgerode to the southern edge and the golden floodplain, he would today ride right across the most beautiful part of the northeastern Harz Mountains to land at the northern edge with the people he loved.

At any rate, he knew that he would find a post carriage opportunity in Halberstadt, which had a connection once or twice a week with the major route via Hanover and Westphalia directly to Kleve. It was much easier—that he had not thought of it himself!—to get from Halberstadt on the northern edge of the Harz to the Lower Rhine than to Nordhausen from the southern Harz. Now he was happy about his brother's letter and that he had not for a moment hesitated to fulfill his wish. From Hasselfelde, not on the big road but the side track to the beautiful lookout points and caves was familiar to him. They covered the whole area of the Regenstein standing, as he now vividly recalled from his youth, on sandstone formations and the famous Devil's Wall.

He could no longer remember his grandfather Lucanus, who had already died in 1737, one year after he had celebrated his golden wedding with his fourteen years younger wife at the age of 79, as he had only been three years old at that time. However, he remembered his grandmother, a née Kuehne, who had a rich and famous library of more than twelve hundred volumes from the pride of the grandparents' houses. It had had a considerable attraction for him from an early age. When his mother, usually with a larger crowd—a selection of six festively decorated children from the twelve brothers and sisters—came to visit their parents' house in Halberstadt, then, to celebrate this always large country outing, they went to the Harz Mountains and usually only travelled a short distance by post coach but from then on the rest of the journey was made by cart. However, the mother was not present at the golden wedding celebrations.

The only thing he did not know was the southern Harz mountains and the places his map told him. Illfeld, the Berneckenstein plateau, surrounded by spruce forests, which he must have ridden through already, offered him new unknown landscapes. The next day he went to the Braunschweig area. He hoped to see the most beautiful part of the whole tour again with the rocky heights and the famous Herrmann and Baumann Caves[51] in Ruebeland. He was currently passing through magnificent beech forests and approaching the destination that had been set for the day.

His first night's lodging in Hasselfelde was already behind him. The next morning, after a blessed dreamless deep sleep, was even brighter than the day before. His horse enjoyed the wonderful silence of the forest and the strong smell of the dewy mosses and the fern-rich ground as much as he did. His gait seemed to him to be quicker and more agile than on the first day, even though the terrain was much deeper than on the previous day. Now he had already passed through Ruebeland and soon was crossing the Blankenburg forest area.

Many a red deer in the animal park fled in a hurry when the sound of hooves on the lonely forest paths frightened them. Old memories came back to him of the time when he had joined the Halberstadt cuirassier regiment as a young officer candidate, when he had often ridden on his brown horse in free periods and still more often to nearby Blankenburg, where the beautiful castle owned by the prince elector family (at the beginning of the century) of the Counts Blankenburg enchanted him anew on this day. One could see from the whole, magnificently kept environment of garden and forests and the never-ending nature reserve that the castle itself was the scene of splendid wealth.

Through the marriage of a daughter of this house to the Emperor Charles of Austria, Princess Christine Elisabeth of Blankenburg was the mother of Empress Maria Theresa, who had become so hostile to his great King. Another Blankenburg woman had been married to a son of Peter the Great—the uncouth Tsarevich Alexei[52].

Regenstein, with its castle ruins of the Counts Rheinstein[53], also offered a rich wreath of legends and historical memories of medieval feuds. Especially one Count Albert von Reinstein, a real robber baron, lived in constant battles with the Bishop of Halberstadt. Captured, freed again and then finally stabbed to death by a Halberstadt captain, Rudolph von Derstatt, this looting count would be the most splendid plot for a novel. Like Philipp, who was trotting along his way and now in the streets of Halberstadt, at the notorious site of the heroic deeds of the eerily beautiful Devil's Wall in the evening twilight, he was longing inwardly to leave this loneliness and to reach the old, towered bishop's town of Halberstadt that day if possible—even if late in the light of the full moon.

So it was in fact shortly after midnight that he stopped in front of the time-honored inn "The Golden Stallion", first taking care, as any good soldier, of his beautiful horse, which had brought him here so faithfully and efficiently. In his heart he was moved with joy to be allowed to rest once again within the gates of the so beloved starting point of his military career. He, a mature man was, almost like a child, looking forward to the next day—to the new, already approaching reunion with his relatives and acquaintances with whom he had not visited for so long— probably about eighteen years since when he had entered the seven-year war.

Surely his patron of the bards and poet friend Gleim[54] was also still alive. Of course, the much-loved war bard, the Prussian grenadier singer, would appear at the wedding and would certainly bring a new romance to the bride and groom. How good it was that he had not missed anything in Gleim's latest production Halladat, published only that year, or the red book that his uncle Lucanus in Breslau revered. He was now able to quote verses from it —but wait—no! He would prefer to greet him with a similar self-made oriental parable full of wisdom.

And so he straightaway tried to scribble the first two lines in his honor:

Hail to my friend, the dearest of the youth.
Hail Gleminde, guardian of domestic truth.
Where would I find a home like yours?
How lovely...

Unfortunately, the inspiration of our tired rider failed at this point, embraced by Morpheus' arm, slumbering gently towards a happy morning, without completing the verses that he had begun. The reception in the circle of the festive house was even more beautiful than he had imagined. It was jubilant and charming when he was allowed to congratulate the lovely bride, a real blonde Germanic woman in her youth, a wonderfully lovely rosebud, surrounded by a whole garland of charming playmates as the centre of the homage—but no less than the teasing banter of his own brothers-in-law in the familiar old living room.

There the celebrated bride was sitting leisurely, just as a spectator in the midst of the wreaths of honor of meandering youth.

"How mother will rejoice at her prompt arrival when she had hardly nourished any hope. She has only gone into town for a short time and will soon return. I think I can hear her already." At which point she escaped his hands to tell her the good news.

After he had paid his respects to the always-kind Aunt Marie, the mistress of the house, he felt the warmth of the family that surrounded him everywhere in the home. His childhood memories came back to life and fluttered around him like caresses of the present, not at all like fading ones from his youth. Only then did he realize deep inside what he had been missing in all those years in Silesia, despite living together with his first brothers, who were faithful to their duties but only rarely were they cheerful—at least in his presence.

The eternally feminine, that's what it was that so easily and gracefully flowed towards him here and so magically captivated him.

Amidst the bubbling chatter and the questioning and answering, the elder sister of the bride addressed him,

"Perhaps cousin Philipp may also remember the French house of Canon Kopstadt?", the elder sister of the bride said to him in the course of the effervescent speech, and the questions and answers.

"I believe my wife Aunt Dore in Hecklingen also knew him, because he is, although much younger, a well-known personality in Halberstadt with his lively enthusiasm for the arts and sciences."

"Just as our poet Gleim is Canon of Waldbeck Abbey, Mr. Kopstadt has become senior canon of the Drübeck Abbey, if I am not mistaken, and our father admires him very much," the bridegroom thought.

"It will be a great honor for me to get to know Canon Kopstadt, as far as I remember, I have not heard anything from him through my dear mother."

Here the talk was interrupted by the entrance of the host, a jovial sixty year old, who welcomed his guest with outstretched hands.

"That's what I call old family loyalty!" he shouted enthusiastically. "As far as the Royal Prussian province of Silesia, dear boy, you have found your way to the old motherhouse. Bravo! This is the eighth son of our dear departed Dore—now comes the time to solemnly hand over the second set of Döring literature to the freeman. But give me some wine, you women! Such a real, genuine right family cousin dies of thirst among you busy cousins. All honor to wreaths and flower—first the welcome drink this hour!"

"Father! Father! You're making poetry again! Uncle Gleim should hear that," shouted the housewife cheerfully to him, while kindly handing the red Burgundy wine to the couple. How quickly the hours passed in the lively conversation with the old and the young, until in the evening the closest friends of the house and the bride's dearest companions with their brothers were expected to attend the amusing opening celebration.

Philipp was allowed only a short break in his inn, to change his clothes for a larger social gathering and, once again child of the house, he helped with the last preparations for the reception of the guests. How many valuable personalities, old friends and new acquaintances, the former Halbestädt cuirassier would meet at the wedding feast! And with what pride the householder and housewife introduced him to their rich circle of friends. Of course, he had put on his beautiful uniform again to celebrate the wedding and showed himself in the full adornment of his former outfit in his now fully mature male beauty and dignity. Without question he was an embellishment to the festive gathering and the mischievous poet friend Gleim would most likely have wished to have sung the praises of this rare and chivalrously outstanding guest in his Anacreontic hymns of praise[55], would it not have been a sacrilege against the bridal couple who were the ones to be celebrated.

But Philipp himself was again quite a part of the cheerful and spiritual circles. His joking courtly conversation was the source of much excitement at the dinner table, as if he were a guest of his own King Fritz and one witty anecdote after the other, which he had to tell, kept almost the whole group in suspense. Also Canon Kopstadt soon found himself among his, albeit silent, admirers and took the first opportunity to find out about the personal details of this cousin of the house. The same seemed to him to be of the same calibre as the philanderers, for he saw the eyes of the girls all around him shining brighter when a smile played around the proudly determined mouth of the man. Especially when the charming and skilful narrator gave himself over with visible pleasure to the effect that his conversation was having.

Nobody, however, was more grateful than the bridegroom's parents for the guest's astounding unveiling, for after the dinner table was cleared, the cheerfulness of the youth was undoubtedly now at its best. The bridegroom at the head first drew the festive polonaise through the hall and it was followed by gavottes and dainty minuets of the popular dance styles of the rococo period in colorful variety. The older guests—that is to say, the gentlemen—were soon sitting in the master's room to enjoy a delicious peach punch. After the bride and groom had been celebrated and the first glass had been emptied to their health and their future progress in the "flowery meadows of life, danced around by geniuses and amourettes," Canon Kopstadt, who was dedicated to deeper research, was eager to learn more about the new imposing "disciple of Mars"

No sooner had he begun with his introductory question, "How, dear friend Lucanus are you..." than the door opened and the newcomer, not yet expressed in the wording of the question, bowed and asked the question modestly but confidently in all directions: "Is it allowed?" and at a nod from the host pulled a chair up to him, in the middle of the stunned circle and placed it right next to the Canon of Kopstadt.

"But my dear nephew Philipp, you don't dance?" questioned the master of the house in amazement. However, Philipp, accustomed to such surprises from Breslau and Glogau, gallantly assured him, "I would love to do it with all my heart, my uncle, but the French bullets in my shot limbs unfortunately do not allow me to do so after yesterday's ride."

Perhaps this was just an excuse for Maria's sake. While the ice had melted and the stage was set for the curiosity of Canon Kopstadt, Philipp was encouraged by the audience to let his favorite topics of conversation open to give free rein to the men waiting to hear it from his lips. It was always a pleasure for him to be able to talk about his beloved King and then to tell the tales about his own victorious battles under the firm eyes and under the leadership of the ingenious young Major General Friedrich Wilhelm von Seydlitz, who was well known there. He managed to tell about the Halberstadt cavalry charge and about his own experiences in 1757 in a very abbreviated form.

However, when they wanted to sound him out how he had fared in the later battles in Silesia and in the Mark, he limited himself to reporting on the victorious defense of Glogau by the King's quick decision to march on Braunau in order to get to the Russians first, as well as on the decision of Berlin in the victorious battle of Kinersdorf, the attentive, sensitive Kopstadt first felt that the story lacked a personal touch, so he asked warmly, "And where has this wartime fate led you yourself, Lieutenant?"

"Into the captivity of the inhumane Cossacks," was the somewhat bitter sounding reply, forcing the excellent man to regret having asked this question. At this point, however, the elderly Gleim, who liked to feed his innocent but somewhat banal mockery, came into the conversation, "What? The little tykes are said to have dared to take on a martial giant like you, young friend — rather — you had allowed them to do so?"

"Whether I allowed it or not, dear Uncle Gleim — I still call you as I did when I was a boy at my blessed mother's side — the cruel beasts did not ask me that. In the winter of 1757/1758 I was still lying on my brother's property with my wounds lame in bed, when the wild hordes, snorting on their little steppe horses, attacked the property and razed it to the ground within an hour. My brothers salvaged themselves to the other side of the Oder but I, without any clothes, as I was — all my uniform pieces were still in Lauerschütz the estate of Uncle Lucanus which they had already devastated in the meantime — only got as far as a nearby grove and collapsed there unconscious as a result of my loss of blood from the loosening of my bandage while running.

"But the wild beasts left neither tree nor bush untouched and hacked down everything in the grove. So they must have found me lifeless there too, because they tied a rope around my body, tied me up between two horses and pulled me through the Oder River. The cold of the river, together with the most terrible pain, brought consciousness back to me. So they dragged me as a war trophy in front of General Totleben[56], who had settled on another estate of my brother.

"After my personal details had been ascertained there, I was taken to the Poznan fortress in Poland the next day with a transport of wounded and held in captivity there for the entire campaign.

"My brother Heinrich tried again and again to get me released but Totleben was his sworn enemy, although my brother was known to him as the lawyer or jurisconsult of the great Frederick as his civil defender throughout Silesia. All complaints and efforts were of no avail and I had to remain in strictest custody in Poznan until the end of the war."

"And what has the king done to compensate you for your suffering?" asked a guest who had listened with pity to the reluctant reports of the splendid scene.

"The King? Our great Frederick? After the peace treaty he discharged me as well as all the other officers he had to dismiss for reasons of economy. As you know, he can only keep the best of the nobility in his small standing army. So I became a lieutenant who had just been discharged with a small pension but with the right to be employed elsewhere in the civil service, as well as the permission to continue to wear the uniform of His Majesty in honor on special occasions.

"Is that all?" remarked the disappointed questioner.

"Thus I have been a privy government secretary in Wroclaw for ten years and at the same time I have been managing my brother's estates as a farmer. Since there is no prospect of advancement in the Wroclaw government and my brother has already sold some of his properties and still wants to sell others, while he owns a convenient town house in Glogau, he advised me to report to the Kleve government, i.e. to the War and Domain Chamber, where the oldest of my brothers has been working as a judicial councilor for almost 30 years. I was accepted there in autumn of this year as a privy government secretary on probation and have now used my vacation and interrupted my trip to Kleve to support my cousin Susanna's marriage tomorrow."

"Again a Tellheim,[57]" Gleim interjected here almost unwillingly, "do we not have the fate of Major von Tellheim, also one of the wounded war victims who were so mercilessly thrown out of the army into the civilian world after the long campaign, in our honored guest before us? Such a splendid specimen of God's creation, the apple of every mother's eye, the heartthrob of all lovely daughters, wanders as a bachelor through the worldly misery, because his pride does not allow him to finance himself through marriage, so to speak. He cannot, after all, start a family from his own meager official salary. How excellently my Lessing has shown all this to the world in his Tellheim — the heroism and grandeur of our great King's officers.

"Now, dear wounded friend, don't let your Minna mourn any longer. Not all Minnas are as energetic and purposeful women as this funny Minna von Barnhelm, who was presented to us by the magnificent Lessing. You have seen the new play 'The Soldier's Fortune' by him, which I think must have conquered all the theatres by now. I don't know the play, but I do know the poet. I have often met with him and his patron, General von Tauentzien[58], in Breslau. It was also Lessing who was commissioned by the general in Breslau to solemnly proclaim the Peace of Hubertusburg. I had just returned from captivity and was forgotten amongst the cheers of the Silesian people."

"With this Voltaire love from the great Frederick it is almost incomprehensible that he could not win this German Lessing for Prussia," Canon Kopstadt took the floor. "After La Croye's death the position at the Royal Library in Berlin had become vacant and I know how eagerly and warmly my friend the colonel Jellius or Guitschard stood up for Lessing before the King. Two or three times he proposed him, until the King resented this unmoved reference to a German by Guitschard, whom he had entrusted with the reoccupation of the position and he committed himself over his head to the French Benedictine Rouanne.

"And what did they end up with in Berlin! A completely unfit, old-fashioned, superstitious clergyman who was a laughing stock for enlightened men of letters."

"Where is the rejected Lessing now?" Another listener warmly inquired.

"I thought he went from Breslau to Hamburg," replied Kopstadt, "because that's where his fine dramatic composition dates from—he is said to have turned his attention entirely to the theater. But Father Gleim will know for sure—we'd better ask him."

Father Gleim, who as the head of the Halberstadt Literary Society[59], was so called by young and old all over the town, had silently been listening to the conversation for a while but now replied willingly.

"The Hamburg theatre era is over for my Lessing too and not without bitter disappointments. However, the Crown Prince of Brunswick, who recognized my friend's value, has appointed him to what is probably the most extensive library in Germany for several years. Lessing is now a librarian in Wolfenbüttel, not far from us. He has already given the world a new work, this time a tragedy, 'Emilia Galotti'[60], which has received great admiration from the critics.

"Right," the old Lucanus interjected, "isn't it the old Roman legend of father Virginius stabbing his daughter Virginia to save her from a lecher? Lessing has transposed this process into the Italian modern age in a stunning manner, especially the dialogue is a masterpiece."

"I am glad that you also agree with the praise of the poet, even if you may not exactly agree with the struggle in the religious field in some other questions that are now very much on his mind. Let us leave that alone today! I would still like to hear something about your new nephew Philipp—doesn't he have any heroic deeds of his own to tell us?"

"Dear Uncle Gleim, this is something that is best kept quiet in larger circles. It seems to me that I have just told you my whole life story and that you yourself could supplement my childhood. You already knew me when I was still playing with a feathered hat and a shooting rifle. In the heat of the battle with my playmates, I crushed the beautiful flowerbeds of your famous flower garden and even smashed the fence. Speaking of that, dear Uncle, how is your beautiful garden these days? May I take the liberty of paying it a visit tomorrow?"

As Gleim then invited the questioner to his home the next day, the subject was directed from the past to the present and Canon Kopstadt nodded silently, with his face marked by finely cut features, as if still thinking about everything he had heard, processing the thought he had mentioned, he remarked to Philipp, "If only this exclusively aristocratic officer corps—and the discharge of such splendid people and such capable men as you young friend here seems to be one, just because he comes from a middle-class family—will not take revenge once again upon the Prussian Kingdom?"

He peeked over as if wondering what his friend Lucanus thought. However, Lucanus did not feel moved to continue criticizing the way his great and righteous King acted and thought. Gleim, however, turned back to the past and patted Philipp on the shoulder, saying with a meaningful look, "I am not going to do that," he said, "all of Halberstadt can still tell stories about your mother, namely in 1736, when your grandparents celebrated the rare celebration of their golden wedding anniversary here, the blooming young parish priest's wife from Hecklingen is said to have appeared, surrounded by her twelve children, to convey his congratulations to the parents. Friedrich Leberecht, the eldest son—already a young parish priest—recited a beautiful poem of thanksgiving and supplication to God for the grace granted to his grandparents, that his parents might also enjoy the same. I only recently came across his beautiful poem here in the Lucan Library. Uncle Wilhelm must show it to you. I myself was one of twelve children but how few grew up. You, however, have grown into a stately giant and you, the youngest, are a special honor to the Hecklingen family, after your previous deeds".

"I would like to be that," Philipp replied modestly, "in any case, my parents too were blessed by God with a long and happy marriage. Although my mother was the second wife of my father, she almost celebrated her golden wedding anniversary and to this day, apart from the eldest, my brother the preacher Ernst Leberecht of Pasewalk, who died last year and my brother August, who died at the age of 25 on a trip abroad, ten of the twelve children are still living and most of them are in good positions."

"Yes, yes, here the Lucanus' and your own lineage are high embellishments of our German bourgeoisie. May God keep them that way at all times." Gleim replied with warmth.

"Here in the library you will also find the wonderfully harsh sermons of your ancestor, the famous cathedral preacher Siegfriedus of Magdeburg, a contemporary of Luther, who seems to have found in the present Berlin court preacher a worthy descendant who is purposeful in his faith."

"My brother Heinrich zu Glogau especially admires him, I am only surprised, uncle Gleim, how much you know about our family." Philipp replied in sincere amazement.

"That's not surprising," Gleim laughed, "since I'm known for my soft spot for famous people."

At that moment the lady of the house entered the circle of men and asked them to attend the tying of the bridal wreath, which the youth over there now wanted to perform. Then the small gentlemen's party rose willingly to attend this beautiful German custom of the *Polterabend*. With a flourish of the musicians, very soon the meaningful game began, to which the gentlemen standing and the ladies sitting, now turned their attention.

The couple's friends, chosen as guides for the bride and groom, opened it by praising the joys of marriage in alternating conversations and then asking the bride to tie the maiden's wreath. They themselves took a small myrtle branch from a basket standing in front of them. Whilst handing it to the bride's next friend, the bride's older sister, they expressed a rhymed congratulation, which she poetically promised to tie into her thread. All the guests followed this example. First the older ones, then the younger ones, until each one had learned his little saying, spoken it impromptu and taken a twig from the basket and handed it to her. Then the wreath winder closed the wreath with a witty speech, placing it on the bride's head and thus opening the final dance.

Of course her fiancé, who had been given the last of the buttonhole twigs, was her dancer. Meanwhile doors and windows were banging outside and a heap of pottery shards, which represented the good luck messengers of the neighbors and distant acquaintances, were flying everywhere. They had to be cleared away at midnight, before the animated guests could start on their way home on time.

The wedding ceremony the next day in the beautiful oldest Romanesque Church of Our Lady was serious and dignified. Only relatives were invited. No friends other than Gleim and Kopstadt, the bachelors, were present, as they were counted as family members because of their long standing.

Before the wedding ceremony, when the venerable organ sounded and Philipp, behind the bridal couple, walked the long aisle between the dark nave and the altar, he involuntarily remembered that 57 years ago, in the same house of God, his mother had walked this same aisle at his father's side. Why shouldn't he also lead Maria home as his wife in this very church? The only thing was that his brother Ernst would have to come from Herklingen and bless her marriage as the successor of his father. And his brother Heinrich from Glogau had to be there, because he had always encouraged him to marry soon. Maria herself, in her childlike, pious and simple Mennonite faith, had not attached importance to the blessing of a clergyman. Even if, in an emergency, the blessing of her parents or her nearest relatives was, as with the old Germanic tribes, a sufficient requirement for a marriage, he would draw her to become a Protestant wife and, for his sake, she would honor and respect the customs of his faith.

Only when the priest gave his blessing to the kneeling couple—Philipp had missed the change of rings, so absorbed in his own future plans—had he awoken from his dreams and was completely distressed by his complete lack of interest in the present. He then joined the crowd surrounding the young couple to congratulate them. He kissed Susanne's hand with the sparkling wedding ring and shook the right hand of the new husband vigorously. He then turned his eyes once more towards the carving of the magnificent late Gothic rood screen, so often admired in the past.

Then he walked out the same way as he had come in, joining the two Canonici who had decided to go to the "Golden Horse" where he himself had taken his quarters. Thus he could invite the gentlemen to take a short rest in its parlor. There Uncle Gleim once again emphatically invited him to spend the whole day with him on the morrow, starting with lunch. His niece, however, had given him special instructions to come early. How pleased Philipp was about this promising invitation and pledged his safe and early appearance.

But the wedding feast did not allow the talkative gentlemen to relax up here for long. They had to comply with their duty and go downstairs to the vestibule to lead the ladies, who had arrived in the meantime, to their places according to the table arrangements. Almost overwhelmed by the scent of the festive table decorated with roses set up in the shape of horseshoes, one quickly found one's way around and soon a colorful babble of voices mixed in with the clatter of plates signalling that the material part of the celebration was now being given its due.

When the first courses had been honored and the glasses had already been filled several times, the more spiritual approach came into play again. Apart from the usual speeches at table, which had to follow a certain order, a charming Cupid appeared in the hall and fetched from his quiver the printed festive poems of the congratulating relatives and friends.

Philipp looked excitedly over to the present leader of the famous Halberstadt School of Poetry. Uncle Gleim finally had to break his stubborn silence, for his name was not found among the authors of the homage poems distributed.

Suddenly, during the last course—the sweet confectionery course—a pink-colored shell wagon pulled by lively butterflies entered the hollow of the horseshoe to the sound of fanfares, carrying a very charming, graceful Erato with a rose-wreathed forehead standing upright in the middle of it. After graceful bows, however, the latter soon spoke an enthusiastic homage to love, and during the roaring applause of the one who had arrived at the conclusion, the butterflies fluttered around to distribute the hymns printed on pink silk strips to all the guests individually.

Then, among the witty verses of the wedding carols was the well-known ornate poem by the poet Gleim. Philipp, who felt his gaze resting upon him, could not help but pay tribute to this noble gesture of homage by gently moving his hands in applause. The celebrated young couple stood up and Susanne put her arms around her dear uncle's neck, impulsively breaking a branch from one of the laurel trees that had been set up in tubs to decorate the banquet hall and then she kissed his forehead, cleverly nestling the branch in the poet's hair.

The musicians accompanied this most beloved impromptu with a fanfare concluding the meal. Everyone thronged to the poet or to the happy couple to share their good wishes and congratulations. No one thought of the graceful Erato any more, only Philipp—who had looked around for her—noticed that the fair goddess must have silently ascended back to Olympus, because the chariot and the butterflies had also disappeared without a trace.

Philipp did not feel obliged to wait for the end of the day's celebration, which had now reached its climax. He and the two Canonici, who had left their overcoats in his room and wanted to put them back on again, had stolen away unnoticed from the festive circle that was still going on in loud eulogies. He longed for a lonely walk in the open air and since the evening in July promised to remain bright for a long time yet but it was now approaching 7 o'clock, he even decided to climb the panoramic Spiegelberg, only half an hour or so away. This was the best way to allow his head, dazed by the scent of wine and flowers, to wander lightly and freely again.

At about 10 o'clock, when the lights were shining everywhere in the valley, he quickly descended his climb and went to his room. He heard that downstairs the last of the hard-drinking wedding guests were still congregated but he was not tempted to have his night's rest cut short.

While sorting the pieces of his uniform, which had been in service again for a longer period of time, the notebook presented to him by his nephew Noth in Nordhausen fell to hand and only now, noticing its artistically interlaced leather cover, he suddenly felt the urge to inaugurate it immediately in memory of this festive day. The rhymes almost flowed into his pen as he thought back to the reflections that had occupied him absorbingly in the morning in the church to our dear Lady and that had become no less vivid in the evening silence on the Spiegelberg. So he wrote:

Love spoke:
And on the altar the bride to God's holy matrimony comes,
Upon the head her new honor a myrtle crown.
But further, it behooves the players now
Of the circle of virgins she now forsakes.
Once again, to bid her farewell, she dresses,
In all her girlish glory.
But not with pearls that spell out tears,
Neither a chain as would be fetters
Not even with rings, when at the altar
The priest the wedding ring shall bless.
No! Put it in her hair with her green crown

Which is the color of eternal trust.
A fabric still, silvery and fragrant
That like a gentle breeze surrounds her all
Shall be the symbol of the sweet magic
The innocence woven around a girl's heart
That in beatitude and chastest purity
Striving for virtue only in nobility.
Therefore let the color pure from its threads,
Light and clear, pious and well its meaning.
The girl's veil is the coronation cloak.
For a young and lovely queen of hearts.
And when her wedding bells do ring
And take her away from maidens many
Adorned in coronation jewelry of love
Proudly the dearest greets her at the marriage altar.
And give her friends warmest wishes
To the grace of God the consort.
The covenant of hearts be blessed by heaven
From this hour until eternity.

IV

Wolfenbüttel

Lessing and the performance of his "Minna von Barnhelm — The Soldier's Happiness"

After the wedding he continued his travels. Reaching Braunschweig already on the first evening, albeit late. This was the city with the Court, from which the King had taken his wife. She was held in high esteem and respect throughout Prussia because of her pious and moral conduct, a respect that she also enjoyed from her husband. There could be no question of the love for the mother of the country, for she had resided in Magdeburg during the seven years of the campaign in order to be closer to her husband and had always received his first squadrons of soldiers after major acts of arms. During the last decade, however, Elisabeth Christine had become the patient tolerator of the King that thought and acted only for his people and his country, especially as there was no necessity for the nascent philosopher of Sanssouci, and she never showed herself at his side.

Her love for him remained untouched by his almost cold formality. She never missed an opportunity, without being obtrusive, to show him again and again the immutability of her high disposition and deeply rooted affection. Her life was filled with works of love but she always drew the envoys of foreign courts coming to Berlin into her circle without ever touching on political issues. Nor did anyone seek her ear, since it was generally known at the courts that she did not have the ear of her husband.

Nevertheless, everyone knew that she was eager to comply with her royal prerogatives, to preserve the hospitality of her court, within the limits set for her.

People liked coming to Schönhausen and they always felt anew that they owed this honor to a royal wife who was seldom wistful but witty and humbly devoted to her destiny, so they never left unrewarded. Elisabeth Christine read a lot and enjoyed reading. She was interested in Reformation philosophy and all sciences, especially encouraged by the daring of the cathedral provost Spalding[61], her confessor. She translated from foreign languages and even translated the epoch-making book "Unter dem evangelischen Glauben" ("Under the Protestant Faith") by Philipp's cousin Wilhelm, the High Court Preacher in Berlin, from German into French. Through this cousin in Berlin he knew quite a bit about her private life. Thus Philipp looked the next morning with warm interest at the vast and extensive castle from which his sovereign had come. He liked the mighty array of older-style conventions that had served the residence of the former rulers — the Braunschweig heraldic creature, the majestic lion on the column that guarded house and courtyard.

When, after a short walk over the beautiful ramparts, he had found his way back to the post courtyard, where his inn "zur Post" was located, he heard there, to his disappointment, that the post wagon was unable to continue its journey that day because one of its wheels was badly damaged and needed to be repaired. The passengers would have to wait two or three days for the next post coach opportunity. What a great prospect! This was supposed to be the much-acclaimed connection from the northern Harz

Mountains! His next question was, "How long does it take to ride on horseback from here to Wolfenbüttel and why was he carrying the letter of recommendation to Lessing in his breast pocket?" Then it was well worth making a detour to him to make good use of the waiting time.

A riding horse was quickly scouted out and within an hour Philipp was trotting along the long poplar-lined avenue that leads from Braunschweig to Wolfenbüttel. From the east and south, the Harz Mountains, which had been wistfully abandoned yesterday, greeted him once again on the horizon. But now he was already quite happy that he was following the advice that had been little appreciated at first, to search out the great poet. He had not mounted his horse, however, without stopping at the nearby market, at a larger castle shop on the corner — he had discovered the castle earlier that morning — to purchase the little volume "Minna von Barnhelm or the Soldier's Happiness" by G.E. Lessing, which he had seen in the shop window there.

His program for tomorrow included a visit to the library, which was well worth seeing, and taking the opportunity to deliver his letter of presentation to the court librarian. The sunny Brunswick countryside aroused his pleasure to the highest degree. Yesterday he had driven by moonlight via Helmstedt past the magnificent fort, along the river Elm and partly at Königslutter through the same to Brunswick. Today he left the Elm to the left and rode in a straight southern line, actually because of Wolfenbüttel, back to Halberstadt. Chance was playing funny tricks on him. Wolfenbüttel, until twenty years ago had been the residence town of the Brunswick dukes of the older line. It was surrounded by the Oker River and the most fertile countryside, surprising the rider with its quite unexpected expanse. He had imagined it completely differently, finding a district town of at least the same size as Halberstadt.

He took quarters in the spacious inn "Zum Herzog von Brunswick". Resting his aching limbs from the ride, he was pleased to be able to immerse himself in his reading after an evening meal, when he heard other guests downstairs in the hall talking about a theatre performance that was apparently taking place in the castle in the evening. He listened attentively. Hearing mention of the play "Soldatenglück" (Soldier's Happiness), he went to the innkeeper, informed himself in detail about whether and where tickets could be purchased, brushed up his clothing as best he could and rushed to the castle without delay. This all took him less than twenty minutes.

All his fatigue had disappeared and the opportunity was too good to be missed. One of the halls of the old castle had been used for such performances many times before, in fact all the time. Yet the intimacy of the tasteful room in which he had a seat in the back row but with a good view of the stage, had made him feel comfortable and full of pleasant expectation. He was not disappointed, it was a play written true to his heart.

This was not a popular, concocted piece. No! That was life as he, Philipp, had lived it, as it had happened in Breslau, in Glogau and afterwards in every Silesian garrison. A piece of national life, yes, it was, as far as the figure of Tellheim was concerned, his own fate. Uncle Gleim had quite rightly judged that, just as with the wounded Tellheim, so it was ten years ago that all the leaders of the dismissed free battalions, among whom there were the most noble, highly deserving men, even though the Prussian officer corps in which they had been, were in the greatest distress. The great King, who did not appear in a play, was the centre of attention as the bearer of a touching, nobly moving plot. Philipp was delighted, even thrilled! The ever-resounding applause that followed each end of the act and the roar at the end, of course corresponded entirely with his own feelings that he would have preferred victory! "Victory!" was called, as in the cheering tumult on the battlefield.

Then the curtain suddenly rose and he stepped up to the ramp, bowing deeply and seriously—Lessing! Yes, there he was, as he had seen him so often in Breslau with Tenentzien, only older, more serious, more introspective—probably grateful for the homage and yet, as if above all external applause. When Philipp saw that some gentlemen were now pushing out of the auditorium through a small side door to the stage, introducing themselves personally to the poet, he was no longer held back himself. He was driven to the great man who had felt his own fate so deeply and expressed it so masterfully in word and action. Lessing was already extending his hand after he had mentioned his name and added "from Breslau" involuntarily from the heart.

"If I am not mistaken, we are old acquaintances. How is your brother, the Justice Councillor in Wroclaw and the other, the excellent philanthropist, of our great Royal Commission Councillor in Glogau doing?" However, Philipp was too emotionally moved and replied boldly:

"May I personally report on this tomorrow because now I am compelled to present my deepest devotion to the poet of Tellheim" and bowing down, he spontaneously grasped Lessing's hand and took it to his heart. The silent and yet so eloquent homage was accompanied by moments of silence on both sides.

Lessing now prepared to leave the hall at Philipp's side and walked towards the wings, standing still for a moment.

"'Tomorrow,' you said? Can't it be later than that? Tomorrow morning I am ordered to see the Crown Prince on urgent business and expect to have to travel to Vienna, where my help is requested for the establishment of an Academy of Sciences. Emperor Joseph and Maria Theresa are behind it and I am impelled to bring clarity about their wishes and my present position."

Philipp, concerned by the melancholy tone and the painful twitching around Lessing's mouth, realized that he was faced with such difficult decisions that he did not want to intrude upon him during his visit.

"Hopefully, I will have the privilege of paying my respects again later. May I now quickly just hand over the letter from Uncle Gleim from Halberstadt. The same wishes to be recommended to his patron and friend, Dr. Lessing."

He handed over the letter, which Lessing thankfully put in his breast pocket.

"Of my good Gleim! Yes, I'll probably visit him in Halberstadt in person—he's at home, isn't he?" which fact Philipp confirmed by a mute bowing of his head, "If my trip to Vienna is settled tomorrow and I get some leave," Lessing added.

Meanwhile both men had continued on into the outdoors. When Philipp wanted to say goodbye, Lessing asked him how he intended to spend the following day.

"I was going to see the famous library," was the answer.

"You'd do better to avoid the walls of the books that often stare at me like tomb walls," sighed Lessing, "rather admire the downright splendid arrangement of the great domed hall. And in the afternoon I advise an excursion to Asseberg, Lichtenberg and Steterburg Monastery. It's a great pity, too bad I can't be your guide."

With this they parted ways, and while Lessing, thinking deeply as he walked towards his residence in front of the library, Philipp wandered even longer, as he so often liked to do, through the quiet streets of the city in a particularly elevated mood. Now he would be a free man tomorrow and today he had enjoyed a more beautiful encounter with the poet than he had ever dreamed possible. This man writes amusing poems and is yet a serious melancholiac. I'm sure he will revive good Uncle Gleim the day after tomorrow. But Tellheim! He was magnificent, true and distinguished. And how splendid was the constable character.

The next morning was hot and sunny, a right July morning with thunderclouds approaching. There the library rooms were a refreshingly cool place to stay. Philipp made himself at home and remained there alone all the time. The librarian seemed to have been expecting him, handing him a small package with this inscription as soon as he entered:

"To the discharged Prussian lieutenant of the Seydlitz Cuirassier Regiment at Halberstadt Philipp Wilhelm."

So Lessing knew more about him and knew his fate! When, in an unobserved moment, he unwrapped the parcel, he found in it only a stapled book "Nathan the Wise. A subscription print, dramatic poem in five acts". Lessing had written, "You win this, my newest opus friend!" on a piece of paper wrapped around the loose sheets of paper. On the first page of the sheets was written, "In memory of our meeting in Wolfenbüttel, on the last of the day of the moon in 1774.

> *Yet the superstition*
> *In which we have grown up, not therefore loses*
> *When we detect it, all its influence on us.*
> *Not all are free that can bemock their fetters.*[62]
> *Gotthold Ephraim Lessing"*

Deeply moved, Philipp carried the gift in his breast pocket. Uncle Gleim, that was worth the ride to Wolfenbüttel, he thought, paying the bill at his inn after lunch and swinging himself up on to his horse, he rode back on yesterday's road to Brunswick without paying tribute to Lichtenberg, Asseberg and Stetebuerg. In the evening he read Nathan's poetry drama in one go upstairs in his inn. Then he opened again the passage where Nathan says:

> *Let each feel honored by this free affection.*
> *Unwarped of prejudice; let each endeavor*
> *To vie with both his brothers in displaying*
> *The virtue of his ring; assist its might*
> *With gentleness, benevolence, forbearance,*
> *With inward resignation to the godhead,*
> *And if the virtues of the ring continue*
> *To show themselves among your children's children,*
> *After a thousand thousand years, appear*
> *Before this judgment-seat – a greater one*
> *Than I shall sit upon it, and decide."*

He wrote these lines in the little book that his cousin Noth in Nordhausen had revered.

On the first page were his verses from the wedding day in Halberstadt. "Yes, Lessing, you are a man! Oh Maria how delicious it will be to read all his great thoughts to you first. Tomorrow we'll go to work, to Rhine, and to you."

Tomorrow, in the afternoon, he had already learned this much—the post coach came through there and continued on to Hanover. That was his direct route—Hanover, Minden, Wesel led the route to the Lower Rhine, where Kleve lay on the other side. Kleve—but on this side Emmerich. The Emmerich of Maria! Hanover the Guelph[63] city did not lure him, but Minden, with the Porta Westfalica! Lord of the Cheruscan historical field of victory over Varus, he wanted to get to know it better and to strengthen and build on it before he went on to the borderland. Ah! Very close, very close borderland to the French! Then he saw the red trousers on Janus Hill running, running as fast as they could. And when the great Frederick just taps on the King's trousers, they run, they run—Pandurs and Frenchmen.

With this mail coach he would probably take Canon Kopstadt to the Rhine with him. Thus he would have travel company almost to his own destination. No! Even that prospect did not tempt him today. He still had to see the cathedral and strew roses for the young bride on her return to her new path in life. If she had still been alive, this would certainly have been appreciated by his mother. How happy his brother Heinrich would be in Glogau when he heard how he had fulfilled his mission here.

V

Minden—Porta Westfalica

It had been a beautiful journey, first through the densely wooded Brunswick country and then through the water-rich flat Hanover, which Philipp had covered in a spacious mail coach that now drove the Brunswick-Minden route without stops. The following morning he was able to board the coach in Brunswick instead of the damaged, not yet restored one. Finally he had passed through the Bückeburg countryside, where the colorful and precious traditional costumes of the rural population had caught his eye, since it was Sunday when people wanted to go to church in this most beautiful state. Also the landscape around was again richly lined with mountains and forests and on questioning he learned from a fellow traveller that the mountain range stretching along the southern horizon was the Weser Mountains.

Thus, he was already approaching the historical site where the great battles of Herrmann the Cheruscan against the Romans had taken place that still filled the heart of the man, whose humanistic education from his youthful days was still in his memory, with pride.

An enthusiastic history lover like Philipp could not pass by the famous Porta-Westfalica with the old cathedral and fortress city of Minden, which Tacitus had described as the one of the Varus Battle, without a thorough picture of it etched into his soul. Now down between the mountains the Weser River glittered in serpentine meanderings approaching us from the plain while it pushed itself through the broad mountain guardians that protect the Münsterland like the columns of Hercules in the north, through which it pushes its way to the old cathedral city of Minden, where soon the post coach would be stopping at the market, disposing of its occupants.

What a pleasure to stretch your limbs after the long day and night ride! Philipp because of his stately size always suffered more than the others when it was necessary to squeeze them into narrow spaces. He soon succeeded in getting a comfortable room in the inn "zum König von Preussen" and after an evening meal, he enjoyed stretching his legs in the streets and alleys of the fortress city in the moonlight.

The distances in the city centre are limited by the fortress walls so he soon found himself standing in the cathedral courtyard of the old bishop's city created by Louis the Pious. How different the squat building seemed to him. The cathedral, with its firm and massive contours that stood out against the illuminated night sky, stood out from the massive sandstone Gothic towers of the Halberstadt Bauweiler that rose up from the ground. Here, a square head rises up between broad shoulders, stocky, almost even a little four-legged in appearance. Almost involuntarily, Philipp thought of the Lower Saxon character, of the even more local character of the Westphalian *tête quartiers* of which he had gained many an impression during his wartime days.

He stopped long in front of this strange balustrade of such massive brick shapes that had looked somehow familiar, turning back after he had just let the impression of the Westphalian stubborn man's forehead, so to speak, take effect on him. He saved himself the trouble of looking at the long side, leaving it to his daytime impression. A superficial glance was enough to show him that there was still a considerable depth behind this façade, which required an in-depth study of the character of the Westphalian.

He strolled along the main streets of the town towards the river, where a bridge crossing meadows rose up to form the transition to Fischerstadt. On this bridge he made a second longer stop, because here the clear silhouette of the Porta Westfalica presented itself to him and reminded him of the pictures of the columns of Hercules in the Straits of Gibraltar.

It was from there that he wanted to welcome the sun on the morning and view the hinterland from the west. After all, this gate meant the gate to the future that lay closed before him with all its secrets, while in the east his past had closed behind him.

All day long he had been thinking about it, as he rolled through the Hanoverian countryside where, from the crisp language of the people he had already noticed in the Brunswicks' language that he no longer crossed the language area of the Harz homeland, which was mixed with Wendish. Rather, he found himself in the strictly preserved uniqueness of the Lower Saxon plain, which had finally led him through the Westphalian Gate into the region of the red soil, where the Saxon tribe had had to drown its freedom in streams of blood and tears in the face of the Franconian Charles.

Over here, the Wittekindberg at the Gate of Westphalia had been the ancestral seat of the noble Saxon Duke Wittekind, who had repeatedly opposed the mighty Charlemagne with his Anglo-Saxon converts in order to protect his Donar's Oaks[64] and Wotan[65] faith until he, too, had finally had to take up the cross and learn to worship God. The sober, four-faced front of the local cathedral church seemed to testify to the aversion with which it actually happened.

Catching himself with such nocturnal thoughts, Philipp tried to tear himself away from the magically captivating silent and still castle landscape, now taking the descent through the honeycomb alleys of the old town and finally arriving back at his inn, noticing the mighty renaissance gable with pictures of buttocks and many other unreasonable picturesque motifs and strange street names. In any case, the nightly tour promised a rich yield for the stopover that he had planned to spend here in the historically important Minden. He resolved to carry out this intention the next morning.

By the time the milk carts started to liven up the streets of the city, Philipp was already on the mountain paths of the Wiehen mountains, the oldest and most extreme of which offer great variety through cliffs and panoramic clearings and lead to the Wittekind Mountains. Deep down in the southwest there were some peaks of the Teutoburg Forest. To the west, Philipp found a long meadow plain of apparently reclaimed moorland. There his future would lie. Above it, however, on the other side of the Weser, wedged in between Teuss and the Hercules Column on the other side, was the Jakobsberg and a wooded hilly area. There he could see the small town of Hausberge.

Minden—Porta Westfalica

The castle hill of the old mountain farm still stands out clearly from the location of the village, even though the castle was replaced by a manor house, the so-called chateau. In the north the course of the Weser in the foreground leads to Minden with its bridges and towers and up here Philipp understood the importance of the town as a bridging place and as a fortress, because it controlled the exit and transition to Northern Germany. No wonder that it was fiercely contested at all times. Beyond Minden, the river makes its way between stretches of forest that enliven a heathland. The horizon, blurred by a fine haze, lets you feel the breath of the nearby sea blowing in over the heathland.

Philipp was wondering why was he so strangely captivated by the open panoramic view here. He had already stood on some far more magnificent Harz sites, e.g. the boulders on some of the more majestic mountain ridges of the Giant Mountains[66]—but that must have been it—so lovely and in its sweetness so simple and uncomplicated in its lines, clearly arranged without much displacement, nowhere had the image from a view embedded itself in his mind this way. In the face of this reality, he ignored the thought of the blood that had flowed in the battle of Idistaviso[67] or the cruel slaughter of 5000 Saxon pagans ordered by Charlemagne[68].

The gloriousness of the present, with its young sunlight and its untouched dewy freshness, made him wallow in an inexplicable feeling of bliss and at the same time a hot longing for Maria. He had felt a similar, inner detachment from all the weight of the world and such a quiet pious exaltation when he had experienced the majestic rise on the solstice day at her side. The view at that time had been almost unique, directed towards the glorious colour harmonies of the horizon and the firmament, while here the picture at his feet had triggered such a miraculous peace and happiness. Almost unconsciously, he pulled out his pocketbook umpteen times to recite the words of his great King's creed to the divinity of the forest valley, which is again revealed in nature. He also had to think of Wolfenbüttel, of Nathan's wisdom teachings:

> *Let each feel honored by this free affection.*
> *Unwarped of prejudice; let each endeavor*
> *To vie with both his brothers in displaying*
> *The virtue of his ring; assist its might*
> *With gentleness, benevolence, forbearance,*
> *With inward resignation to the Godhead.*

How splendidly that was said. Once again he stepped onto the steep slope where the Wittekind Hills fall down to the Weser loop. Just at that moment the sun was shining down on the small town of Hausberge, nestled in the darker, wooded hilltop. The modest little church behind the Hausberge, on another ridge, stretching out with its pointed turrets pointing towards the sky, seemed to offer a quiet, harmonious connection to the musings that had just fulfilled him.

As he then began the descent, in order to get to know the cathedral church in Minden[69] in the light of daytime, he took it upon himself to find out more about the Hausberge, the name of the most beloved Weser town. Surely the history can be found in a library of the city. Everyday life was beginning to bustle in the city and especially in the market, where the country folk in their colourful traditional costumes on their carts with trading goods were streaming out. He found himself on the cathedral square in front of the long side of the church and was almost blinded by the quite unexpected beauty of the magnificent windows coming towards him.

Here, however, he was able to see how the long building had been constructed at different times and how successfully the Romanesque front façade of the transverse building closed the transitional Romanesque to an early Gothic one. The interior of this peculiar exterior design, which he was almost inclined to regard as an aberration of taste, reconciled him with it as soon as he entered the church—just as one does not attach any importance to the exterior garments after the acquaintance with a noble soul. The light and air of an immeasurably wide, wonderfully structured hall flooded around him here. The columns, but even more so the windows with their early Gothic, round-shaped skylights, seemed to fit so harmoniously into their striving for the sun in the sky that he was prepared to bow down in admiration before the high art of the architect's judgement. He could not get enough of the finely structured balustrades and the wonderful refractions of the light effects of the windows produced by the artistic network.

The sexton who led him around urged him to keep moving but Philipp, accustomed to deepening his impressions and not tiring his senses by observing things closely, paid him his fee and took with him the sublime impression of the light-filled and bright-radiating interior. He was quite unaccustomed to this image. He had been taught to admire the great cathedrals, with their heavenly striving outer Gothic style. On the inside, however, he was always disappointed by the gloomy twilight enveloping the senses that the Catholic religion, from whose time the magnificent buildings originated, had created as an atmospheric moment for inner reflection.

It was here that he had encountered, almost for the first time, a radiant church interior. His Protestant sense, which yearned for enlightenment but not for mysticism and obscurity, had almost experienced an hour of consecration in this place. He now looked at the bare gable surfaces with completely different eyes, knowing that they had their important purposes and that a great master had been at work here. "Happy is the cathedral congregation, who decided to build such a temple of light for their Sunday edification," he said to himself.

The more Philipp got to know the Westphalian Gate fortress city Minden, the more he felt attracted to it. He had heard from his innkeeper that the Cathedral Dean was a Baron von Vincke[70] from the old Minden knighthood, who had entered this dignity about 15 years ago at the age of 21 and who enjoyed the very special favour of the great king, who always used to stay in the Cathedral Deanery when visiting his Westphalian province.

Von Vincke maintained contact with the most important and highly placed persons and practised a very generous hospitality, so that the winter months, which he always felt obliged to spend in Minden, were thus the meeting point of a rare, distinguished selection of important spirits. As he had expected, at one of the bookshops located near his inn, Philipp found an extensive brochure on the prehistory of the little town of Hausberge and he missed many pauses for rest when enjoying the fascinating reading to memorize the meaning of the particular spot each time it was presented to him in the sunshine.

To the same extent that during his evening hike the impressions of his immediate surroundings faded into the background, his great inclination to explore the historical development of what happened came into the foreground and gave him the guideline for the arrangement of his next daily program.

How could he leave the area without having seen the army campaigns of Drusus and Varus against the Germanic tribes here in the landscape? So he found himself again the next morning on a hike over the ridge of the Süntal, this time only in the direction from where he could see the course of the Weser upstream the furthest. Scholars were still arguing about where the camp of Varus actually was in the year 9 B.C. when he left to join the strong barbarian tribe of the Germanic forces, who under their younger prince son Arminius had united with other tribes to break the Roman oppression.

The whole North Sea coast had already been subdued and Drusus had made the Rhine his strongest base of operations by establishing fifty fixed camps and forts, from where he now threatened the northwest of Germania. The encirclement began as a part of German history and when Drusus died, his brother Tiberius fortified his work and a new Roman province between the Rhine and the Elbe seemed to be emerging.

There was a sudden change, however, when Quintilius Varus took over the command here. He came from a country where the people were accustomed to servile obedience and it is understandable that his introduction of a foreign law by corporal punishment aroused relentless fury in a tribe of free men. Only there was no leader to take bloody revenge on the oppressor until Arnimius carried out the task of liberation.

The Roman camp is said to have been located at the Westphalian Gate, to which Varus refers to as the path of death. For from here he moved with his three legions to the Teutoburg Forest where he and his mighty retinue met their doom.

Philipp had now gradually wandered around the whole area of the Wittekind Mountain and could well imagine that the plain to the south had served the Varus army and where they had set up camp. Now he went down to the valley to see the place on the other side of the river, where the Cherusci awaited the arrival of the largest army the world had seen. It must have been a magnificent view when in the morning of the day of the battle the new legions had to wait for the enemy and marched up.

For miles around, the eight legionary eagles and the shimmering forces of the Roman decimation troops shone in the morning sun in the middle of the front, while the allies formed the flanks. Tacitus described all this very vividly, and it had left such a deep impression on Philipp's young mind when he was at school, that he was able to put himself in the picture here and there, right into the landscape. There was no doubt that the German army had chosen these steep cliffs to the south as the most favorable city for the defense they were now facing.

VI

Kleve

Now at Wesel he had seen the Rhine for the first time. Twice a week the postal connection went from Minden first through the lovely Westphalia, then behind the city of Hamm through the black sooty region beyond the border fortress. Yes, it was a broad majestic river but no trace of romance was to be discovered here. So he lauded his Oder near Breslau with its magnificent bridges, the romantic cathedral island, the countless towers and wall formations on both sides of the river that was animated by ships and barges carrying a whole travelling market across the waves.

The wide expanse of water of the Rhine, on the other hand, which lost itself in foggy plains to the northwest, was barren and boring. Here and there, only a church tower in the distance allowed the thought to enter his mind along the way that more people lived in the south, where he came from. The big rafts with cabins built upon them were meandering along, telling us somehow that they had either already travelled a long way or still had another long way to go. Wesel, the town which had one citadel at the upper and one at the lower end but which had otherwise settled more inland, could be compared to Glogau in one respect. Rather than the soldiers' processions with their firm steps and the gates to all directions, the larger squares with the planted canons, the main streets widening towards the market to which the more angled alleyways led and the Prussian type of fortress in the western border area seemed to him to be just as much a part of it as in the east.

Only the race of people struck him as being very different. It was precisely market day when they stopped in Wesel for a night's rest. On his wanderings through the town he talked for a while with the peasants from the surrounding area, who were offering their goods for sale at the market, observing their trade and barter.

Here were the Polish natives of Silesia, vividly gesticulating, fantastically dressed in a fur cap, velvet vest and knee breeches, often betraying the most abject poverty but always with boots of impeccable cut and fit. With panniers and baskets, carts and hand carts were piled up and had been dragged there in a motley array of often unbelievable junk, guarded and praised by fiery-eyed women dressed in the most garish colors. Here were buxom women in snowy clean headscarves, clean calico skirts and aprons with wooden slippers, lumpy clogs and thick woolen stockings as footwear. Their baskets were covered with dazzling white cloths in which the butter chunks and eggs rested. They were ponderous and clumsy in their movements, slow and loud in their speech. This was pure Lower Saxony, without any mixture of Wendish and Slavic tribes that could be so striking in the East.

At Wesel he went over the island of Büderich to the other side of the Rhine and via Xanten and Goch to Kleve. He was quite astonished to unexpectedly find a hilly town here in the Rhine lowlands. The mail coach arrived from Xanten first at a small, triangular square in the town and Philipp saw here immediately on the left the "Van Gelder" Inn that the innkeeper in Xanten had recommended to him. Here he got out and ordered a room. As usual, he first strolled over the nearby bridge close to the inn after supper for an orientation walk through the city, immediately noticing in the reflections on the water to his left, the roofs and tower of the castle. On reaching the main road, he immediately took the path that led uphill to the height from where the square tower welcomed him.

Look there! Even before he had reached Burgstrasse with its ascent to Schlosshöhe, he read the street sign "Stechbahn" on the right and, turning off into the side street, stood naturally still in front of the illuminated windows of his brother's house. A strange feeling crept over him. He had not seen this brother now for some twenty years. He hardly remembered him, for he had been a fifteen-year-old secondary school pupil in Halberstadt when his brother had said goodbye to him there on his journey to the West. Here he was now standing in front of his front door and was itching to walk into the house. However, he did not dare to do so at this hour of the evening. Tomorrow morning yes! Freshly powdered and in the correct visiting suit! So he strolled back again, left the castle without looking at it and after the long journey he soon lay gratefully under the roof on his bed.

How cheerful and warm-heartedly his sister-in-law greeted him when he arrived at noon the next day! His brother was still at work at the government.

"Your brother-in-law in Glogau let us know about you a long time ago and will be happy to know that you are now well established. My Carl was afraid you'd be recruited for the West Indies, there are so many recruiters in this country."

"What do I hear? He is still in the country after all!" A male voice was heard in the hallway and, with both hands stretched out to him, his brother was already standing in the doorway.

A slender, small figure, which one could well believe his almost fifty-five years, looked up at him towering high above him with an expression of obvious pleasure.

"So this is what our wild warrior looks like—I imagined a Herculean one—and you certainly are! I pictured you as a farmer since you have always worked on the estates but you are much more a royal lieutenant than an administrator. In fact, you are an elite specimen of a former cuirassier."

Philipp had to put up with being a kind of exhibition object for the children at first and in the evening again for the colleagues and neighbors who were quickly invited to come. He was not unpleasantly touched to notice that his outward appearance was on display in front of all these highly distinguished officials and that he had, so to speak, done well at his first debut.

How long had it been since he had left the Golden Meadow he wondered. At that time it was the beginning of summer—the wedding had been on July 10, in Halberstadt. The harvest carts were already driving in the grain. The middle of August had come upon him without noticing under all his sights and experiences. He puzzled why he had not found any news from Questenberg among the messages he was waiting for. It seemed that Maria had not wanted an exchange of letters at all. Perhaps she wanted to examine her feelings once more, without being influenced. Or maybe she wanted to test his loyalty. Perhaps his quick farewell had caused distrust in him at the time. How little did he really understand this wonderful, or perhaps even perplexing creature.

Anyway, he did not want to miss any opportunity to give her a happy, bright life here in her homeland—as far as he was able to. He was going to cross the Rhine the next morning and go to Emmerich. Somewhere he would be able to hear from her congregation members whether there was already news from the pastor and whether the emigrants would really be moving in the fall.

He was reluctant to show any sign of impatience among his own people or even to let it be noticed at all. Until now, he had kept his secret closely guarded and it seemed to him a breaking of trust to impatiently or worriedly ask for news. It was a radiant August day when, at about ten o'clock in the morning, he boarded the ferry down by the Rhine, which carried the traffic between the two riverbanks. A lot of country folk went over with him and he tried in vain to find a similarity between their language and his German idiom—he could not even echo the Silesian dialect he was familiar with. He abandoned his efforts and positioned himself at the front of the broadside to let the fresh Rhine air and the views of the region waft over him.

How little it offered in the way of stimulation! The large wide expanse of water with little life, the flat shores, only the disappearing heights of Kleve that he had left behind him by walking a longer distance, as well as downstream the little town of Elten with the Eltenberg limiting the horizon there. Emmerich itself, which was now approaching, certainly had a Dutch character. With its low brick houses it was a good distance away from the river itself and the street that ran through it, which widened to two church squares, offered only grocery stores carrying Dutch inscriptions that completely revealed the border trade there.

Philipp asked the way to the Mennonite church. There was no such church, for the congregation was small[71]. As far as the shopkeeper, with whom he had inquired, thought he knew, they had all moved away or emigrated completely. Where the clergyman of the congregation was living, was now Philipp's new question. Soon he was knocking one polished door hammer after another. In the house where the Mennonite pastor should have had his apartment in the corner of a small square not far from the large Reformed church, there was no movement and the door was not opened. The shops were still closed so apparently the pastor and therefore Maria had not yet returned from Questenberg.

He now went further down the street and searched inconspicuously for the personalities he was looking for in the larger inn where he ordered refreshments. But everything was in vain. All that was known was that the Mennonite service, which was held in a little saloon at the other end of the small town — it used to be a barn that had been converted into a prayer room thirty years ago — had not taken place since the spring. No one knew any details because the small congregation did not associate with anyone other than its own members of faith and they kept themselves to themselves.

That was precious little he had found out today on his first research trip. Quite depressed he returned to the river to use the first ferry departure to return home. Now he would at least have got to know the house in which the pastor and therefore Maria had spent her life. His bitter consolation was that the next time he knew how to find the way easily without questions. It was strange that no one had been able to tell him when the pastor was expected back. It was a peculiar thing about such a religious segregation and as renowned as the Mennonites were for being quiet, unassuming, and industrious citizens of the city, they were a peculiar, inaccessible people and he had made this experience here on the spot.

For the time being, however, there was nothing to be done to change this. After all, the landlord of the "Sonne" in Questenberg had told him September, not August, when there had been talk of the pastor returning from Russia — so he was only being punished for his own impatience. Yet he wondered why the innkeeper had not written to him here in Kleve yet. Certainly, after arriving in Nordhausen he had faithfully kept his word and told him about Maria. Only it had taken him a little longer than he had thought and the letter from Questenberg had been delivered to him only on the last day in Halberstadt by a postal service that only made a weekly trip back via Aschersleben to Magdeburg. He had gained a connection to Halberstadt at the first mentioned place.

Then the good host of the "Sonne" had told him that Maria had already calmed down completely and that Gote was now diligently giving her a hand to learn how to cook and do the dishes, of which she had received little instruction until then. She sent him her best regards and asked him not to write to her any more, nor to expect any letter from her. She now knew what he had meant, and it was good that way. He would probably have a lot of other things to do and she wanted to use the time well to learn a lot more.

That had reassured and delighted him three weeks ago when he received the letter because now he knew that the dear girl was back in balance and that he was free for all the first experiences he still had to overcome here on the Rhine. However, now that he was here, there were no such experiences at all!

His brother had received him far more warmly and kindly than he had imagined from this elder, him being the youngest member of the parental home, who had remained completely alien to him due to distance and time. The lighter tone here on the Rhine, where Frederick's wartime life had not taken place, was also at home in the Stechbahn and his sister-in-law in particular loved the humor and the sometimes even hearty jokes that were not only told to her by her schoolchildren but also from the office of her dear husband. She appreciated everything that contributed to the cheerfulness of her circle. He had already noticed that the Dutch influence was a healthy, though probably extremely coarse one compared with the one he was used to from the eastern borderland of Poland with its smooth, spirited politeness and elegance.

Everyone here was quite broad and heavy, clumsy and drastic. He always had to think of the local wooden lumps on the feet of the population, against the fur-trimmed high boots of Breslau and Glogau — this was the most characteristic feature of the novel things here and the familiar ones there. His brother and his sister-in-law immediately persuaded him to have his luggage brought to their house from the "Van Gelder" inn, where he had stayed as a precaution after the advice of his brother Heinrich, and occupied the room at the back of the hillside garden. In August it still emitted the sweet apple smell of the long consumed winter supply and on its floors, the wall shelves and in the bay window Gertrud's fruit jars were delicately arranged, already revealing the contents of her newly filled "preserves" through meticulous labelling.

That was the hallmark of every guest room on the Rhine. It was also used to accommodate the often, dear visitors from the family but also the more rarely seen, secret food supply of the mother of the house. The expected new family member was not due until January of the following year, so Gertrud enjoyed the most active mobility and her bright laughter often sounded during the day from the children's dormitories in Philipp's little hermitage situated along the road. Downstairs on the ground floor was the good parlor, that is to say, the two of them, one at each end of the house. They had windows to the front and to the back and in case of larger social gatherings they could form a room—the so-called "hall"—that also contained the spinet and was furnished with smooth, dark parquet flooring.

It would not be long before it would be a much sought-after room for the young men's world at important ball celebrations in honor of the daughters. For a company that would later rent out ballrooms did not yet exist. At present, the most beautiful and most attractive events for young people were always reserved for the city's most distinguished families in their own homes.

Next to this room was the father's sanctuary with the bookshelves and desks, because usually every higher civil servant had his private secretary who handled the home work for him. Brother Carl August had the advantage of having two rooms available for his own purposes, so that he was always the sole master in his study facing the street and his secretary occupied a bright back room with shelves opposite him at a certain hour every morning and left just as punctually in the evening.

In the middle of the house were the front door, staircase and exit door to the courtyard and garden. In the other half of the house was the spacious kitchen with pantry to the rear and the large dining room to the front, leading to a private room for the mother. Her sewing table stood there on a raised window seat with an armchair in front of it, and of course there was a small double-sided outside mirror — a so-called "Peephole".

The house, however, did not end there, there was a narrow second corridor between the mother's parlor and the neighboring house, which was needed for larger heating, kitchen and cellar supplies because at its rear end was the narrow dark stairway to the underworld. It was also necessary for garbage collection from the yard but was usually closed tightly to the street. Where it ended in the yard, the high upright small cellar for the rubbish, the wood and coal crates and the doghouse were attached in the most practical manner.

In front of the rear windows of the hall, however, the most popular room of all, truly for a larger family in the most conveniently arranged dwelling house, namely a wide balcony terrace that also formed the flat roof of the washhouse.

This terrace, which in summer proved to be an even more intimate, atmospheric place to sit and enjoy summer punch, almost reached the rear garden fence. It rose steeply up to an elongated but not very deep courtyard where only a narrow strip formed the garden land of the houses along the lane. The larger gardens with old shady chestnut trees, lime trees and also fruit trees belonged to the houses from the Schlossstrasse, to the left and right to those on the rear road. But in their larger complex they formed a magnificent breathing and visual supply of air and light for the residents. There now lived in the houses all of the father's neighboring colleagues, for the main street led directly up to the palace, the Schwanenburg, where the High Tribunal Court and the Domain Chamber etc. had their seat. The gardens were naturally the target and playgrounds of the children of all the civil servants that grew and flourished by the dozen in each of the families.

For Philipp it was a blissful recollection of his own youth in Hecklingen with his father's parish garden that was similarly populated and now so quiet. Once he had watched here from the window the blossoming schoolgirls and high school students or the still small A-B-C upstarts of both sexes playing happily. Then he realized how he had been neglected in his childhood. He was sent to university at an early age, soon entered war life with battles and imprisonment and then went into the office of Breslau and the administration of the fraternal estates. He had not quite tasted the most delicious treasure of his life, his innocent youth. Instead, alongside his older brothers, he was immediately driven into a serious straitjacket.

Perhaps the young people down there in Sethe's[72] garden would end up doing the same. He noticed that he had lost the criterion or had never possessed it for the transition from boy to youth and from youth to man and that is probably why he felt strange and abandoned in their midst, in spite of all the really pleasant kinship of his own. What he liked best was to linger with all the loud, romping youth.

He immediately used the next few days, however, to pay his respects to the parents of the noisy crowd down there and especially to those superiors, whereby he had to begin his new official duties in six weeks, after their holiday period. He also visited his brother's family doctor, a man who, according to his brother — but especially according to his sister-in-law — deserved his utmost respect.

This Dr. Schütte[73] had established himself here in Kleve as a 25-year-old young beginner almost fifty years ago in 1725. But he was a splendid specimen, which one could take for 54 at his 74 years. Dr. Schütte was the actual founder of Kleve as a health resort that as such enjoyed great popularity, especially among the neighboring Dutch.

Here they were able to find, elevations and hills, even mountains granting them wide, delightful views into their own country, overgrown with forests and the most beautiful bushes. This was just beyond their national border, as inhabitants of the lowlands with their two large arms of the Rhine — the Rhine and the Waal River. Through the immense delta that extended its waterways to the mouth of the Meuse near Antwerp in innumerable canals, the inland cities were provided with water connections for the transport of trade.

Dr. Schütte in 1741, that is, immediately after the great King took office, had the depths of the kingdom of Prussia examined by miners here in the far west and had succeeded in bringing to light a ferrous well with healing properties and a mineral spring. Naturally, it was not without first being subjected to taunts and ridicule from the city's incredulous wise men. His discovery, which led to the opening of the first spring spa on July 17, 1742, enabled him to gain the ear and support of the city and later the royal authorities.

In 1742 the number of people drinking from the healing springs was eighty-five and by 1743 one hundred and thirty. Then it was one hundred and eighty person and so on until it was thousands. Not only the large and small towns of the Netherlands but also the rich merchants of the Dutch colonies in the West Indies knew how to utilize the healing springs in the vicinity of their homeland. No less so did their own Rhine compatriots from Düsseldorf, Aachen, Cologne and Wesel.

A natural inlet of the mountain range since ancient times had an amphitheatre and pleasure garden with beautiful installations, grottos, marble sculptures, fountains and the like (from Moritz von Nassau[74], the great benefactor of Kleve in the 16th century). Since the discovery of Schütte's springs, the double significance of an unusually graceful spa garden had been achieved. Because it was possible to attach the fountain house to the amphitheatre on one side, while the first bath and spa house were on the other side, with arcades and terraces, further enhancing the decoration of the charming mountain building.

It was crowned by the Sternenberg, as the highest elevation was called, where radial paths carved out of the forest, starting from the mighty lime tree, allowed the most beautiful distant views at its end. In general, the view of the landscape that could be enjoyed here was of considerable magnificence. One morning, the old court physician Dr. Schütte could not resist personally showing him his spring installations as well as the beautiful mountain promenades and avenues as works of art of the former Nassau governor Prince Moritz. For a long time, Philipp reconciled himself with the choice of this unique Kleve, embedded in a magnificent landscape, as his future hometown.

"You don't know, Mr. Court Medical Officer, and you can't even imagine how much I owe you for this walk," he addressed his old guide with true enthusiasm.

"You must know, I'm a child of the mountains, grew up on the eastern edge of the Harz Mountains and was almost desperate about the endless grey fog that the much praised but only so horribly bleak and scary looking Rhine River had to offer. What I see here, however, is one of the truly enchanting crowns of creation. On this side of the Freudenberg or Sternenberg and on the other side of the Eltenberg, they seem to form a much more majestic Porta Rhenania here on the border of the Prussian lands than the Porta Westfalica Mountains on the Weser, don't you think? They may not have such an ancient and bloodstained heroic history as the battlefields of Drusus and Varus and later of Charlemagne and the Saxon Duke Wittekind but the entrance gate to our German fatherland is wonderfully magnificent. I am deeply overwhelmed."

"You are mistaken," the doctor now took the floor, "this Rhine Gate here also has its bloody tradition from Roman times. Our old town Clivus, hilly, named such because it lies on three mountains, or derived from clover because it reminds of the cloverleaf, was founded by the emperor Trajan and was called Colonia Ulpia Trajana. Hadrian extended it down near Kellen to the Rhine. Under the emperor Diocletian it was later completely ruined by wars and by the flooding of the Rhine, which was used as a means to an end.

"Later, when inhabitants returned to the area, it was enlarged from its Central Gate to the Bridge Gate but was heavily surrounded by the Romans and Franks as a border town of Germany. Even the long hall with the short tower on top of our Swanenburg Castle[75] is said to have been built by Julius Ceasar after the city of Rome was built, before the birth of Christ, as an old inscription up there somewhere says. Roman memorial stones with inscriptions, urns, cinder pots, copper and silver coins were found by Prince Moritz everywhere when he was having the land ploughed, and they were later buried near his tomb".

Eager to learn, Philipp had listened to the narrator and now knew whom to turn to in his fondness for the historical past, development and teachings. They soon returned over the Sternenberg to the Nassau Gate and walked under a shady avenue of lime trees along the ridge leading to Xanten. Finally upon the Sandberg they enjoyed an even wider view almost like the previous one. From up there they looked down on the water tributary, called Kermisdahl, with its sparse pastureland.

VII

Journey to Düsseldorf

The next day was dedicated to a few more visits to fellow officials and in the evening everything was arranged and packed and brought to the new lodgings, so that Philipp could start his trip to Düsseldorf according to the program. It was quite a distance to get there, the journey went via Xanten and Krefeld and everywhere in the larger towns the postilion at the front of the coach was happy to make a longer stop to allow the passengers plenty of time to take their meals.

In Xanten, Philipp was amazed at the extent of the market square with its beautiful medieval town hall and he never tired of admiring it.

"But sir must first see the cathedral," said the landlord of the "Drachentöter", proud of his hometown. Philipp was pleasantly surprised by the splendid city gates he had already passed through and now here in the royal square and by virtue of a special tip to the hard-drinking postilion, he was given a whole hour to take a look at the nearby cathedral church.

Such a small town and yet such a magnificent building! What power, what wealth of the Roman Church was expressed in its churches! He had sought access to it from a narrow street in the city and, being built into a quiet narrow street with walls and towering gables, he only realized the full magnificence and majesty of the holy building when he found a doorway to it and entered its interior. Right in the nave of the enormous cathedral there were carved altars of such outstanding wood carving art as he had never seen before. The baptistery in a special side apsis was also a novelty he had never seen anywhere else. How light and spacious it was, and tastefully furnished! How he would have loved to spend an entire afternoon here, immersed in all the altarpieces and altars that were placed in front of each column and that formed special rooms in the middle of the nave. He had always loved to focus his contemplation on these innermost expressions of the various folk feelings even as a child.

Time was pressing and he had to move on. Approaching the exit through the main portal, he saw the entire length of the cathedral facing an open space and was able to let its dimensions and structure have their effect on him. He quickly returned to the inn "Gasthaus zum Drachentöter", where the landlord intercepted him to show him his own banquet hall. Here he found wall paintings depicting the entire Siegfried saga and it occurred to him just in time that the German hero of the saga and lindworm[76] slayer was supposed to have been born here in Xanten. This city was a figurative element in the oldest medieval poetry, around which one of the most poetic veils of the first German heroic songs had been woven. Kleve, the city of Lohengrin, Xanten, the city of the Siegfried legend! He considered what other things he would get to know that day.

The trip to Krefeld was not very eventful and lulled him into a pleasant afternoon slumber. The mail coach was then rattling through the town of German ribbon weavers and the silk industry and the postilion seemed to have no sympathy for them. He seemingly wanted to catch up on the time he had allowed himself in Xanten. Soon the travellers were in Neuss, driving over a mighty long pontoon bridge to the city of art and the muses, Düsseldorf as the lights were already flickering everywhere and the long summer's day was approaching its end.

At the inn, "Breitenbacher Hof", which the postilion had recommended to him as cheap and popular, Philipp found just the right accommodation for his purse.

From early in the morning the next day he could already get a picture of real Rhine folk life. His inn was situated in the middle of the market with its comings and goings, questions and answers. It was a trade and exchange day on the main day of the weekly market, so that he felt moved to look down and listen anew at his open window, directly above the front door. Nothing could give such a clear picture of the folk character as such a market bustle!

Finally he had to tear himself away, since the meeting shortly before lunch with Chamber Councillor Fritz Jacobi was the purpose of going there. He had quickly inquired about the way to the distinguished Hofgarten neighborhood and soon found himself in the anteroom of Gleim's friend. He had given his letter of recommendation to the girl who had taken his own business card to announce his arrival and when, after the necessary waiting time allowing the letter to be read, a side door opened and a refined face smiled at him. He had the impression that Gleim had a well-meaning admirer here.

"You are most welcome, my dear friend of our dear old father Gleim, so highly recommended to me. Please accept it as kindly as it is meant and I hope you will not be disappointed. In fifteen minutes I'll be going to my wife, who is always expecting me at this time of day on Saturdays at our estate in Pempelfort and I'll have *à la fortune du pot*, with the Saturday *boeuf à la mode* – English: 'Beef with parsley potatoes'". You will then tell me and Betty[77] quite a lot about your visit to Halberstadt and if you give us the pleasure of being our guest in the countryside, we will tell you about a recent visit we received, which you will certainly enjoy sharing.

Philipp was quite surprised by such a fountain of hospitality streaming towards him and did not know at first why he was receiving so much kindness. He could find no words at first and answered only with a silent bow.

"So please agree to join us," and with this Philipp felt involuntarily compelled to give his consent to the privileges offered to him with a warm shake of the hand.

"Please take a seat for a moment while I finish locking up and tell the coachman that we'll be stopping by your apartment and taking your luggage with us – it will be the easiest thing in the world."

With this, the speaker went back to his room, and Philipp considered how he could pack up the few belongings in his inn, which he in the manner of a soldier had taken just for a two or three day trip. But everything went like clockwork upon the Jacobian command and within an hour Philipp was already sitting at the side of the wife Betty, a born Dutchwoman, cheerful and radiant, deft and natural, who immediately filled everyone around her with warm comfort.

Philipp reported about his pleasurable hours with his uncle Gleim and the recollections from his childhood together with Aunt Gleminde and told about the poet's latest triumph with the wedding caprice—the surprise by the unknown Erato.

"That's him all over again in his youthful, purest manner, yes, one can safely say 'child's mind'. A whole anachorite—someone who withdraws from society—with all anacreontic inclinations, unworldly, childlike, sensitive in his monastic home, as he surrounds himself with all contemporary writers *en effigie* but does not tolerate any contradiction from them.

"Pictures are the most exquisite partners for this—that reminds me, I promised him mine. He has owned my brother's medallion for several years. But my brother Georg himself escaped from his singing student companion Gleim this spring and now publishes a quarterly for women here in Düsseldorf, to which father Gleim still faithfully contributes."

Mrs Betty had her brightest laugh ready to accompany him when her Fritz talked about the blessed days in Lauchstädt, where Gleim had awakened his brother every morning with a new song and Jacobi then felt that the sun around him was gilded with more glory than ever! Yes, he felt the room become a temple, he felt the closeness of God and was sure of his consecration.

"But you will get to know the highly gifted man, who also lived in Halberstadt for five years, in persona, because my brother is our regular Sunday guest."

Philipp had become a little uneasy when he heard his host speak of his uncle Gleim, who was so dear to him, in a somewhat ironic way and he was glad when Jacobi now began to speak of his cousins Lucanus, especially praising the great merits of his father and his mother's brothers in founding and maintaining the famous Lucanus Library[78].

"And as Father Gleim writes to me, you yourself are of Lucanus stock," he then asked Philipp and when the latter explained that Simon Heinrich Lucanus[79], the founder of the library, was his maternal grandfather, his host patted him on the shoulder in confidence, first rising from the table standing before his wife, "Then come with me to my realm, where we will smoke a real Batavia from my dear wife's very own fraternal colonies, for you are worthy to be told now about my friend Goethe."

Philipp obeyed, bidding farewell to his neighbor and hostess with a kiss on the hand. Coffee was served with the cigars at the host's house and soon the two men found themselves alone in a room with its art treasures reaching almost to the ceiling, far more like a museum than a workroom. Jacobi immediately opened the window and the door leading out onto a veranda, letting in the warmer August air.

"I want to warm you up, my dear Lucanus grandson, as I introduce you to the greatest genius of the present day."

"A greater genius than our Prussian King Frederick?", interjected the former lieutenant, who was rising to his full height, modestly yet confident of victory.

"Frederick is the greatest *ruling* genius and more correctly, Goethe is the greatest *poet* genius."

"But the poet is still so young, and one doesn't know how he will develop," replied Philipp to Jacobi, already more courageous than before and considering him a philosopher.

"Didn't Frederick also commit his greatest genius when he entered the Silesia of Maria Theresa as a young king," he replied and Philipp found it more tactful to remain silent again at this point. In his opinion, the taking over of Silesia during the next twenty-three years had required much greater genius than the first bold invasion but the older host should politely be deemed right.

In the meantime Jacobi had put a book in front of Philipp, asking before opening it, "Have you read Goethe's Götz von Berlichingen?"

"I'm afraid not," replied Philipp openly, "after reading what Frederick said about it, I had no desire, quite frankly to buy the book and I have never been to the theater in recent years—but I must retract this, because I saw the Minna von Barnhelm play in Lessing's presence in Wolfenbüttel only recently and was thrilled!"

"Have you spoken with Lessing?" Jacobi asked.

"Yes, I had a long talk with the great man and he gave me his latest poem, 'Nathan the Wise', in farewell."

"What did Lessing say about this latest book by Goethe? It is not surprising that Frederick, in his preference for French literature, did not even appreciate a rising German star and judged 'Götz' completely unjustly but it is incomprehensible that Lessing also punished 'Götz' with contempt. Did he comment on the Werther book?"

"No," replied Philipp sincerely, "there was no longer any opportunity for that. Lessing had a call to Mannheim the next day, and I traveled here by the Rhine."

"You don't seem to know 'The Sorrows of Young Werther'[80] yourself? I would like to give you this proof copy from him. Goethe sent me several proofs from his publisher that he didn't want to see sold, because he later changed all kinds of things in them. I believe it concerned his friends Kestner in Wetzlar but for readers who do not know that family, the original text is perhaps all the more truthful. So read it with the interest it deserves."

After Philipp had thanked him warmly and delightedly for the valuable gift, Jacobi told him almost without hesitation of the visit of the poet genius in June of that year, stopping only now and then to animate Philipp to help himself to the smoking supplies or the liquor.

"He sat in the very same chair in which you are sitting, arriving here one day, quite unexpectedly, on a Rhine journey which he had undertaken from Ems with Lavater, the Swiss and unusually benevolent prophet as well as the pronounced rationalist and ruthless teacher of education, Basedow, in response to one of his high-spirited inspirations. What a strange trio! The two old men, however, were strangely attracted by the fire of youth and unconsciously this man exerted an almost conciliatory influence between the two ideological extremes.

"We spent all too many divinely happy, exuberant days here. Goethe was beside himself with effervescent gaiety. Dances, serenades, rides and masquerades kept him constantly on tenterhooks. In between, he would dash up to the two saints and rave piously with the world-forgotten prophet or delve into Rousseau's freedom issues with the original philosophers. Goethe literally intoxicated us all. He contacted my wife immediately by letter, because she was absent when he was here. What did he say to her? 'Your Fritz, Betty, my Fritz. Not introduced, marshalled, excused—we just turned up unexpected in front of Fritz

Jacobi! I and he and he and I—before a sisterly gaze could preconceive what we should and could be.'[81]

"For my sister Lotte was with me at the time representing Betty. From here Goethe travelled with my brother Georg and me to Elberfeld to Jung-Stilling[82]. He sent for his dear old friend and fellow student from the Strasbourg period to the inn where we were staying by sending for Dr. Jung on the grounds that he was ill. Then he lay down in bed, thickly wrapped in cloths and when the doctor took one hand hanging out to check his pulse, he was suddenly embraced by the rising, hooded monster and recognized, rejoicing, the loudly laughing bosom friend.

"Later I accompanied him from here alone to Cologne. Basedow and Lavater had already spread out in different directions and met again briefly in Ems. The days in Cologne, when I had him to myself in the evening, over the still flooding waters of the Rhine with the glittering moon picking out the Siebengebirge far above the horizon and forgetting reality, he sat there on the corner of the table and recited his latest romances to me, 'There was a king in Thule' and 'There was a Rascal Bold Enough', and I felt as if I was receiving a whole new soul."

Jacobi was silent and Philipp's spirit resonated with his, for he experienced how powerful the poet had seemed to his guest. What else could one speak of now? Philipp stepped silently to the window with his present and began to leaf through it.

"Why don't you sit on the veranda outside where there is better light—I'll have a look around the stables in the meantime and pay my people off. Pretend this is your home."

Now there was nothing Philipp liked better than to get some fresh air and with his copy of Werther in his pocket he soon found a shady path that led to a small birch grove. He now considered his further dispositions. He had been brought here completely against his intentions but he felt more at home already and confessed to himself that these qui pro quo with the great spirits—he thought involuntarily from Halberstadt to Wolfenbüttel and now here to Düsseldorf—had already compensated him to a large extent for the many intellectually impoverished years in Silesia.

He thought to himself, "Who, like him, was allowed to come into direct contact with the brightest stars of the spiritual firmament?" This young Goethe, whom Jacobi, in his skilful and fine differentiation, had already placed at the side of the great Frederick, whom he had already heard women rave about in Breslau, had to be a special figure after all. And he, Philipp, had been sitting in the same armchair today as this genius!

After his pleasant walk, he found his guest reading the newspaper on the terrace in front of his 'museum'.

"You have just enough time to read the reviews of Goethe by Friedrich and von Lessing here again. I picked them out, because I collect all such things—and I ask you then to form your own opinion of the idol—I have given you Goethe's dedication copy to me. I hope you have not yet come far in the Werther. I would like you to slurp my genius bit by bit, at least as far as his greater works are concerned. The man reveals himself exactly the way he develops himself and the things he experiences and has to get rid of. He is extraordinarily productive and his father's wealthy circumstances at home in Frankfurt allow him to enjoy an extended break from a real working life. His mother would like to see him most of all connected with the nooks and crannies of literary intercourse he is engaged in by marrying a pretty and homely girl who suits her as a daughter-in-law and the engagement is now the madame councilor's most zealous endeavor. But I believe that her bird Wolfgang is not yet thinking of being locked up in a marriage cage. He loves the floral necklaces only as a lovely pastime for the time being."

In the meantime Mrs. Betty had joined them to get them to come for dinner. Hearing the last words just then, she said, teasingly embracing her husband from behind, "As if these floral garlands didn't exactly love older poets and worldly wise men either! By the way, I have even wound a wonderful wreath of cyanine myself, taking it out of the field to decorate your great favorite painting with it. You know, he will celebrate his twenty-fifth birthday soon — he is still twenty-four years old today and that is much too early for marital fetters. Surely, Lieutenant, you'll admit that?"

"Do you know that I have already turned 40 years of age without having put them on," Philipp agreed with the mischievous hostess, thinking to himself how seriously he was now occupied with such thoughts. "May I take the liberty of asking whether the Privy Councillor is also engaged in family research like my uncle Friedrich Lucanus," Philipp now introduced the dinner conversation.

"My brother in Glogau also has a great passion for this subject and I especially ask if your family originally bore the name Jacobs and still has relatives of that name."

"My wife can give you better information about that. She likes to deal with such family matters." Mrs Betty listened with interest.

"A gentleman down from the Dutch border once asked the same question. Remember that, Fritz. You used to call him your cousin from what's-its-name and it turned out that he and my husband—the gentleman's name was Jacobs—had the same ancestors.

"You have, as I always tell you, a wonderful memory, Betty—a real elephant's memory, which, as you know, doesn't forget anything that happened years ago. Now I remember the cousin from what's-its-name very well. He was with us when we were still living in Zitadellstrasse as a very young married couple and we made great friends with him and his wife. Unfortunately, we never heard from them again."

"No, and were very surprised about it," Mrs. Betty confirmed the last remark, "because I still gave them letters of recommendation as Jacobi relatives to my brother in Sumatra, since they intended a trip to Dutch India.

"Yes, and the cousin of what's-his-name had such a nice Dutch wife, almost as nice as my Betty, who always travelled with him and had her child, I think a daughter, since she was a Mennonite herself, brought up by the Mennonites."

"Everything is exactly right," Philipp vividly recalled, "we mean the same Jacobs."

"Do you know this cousin better?" Fritz here asked interested. "In fact, I owe him my first acquaintance with Spinoza, whose teachings I am still very fond of today.

Spinoza's boundless unselfishness, in which he virtually revelled, his consistency…"

"But dearest Fritz," interrupted Betty, who was well aware of her husband's admiration and a slight deviation from the subject when a sinking into philosophical systems beckoned, "let us hear what our guest has to tell us about our relatives who became quite dear to us at that time. Do you bring us greetings? Where are you staying?"

"To my sincere regret I must tell you that both have long since met their deaths in the waves of the Rhine."

"But why the Rhine? — They seemed to be such a happy and wealthy couple," Fritz continued probing.

"On that same voyage, on their return home, they were run into the ground by an outgoing ship in the fog and everyone on their ship drowned."

"Lord in heaven," cried Betty here in horror, "so that's why we never heard from them again. And what has become of the daughter?", she asked after a pause.

"She is my bride," it came firmly and seriously from Philipp's lips. It was the first time that his secret had slipped out — and he was initially surprised by himself.

"Your bride? My niece — your bride? And Lieutenant, jeez, nephew and you didn't say that till now?"

And with an almost pleasantly refreshing cordiality after the painful turn the conversation had taken before, Jacobi grabbed the bottle and filled the glasses, "Come a toast to my dear nephew".

"Philipp" came to his senses and rose to toast with the new uncle, visibly excited and happy. "So my dear nephew Phillip, your bride is my niece…?", "Maria", Philipp added, again this time very radiant.

"May yours and our Maria live!"

"Three cheers and may you be blessed!" agreed Betty, and since the simple Saturday meal came to an end in a surprising and animated manner, Betty energetically ordered, "But now come with me to my lady's chamber, for now Philipp's nephew must confess," and so they went out another side door into Betty's realm.

The first thing that caught his eye there was the garland intended for Goethe's painting that Betty now picked up as if in triumph and put over his shoulder as a sash. "Philipp as Maria's much-loved, I welcome you!"

Would the celebrated man ever have dreamed of such a thing happening here on the Rhine?

Thus the very same evening, in front of this splendid couple, he opened his heart to all his worries and when both Uncle Fritz and Aunt Betty offered him almost simultaneously, "If you'd rather take your Maria now, we'd be only too happy to keep her with us until you can take her home as your wife," he wept tears of emotion, tears of joy and accepted the offer with gratitude.

The next morning Fritz Jacobi received him for breakfast after exchanging the usual inquiries about his condition and night's rest with the question: "Dear nephew Philipp, as far as I understood, you come from the Harz Mountains and your father was a royal Anhalt preacher in the foothills of the Harz. Are you now also related to the royal court preacher of your name in Berlin, the author of the *Vertheidigte Glaubens des Christen* ('The Defended Faith of the Christian'), that epoch-making book, which because of its almost philosophical frankness has made so much noise and whose court preaching, originating from his father, has remained untouched during Frederick's entire reign, despite all the hostility of the orthodox? For this brave man of God is my guiding star, and Lavater and Graves revered him in the same way."

"August Wilhelm is my cousin, his father and mine were brothers," Philipp explained adding, "The son of the court preacher is now married to the daughter of the famous Spalding and works in the same institution in Magdeburg from where our great King Frederick's father brought August Wilhelm shortly before his death to Berlin. The son will certainly sooner or later join his father in Berlin and one day become his successor.

"Thanks be to God that our royal house knows how to secure for itself such bright, enlightened and yet faithful men," emphasized Jacobi, "even though the King is probably not a church believer."

"He is a powerful protector of the Protestant Church and does not tolerate Catholic domination. In Silesia we have truly come to know this in the most excellent way. Our Lutheran Reformed Church in Glogau, for whose reconstruction after the Seven Years' War no funds could be raised, was built almost exclusively from the King's casket, despite the fact that the Church Council had not even considered Frederick's choice of location. To regard our Frederick as an atheist at all is the greatest injustice that can be done to him. All his polemics are directed against atheism, not to mention his virtuous life and actions".

"But surely the queen gives your excellent cousin her strongest support?" Jacobi interjected here.

"Far from it, dear Mr. Uncle — the Queen, in her not altogether easy position, has her main attachment to my intrepid cousin and the Cathedral Provost Spalding. When would Frederick ever have allowed a woman to influence him?"

"However, three ladies on the European thrones must have given him enough trouble in return," laughed Jacobi.

"But you know, dear nephew, I don't want to hear you calling your uncle, *Sir* in future. Here on the Rhine we have long since discarded the stiffer formalities. A Lucanus grandson, a Jacobi bridegroom and a Sack cousin — to them I'm simply Uncle Fritz, today and always. Amen."

How quickly Sunday had faded away here among the stimulating and spiritually vibrant people! Georg Jacobi — more of a weakly aesthete and a little over the top, with contemporary tastes and the sentimentalities of the gushing poets and intimates of Gleim — appeared in the afternoon and soon made friends enthusiastically with Philipp because of the Halberstadt connection. Even if Philipp preferred his uncle Fritz by far, he could be extremely satisfied with the reception he had found with both Jacobi brothers.

The next morning he immediately wrote a detailed report about it to Uncle Gleim. He wrote nothing about the Goethe enthusiasm that reigned here, because this name had never been mentioned in Halberstadt.

Nevertheless, there could be no talk of leaving on Monday, as he had planned. Philipp did not want to offend his hosts and new relatives from the outset. Today and tomorrow there was also a Kirmes[83] festival in nearby Ratingen and he had to promise Georg Jacobi that he would pay homage to the Rhineland customs and take him and his wife on a merry-go-round.

Thus it turned out to be five days in Pempelfort instead of two when Philipp finally broke away from this genuine Rhineland house of cheerful sociability. After he had immersed himself in the Götz book while his uncle was busy at the chamber in Düsseldorf, he became quite enthusiastic himself about the combative figure of this robber baron, marvelling enthusiastically at the young creator of this distinctive figure and the characteristic and finely observed secondary figures of the play, already now as a rising German genius, like the Jacobi Circle.

Lessing had then delivered the epigram: "He fills the guts with sand and sells them as ropes. Who? The poet who puts a man's life story into dialogue and writes the thing out as a drama?"

"Voilà un Götz de Berlichingen qui paraît sur la scène, imitation détestable de ces mauvaises pièces anglaises et le parterre applaudit et demande avec enthousiasme la répétition de ces dégoûtantes platitudes."[3] Over and over again he read this criticism of his royal master just as head-shaking as that of the great Shakespeare glorification in Wolfenbüttel. What did the two of them have that they didn't like about the German poet? That he was a German? But wasn't Minna von Barnhelm an equally German play? Philipp had no idea that Lessing had previously written Miss Sara Sampton, a play based entirely on Shakespeare and that Minna von Barnhelm had only been written by him after Goethe's Götz. He himself was immediately taken with the two masterpieces—perhaps as a Frederician cavalier he was

---

3 "Here a Götz from Berlichingen appears on stage, a despicable imitation of those bad English plays and the audience applauds and enthusiastically asks to repeat these disgusting platitudes."

even more inclined to the Minna but as a distinctive free German from the Harz Mountains, Götz was a hearty core figure to whom even he felt related.

Accompanied by the blessings of his hosts and not without their repetition of their offer concerning Maria, he arrived at his new lodging in Kleve on Friday evening, with the intention of settling in tomorrow and visiting the fraternal family on Sunday. He first had to figure out exactly how to justify his prolonged stay without discussing the Jacobi kinship episode. Halberstadt and Berlin, Gleim and Goethe, he had plenty of material to report. Also, that the Jacobis wanted to take him on a trip to the Rhine the next summer, to Mainz and Frankfurt, to show him the beauty of the river—the Lower Rhine was not the celebrated romantic part—that was another point that he had to keep quiet, so as not to upset his brother too much. No sooner had he entered his rooms than he rang the bell and asked if there was a letter for him. Yes, it was said that the Justice Councillor's office had said that it had received several letters for the lieutenant. One look at the clock and he was already on his way to the Stechbahn, reassuringly seeing light in his brother's room.

"I'm back again, I just wanted to report and hear how things are going with you," he greeted the astonished brother and heard from him that not much new had happened in the days of his absence.

"Only that there are three letters for you, which I did not like to send down to your lodgings," and with that he handed the sealed letters to Philipp.

He immediately flew over them but there was not one from Questenberg among them. He pocketed them, signed up for coffee on Sunday and said goodbye again. A letter from his brother in Glogau, one from his cousin Lucanus in Halberstadt and the third with a postmark that was foreign to him. That much he had glimpsed and hardly back home alone again, he opened the latter first.

A signature he did not recognize! He was reading, "It surprised us very much to learn from the Lieutenant's letter to our father that he has not yet heard anything about the changes that have taken place here in the last few weeks. My Lotte's father died suddenly on July 10, from a sudden stroke, which afflicted him in perfect health. My bride and I want to get married in the month of September, when I have accepted an applied for position in Wippra, where I have to start my new vocation right after the autumn holidays.

"The Sonne Inn is to be leased out and there are already two prospective tenants for the house. Gote is now with her brother or is coming to us later, something she has yet to think about. Soon after the Lieutenant's departure the Pastor came through here with very good news from Russia and took Maria Jacobs back to the Rhine, as had been agreed with our blessed father. He wanted to visit the Lieutenant in Kleve immediately.

"We therefore thought that the lieutenant knew about our pitiful loss and were surprised that we had not heard anything about the Rhine. It all came so suddenly for us and my poor bride is still very depressed. That's why she hasn't written to Maria again since our father's death and is still waiting to hear from Maria. We hope to hear good things from the Rhine soon and until then,

I remain with the utmost respect,

Your obedient Servant,
Martin Ender, Teacher."

Philipp had read the letter over and over again and when the morning sun shone brightly into the room, his head was still deeply sunk onto his chest as if he had turned to stone in the same place.

VIII

Kleve

After the hot day's ride in the mail coach, his brain had become quite stupid from all the gloomy brooding and soon a sound sleep conquered him. There were two knocks on the door. The third time he woke up and had to think about where he was for a while. "When do you want breakfast?" shouted the voice outside. "In half an hour," changing his clothes and washing in the fresh water allowed his aching body to feel more comfortable. After another hour he was on his way to the ferry to Emmerich. He blamed himself for having searched far too superficially the other day and when he was still standing in front of the closed shutters of the house, which lay there just as desolate and deserted as he had remembered from the other day, he decided to go to the pastor of the Reformed parish, who surely knew where his fellow minister of the Mennonite community was.

He was dispatched somewhat cold and agitated by the clergyman, who was disturbed from preparing his Sunday sermon in his dressing gown and pipe.

"The Mennonite community has been disbanded since the spring. I know only in part, from the head of the Mennonite community himself, that its members had joined forces with those of other communities and an offer from the Empress of Russia, which granted them full freedom for their, so to speak, non-patriotic religious beliefs and their own land on the Volga. They were tired of the continual harassment of the Catholic priesthood here, who chafed at the closed sectarians, who for their part had unobtrusively cultivated their land in the surrounding area. Just four weeks ago, they had arranged for their houses and land to be publicly auctioned off. With the proceeds they would be able to get twice as much abroad. The agents from Russia granted free travel and the pastor, who had looked at the conditions in Russia, could only have recommended the move.

"The Mennonites themselves, including the pastor, are no longer here—the city had the auction carried out. Surely they will be informed there how the matter has proceeded. There were perhaps a dozen families who did not have a church, only one prayer room, which the city has auctioned off. The people lived so secluded—I don't think anyone can tell you much more about them but as I said, perhaps the town hall will be able to give you more information."

Philipp said goodbye gratefully for the hint and was soon in front of the mayor. "Yes, the pastor embarked last week with his whole flock, and two hundred people from all kinds of German and Dutch Mennonite congregations in Bremen. He thanked us very much for our favorable proceeds and in his letter he also said that in three years he intended to visit his homeland again."

"Can you tell me the place of residence of the Mennonites in Russia?" Philipp asked quite distraught about what he had heard.

"Did he leave an address here?" asked the head of the city to his clerks.

They all shook their heads stupidly and uninterestedly. No one knew about it. When one of them saw how disappointed Philipp was standing there, not moving at all, as if he had to find a clue here after all, the man remembered that the agent had lived in the inn "Zum grünen Baum", and that it was possible that he still lived there.

Philipp almost jumped down the stairs, as if the agent would like to escape him again the next minute. However, even this search was fruitless—the agent had left months ago, and when it was checked, he had not even signed the guest book.

This Emmerich was a horrible city, full of liquor stores, cheese and chewing tobacco! He thought to himself, "Who, in this world-forgotten corner of the earth could I still question here? Should I really leave here today, just like a fortnight ago, completely ignorant?" Maria had already been here on the Rhine six weeks earlier and he found every trace wiped out, while he had so surely imagined the two of them just here as a happy, reunited couple. Where, he wondered, in which house here was she waiting for him. Finally he indulged in this new hope and went from inn to inn to see if a demoiselle Maria Jacobs was staying there.

Yet he was always faced with the same negation. The ragamuffin boys who were following him were growing in number and through their brazen imitation of negative replies, he realized that he was already the target of Emmerich's feminine curiosity behind the windowpanes with their little spy mirrors. Now he suddenly focused on all those heads and pairs of eyes, wondering if Maria was not among them. He was shocked by the often horrified expression of the fleeing beauty who must have thought he had come from the madhouse.

Then he desperately gave up searching and walked towards the ferry's landing place, looking for ways to achieve better results next time. Then he remembered to buy a newspaper before going home and while looking through the advertisements, he thought that it might embarrass Maria to see her name printed in it as wanted and conversely to announce his presence to her.

He considered what the most conspicuous way of doing this would be. He would place an advertisement saying that he was looking for a house or a farm in the area to buy, putting his full address in Kleve in large letters below. He wrote the text of the advertisement as soon as he had reached home, when he discovered that the Emmerich newspaper was being printed and published in Kleve. His name, as the same as that of the brother known to the city, would certainly be read in Kleve. No, that could cause inconvenience! For that he had to get the permission of his brother first. He just did not want to do the wrong thing!

Then, like the night before, he was attacked by the ruminations about Maria's motives in all her mysterious hide and seek, wondering why, if she was so close to Kleve, that she did not write to him. Now he began to suspect the Mennonite pastor that he not only was in love with the beautiful, spiritual girl but that he had stolen her from him and was now kidnapping her. Carefully, on Sunday, he sounded out his brother to see if a gentleman had already asked for him before he himself arrived in Kleve but was only affirmed in the negative. In his pitiful state of mind, he resorted to reading the Jacobi host's gift "The Sufferings of Young Werther".

There he hoped to encounter a hero like Götz and to gain self-confidence and strength from his primal power and ardor. it was not clear to him what kind of a soulful, soft and upsetting book it was. He kept looking at the name of the author wondering if Fritz Jacobi not been mistaken and given him a work by his brother Georg, for whom Goethe had perhaps written a preface. No! It clearly said, "by Wolfgang Goethe."

In the book, the small-town circumstances of Wetzlar were masterfully captured with its focal point of the War Chamber Court—it could just as well have been Kleve, with the importance of its civil service. Instead of being strengthened in his male determination, however, he was drawn into an even deeper and more passionate love and suffering pit and was unable to think clearly about his own situation at all in the following weeks. He was often close to getting himself a gun and putting an end to his self-tortured life. Yet then he remembered all the amusing swings and pranks of the sunny shining godlike figure of the author of the Werther book. He remembered that Jacobi told him that the young poet could only describe self-experience, which he himself openly admitted, at the same time bringing Werther's love emotions to the point of suicide in his novel. Philipp's thoughts were swinging from one extreme to the other.

From his fury towards this young windbag Goethe, which exceeded his strength and wisdom as a disheartened warrior, he drew an astonishing power to banish the image of Maria completely from his life and to shape his new existence in this way, as he had envisioned when he said goodbye to his brother in Glogau, standing with his siblings at their parents' graves and still having no idea about Questenberg and what was happening there.

Only the last two months of this summer were to be immersed in those thoughts. If Maria did not ask about him, she showed herself to be stronger than he was against this pernicious sentimentality of the passion of love. Surely he would be superior as a man to a woman! Well, may she be happy with her life—in which he thought of the Mennonite pastor—just as Lotte was happy—he was truly, like Goethe himself, not a Werther weakling. Now he recognized in the poet the genius that Jacobi held in such high esteem and every time he threatened to fall into questions about Maria's fate, he conjured up the Frankfurt hero of life who defied the love of women. He certainly kissed more often and forgot but the world admired him.

The deeper he threw himself into this way of thinking, using his willpower, the more it grew again to the gigantic dimensions that had so often been admired in his work and creativity in Silesia and which had earned him the special affection and trust of his uncle, President Johann Heinrich Lucanus. It was to this man of honor, who protected him out of his grave, that the appointment to Kleve was successful and it should be his endeavor to do him justice.

In the Stechbahn nobody suspected what fights had already rummaged through him here, what means of overcoming himself he was striving for. The splendid physician Schütte in his widowhood was an excellent support for him. Not that he had confided in him, no, on the contrary, he felt that by not doing so, this man was what he needed. Around the time of Martini, he entered the government. His brother often shook his head, warning and grumbling about the monstrous work mania that Philipp revealed rebuking him for never showing his face in society and for not even allowing himself to be admitted into the circle for the winter pleasures.

Most of all, his eldest nephew Friedrich Gerhard, now almost seventeen years old, joined him in the circle at the Stechbahn, as did little Sophie, aged twelve, who already clung to her uncle in a more confidential manner and secretly let him help her with her schoolwork. Friedrich Gerhard liked to hear his uncle tell about Silesia and was soon to visit the University of Göttingen and then Frankfurt Oder but was already striving to go to Breslau as a trainee teacher. He calculated that this goal could be achieved in just less than four years.

Philipp rejoiced in the young man's striving and walked with him many a Sunday afternoon through the Tiergarten and the now desolate grounds around the sanatorium, down through the suburb of Rindern to the Rhine or along the Kermisdahl to the Schenkenschanz where many a battle had taken place over the centuries, about which Friedrich Gerhard was eager to relate.

He liked to drive with the elderly Doctor Schütte in the wider neighborhood. They extended such trips over the Dutch border to Nymwegen and Sophie was regularly allowed to go with them. She pricked up her ears when the physician explained to her uncle about the antiquities and treasures of paintings that were usually the goal of the journey. In Nymwegen, they looked at the rooms and tables in the town hall where the Peace of Nijmegen[84] was signed in 1678, continuing up to the Belvedere, where they could see the Waal, the Rhine, the Meuse and the Issel, the charming area around Arnhem and the many surrounding villages, forests and fields.

The Valkenhof was the destination on another Wednesday afternoon, where on the nearby Mockaheide once in the battle of 1574 the Spanish armies of the Nassau Oranian counts of Ludwig and Heinrich had been attacked and massacred on the nearby Mockaheide[85]. Also Cranenberg, which a hundred years ago the Elector of Brandenburg Friedrich Wilhelm gave to his doctor Arnold Fey because of a cure favourably performed on him. Fey had only been its master for four years, since he had died childless in 1679, whereby this small town was returned to Brunswick. The beautiful Reichswald forest was often the destination of trips and hikes, as long as the autumn foliage still pleased the eye.

Philipp had written to Düsseldorf, thinking of Madame Betty and the pleasurable days in Pempelfort that had now been exchanged for Jacobi's city apartment.

At Christmas an invitation came from Fritz Jacobi. "Betty missed all the news about Maria in your letter. If you are already married, bring your wife—otherwise you are welcome to the party alone. The children are looking forward to seeing the giant uncle."

The first Christmas in 1774, however, belonged to the fraternal circle on the Stechbahn, where he had promised to celebrate a real German Christmas with the parents of the local children.

"I'd like to come to you between the years, around the 28th about Sunday, but alone, and I will tell you everything," he replied to Düsseldorf, allowing them to conclude that there were new difficulties between the lovers.

Philipp described his second futile search in Emmerich and the whole change in his mood since reading the Werther book and comparing it with its author. He went on to tell how he himself, while waiting for further developments with regard to Maria but rather than rushing, had decided to let them rest, Fritz Jacobi was silent with consternation and his wife Betty looked at him with great amazement—but like her husband did not question him further.

Later, when she had him alone in her chamber, she suddenly asked him whether he had not already thought that he himself had thrown Maria back into the arms of a former admirer by pushing aside her request to take her from Questenberg. Certainly, he had remained in harmony with the commandments of custom and with the man's endeavors to give his wife a home and a position in life, but the orphan Maria, in her helpless isolation, strengthened by the death of her uncle in Questenberg that occurred so suddenly, wanted to emigrate with her former co-religionists.

"Yes, but she knew where I was and was waiting for her, why didn't she trust me and then write immediately?"

Betty understood the situation of the poor girl from the woman's perspective and took her actions to be quite natural. The connecting link, the uncle, who recognized Philipp's care and interest, was no more—her shyness and female reserve had forbidden her to impose herself so soon on him, who refused to let her travel with him. The poor creature, the poor woman, went through Betty's mind again and again—even if she had so much veneration for her Fritz on this—no! She could not empathize with the men, she could not even agree with them.

"Will you allow me, in my turn, to help you now to seek Maria? I know many Mennonites in my homeland where Menno was born a Dutchman. There they do not live as isolated as they do across the border and maybe through them I can learn more about her fate. Poor, poor Maria"

He obtained the promise not to let anything be said about this in Kleve, where he was so bitterly struggling to find his own way to renunciation and work. He was not permitted, he felt, to let his feelings—they were still so sore inside—become master of him again. His mother had already once fought this soft, deep emotional predominance within him and had therefore gladly seen him so joyfully intoxicated by his profession as a soldier.

While reading the book about Werther, he had newly recognized the danger in himself and had happily grasped the defensive weapons in Goethe's human model at the last moment. Strange this change of opinion, which he encountered here! Madame Betty had previously agreed with him that he could not possibly have taken Maria away from her relatives—this time she had expressed herself in a completely opposite way.

He himself had found it difficult to come to grips with his soul and had hoped to gain even more strength in Düsseldorf. This had not been the case—both Jacobis had actually disappointed him quite a bit this time. Moreover, he had felt immediately upon his entry that the beautiful unbiased balance between Fritz Jacobi and Betty was also disturbed and that he had been needed as a stopgap, so to speak.

He liked to turn the conversation to the literary friends of the house and asked what Genius Goethe was now working on. "One hears and sees nothing of him," he received as an answer. The Weimar princes Karl August and Konstantin have recently been in Frankfurt and are said to have persuaded Goethe to reconcile with their Wieland[86] in Weimar on whom Goethe had unleashed a sharp satire in a letter under the influence of a wine-soaked mood. Then he lost his old patroness, Klettenberg[87] through death, which is said to have affected him.

"You wanted to write to him on New Year's Day," said Betty but Fritz didn't hear it and was taciturn. Philipp was glad to have fixed his trip home for Monday morning, even though he had to appease the sad children of the house with sweets.

The New Year in Kleve saw the beginning of increased work which he surrendered to with even greater satisfaction. Ice-skating was a busy activity on the Kermisdahl, but Philipp merely had to be satisfied as a spectator and admire Friedrich Gerhard and Sophie, because his war scars caused him much trouble in the humid climate of the Rhine valley. Friedrich Gerhard moved to the university at Easter and his second son Carl moved up to the first class, because although the Protestant high school in Kleve was a rather primitive school institute, it paid five teachers and dismissed the pupils first when they were ready for the academy.

On January 26, Gertrud again had given her husband a healthy son and brother Heinrich in Glogau, who complained a lot about his health, had donated eleven ducats for distribution among all the children, including the expected one, on this joyful occasion. Then at Easter there was a merry baptismal feast and Philipp, as a confirmed bachelor, naturally had to endure a hail of insinuations from the neighboring women.

Nevertheless, he suffered all of it and since he knew how to find wit through his sense of humor, nobody noticed that in his deepest soul the little arrows hit a still sore and aching spot. He had heard nothing more from Betty about the results of her research and what he learned about Halberstadt from Düsseldorf was not very encouraging.

Meanwhile, Goethe's literary friends had leaked something to other circles at the nightly meetings in Frankfurt's Circles. He was working on a play that would have the Spanish crown prince Clavigo as a hero. Others reported that his productivity was boundless—he had created a new play for lovers, "Stella", in which he dealt with the problem of ménage à trois[88].

Well, he has a living example in his friend Jacobi. When Philipp read this passage in a letter from his cousin Johann Heinrich, he became pensive. This probably explained the tension between the spouses that he had felt at Christmas, and thus Betty's partisanship for Maria and the somewhat reproachful tones for his departure from Questenberg. After all, the death of Maria's uncle was not an obvious reason for their mutual betrothal. After the last conversation in Düsseldorf, he had recalled all the events in Questenberg for days.

Yes, Gote had probably once indicated to him that the Mennonite pastor seemed to venerate Maria very much but that this was the case on Maria's side, which could be dangerous for himself, had never occurred to him. Just as the congregation had entrusted Maria to the travel protection of the pastor and yet she had also made the decision before he, Philipp, came into her life, to return with him, so it was that the pastor had to bring him his bride on the Rhine, now that the situation had changed.

The uncle, a clear-sighted man and father, had also judged and fully agreed with him that Maria should stay with them, as their closest relative, until the return of the pastor in the fall. He had explained to him that she was the bride of another man and would give him her address in Kleve. He had also promised this to himself and Philipp was allowed to assume that the honest man had kept his word.

Maria must have changed her mind—otherwise it was not possible. Her love for him had been an intoxication from which she had awakened, her heart had belonged to her fellow believers and she had remained faithful to them. Even if she had listened to the pastor, that would have been her free decision—she was much too determined a person for that. Maria had become Charlotte Buff[89] in his musings—only he was not a Werther but a Götz.

In spite of everything, he had one of the Mennonites who remained there investigated through an art weaver in Kleve, whether among the emigrants there had been a Marie Jacobs or the pastor as a married man. Through his connections, the weaver had been able to scout out the ship's office in Bremen and inspect the passenger lists there. Shortly after the christening at the Stechbahn, Philipp had visited him again and found out from him that the pastor had been a single man without a wife and that no demoiselle Jacobs had been found among the names of the emigrants.

So Betty's assumption was refuted. For him, however, Maria's Charlotte Buff resemblance was not explained and the mystery of August of last year became unsolvable, taking possession of his mind again. He started to wonder whether she had done some harm to herself and whether she was lying at the bottom of the Rhine like her parents. Surrendering to this assumption could drive him insane so he immediately rejected it, she would be much too pious for that, he comforted himself.

All the brooding, questions and research did not help, only work. However, despite all his activities at the administration, he longed for more physical exercise and again began to pursue the idea of acquiring a country estate. His mother's second-to-last uncle, Friedrich Lucanus, in Halberstadt, had, as his brother had heard from Glogau, bought Quaritz, a property he knew very well, as a bachelor at a much greater age than himself, and had farmed it.

Philipp hoped perhaps to hear now at his domain chamber about a free lease. If he considered the idea more thoroughly, he was forced to reject it again. In order to be able to afford the lease, it would have to be a more lucrative estate—he did not have the means for such an undertaking.

The summer flew by while searching and looking at the few farmsteads that were offered for sale. He always called on his dear old friend, the physician, when such offers were to be examined and almost always the physician had to advise against it, since either the house or the fields were in the Rhine area, where the danger of flooding was too great.

"Dear friend, you may only buy here in the spring, unless the property is on the heights beyond Xanten," Dr. Schütte said to him. They often would have a nice trip but regularly came home without having achieved anything. The walks with his nephew Carl had gradually fizzled out. He was not as talented and lively as Friedrich Gerhard and was about to take his final examination next spring.

Thus the year 1775 had passed away and 1776 brought his brother new additions to the family. This time no ducats had come from noble brother Heinrich in Glogau. Even though he had earlier urged his brother to increase the family in his letters, he might now have thought because of so many sons, "Enough is enough, cease now with your blessings!"

The new offspring, Max, probably had four baptismal names but only godparents from afar, for whom, except for Brother Philipp, court clerks had to practice as substitutes. There was no baptismal ceremony, only a family coffee together. That had taken place in August, all gathered on the terrace, when baby Max was 6 weeks old and it was approaching September.

"I think, Herr Lieutenant, I know a farm suited to your needs," Dr. Schütte had murmured to Philipp at the first undisturbed opportunity, smiling and rubbing his hands.

"I'll pick you up tomorrow afternoon, no need for a carriage — the estate is very close to you, close to Gnadenthal."

Gnadenthal, however, was the castle-like property[90] between the spa facilities and the zoo and belonged to the gentlemen of Blaspiel, who held an almost princely court.

Around the time of Martin's Day in 1776, about four weeks after this hint, Philipp was the lucky owner of the estate Endhuisen in Rindern, in whose district Gnadenthal itself lay and which was directly adjacent to almost the same spa facilities.

The purchase remained for the time being a secret between Philipp and the physician, the present inhabitant still residing there until the spring of 1777. Since it was only just under an hour's walk from the lodging house, where Philipp was still living, almost no evening went by after the hours of government work, that Philipp did not deal with the foreman already at Endhuisen about the winter sowing and other autumn cultivation in the fields and the domestic preparations for the coming year.

Now Philipp was in his element and his soft big brown eyes regained a glint of joy, which was only noticed at the very beginning by his sister-in-law Gertrud, but which, according to her supposition, had since been lost. Under the Christmas tree in 1777 in the Stechbahn lay a thick chunky cardigan and he felt as happy as if he had been given a bag of ducats. He returned the favor to his sister-in-law by asking to celebrate her next birthday in his own way.

"I can only permit it if I may also be present," said the Justice Councillor to his lovely blushing wife. Thus the

May 22, 1778 was already promised to Philipp Wilhelm under the festive illuminated tree on December 24.

"He's so radiant with happiness," Gertrud later said to her Carl August, "watch out, he's got engaged and wants to get married in May."

"Engaged and he? Then he wouldn't be here today," the Justice Councillor reasoned.

"Old Schütte looked up at me today so exhilarated, winking at Philipp as he made his request. I'd rather think he's marrying his old Veronica in May!" Then the whole Stechbahn company laughed and joined in the mother's golden merriment—even the little baby boy crowed along with joy in his new cradle that the Christ-Child had pushed into the Christmas room, the old wickerwork cradle having become obsolete.

He often asked himself if he had banished Maria from his heart completely, especially when a new season came up and his heart was filled with an unquenched longing to ponder his strange destiny. No! But as a rejected suitor, in order to move forward, he gave his emotional world a different, a Lucanus not Sack direction, saying to himself, what he had so often tested against the Polish women's curls as the best protection, that he was—like his mother's brothers—yes, like Uncle Gleim, destinated not for love but only for friendship.

When May 22, 1778 approached, it looked very busy at the manor house Endhuisen. Since April Philipp had moved in there, he had taken over the foreman of the previous owner and in a relative of Dr. Schütze, Veronika, he had acquired a housekeeper. She was more of a farm manager and was in charge of the household, milking the cows herself and running the dairy farm. The main income of the farm consisted in the sale of milk and poultry, especially ducks.

The fields had in former times been part of the large Endhuisen estate but with many changes in ownership had gone from one financial disaster to the next. The fields and meadows, arable land and pastures which Endhuisen had kept were only enough to grow the necessary crops for the cattle, the rye for the bread of their own household and to breed so many cows and pigs that milk for the daily sale of milk and butter came out of the milk chamber. The cash profit after deduction of the costs that guaranteed the improvements for the next year was improved by slaughtering the ducks and geese in autumn.

The pigs delivered the meat for winter and summer and a hunting license also still belonged to the remaining assets. Thus Philipp could mostly pay homage to the huntsman's blessing together with his neighbor Blaspiel and other noble landowners.

Today, on Saturday, May 21, 1778, his people sat on the cleanly swept threshing floor and wove oak wreaths from the Reichswald foliage that the state forest ranger had provided. On the morrow Philipp wanted to pick up the whole family of his brother for an excursion into the surrounding area and in Endhuisen they were to be the first to visit his farm. He had also invited the Jacobis from Düsseldorf with their children but Fritz did not mention that he was coming until the next day, when he planned to pick up Betty. Philipp had a guest room for Betty and a room for the children prepared and had given his parlor to the

Jacobi sons. He himself had reserved his old quarters at the inn.

The meals took place in the hospitably decorated barn. It was all excellently prepared. The physician's old housekeeper had taken care of everything material and the good old Doctor himself had a great time at the feast, which could not have been greater if it had been his own wedding. The tall Military and Domain Secretary, for that had been Philipp's title since the autumn, was enclosed by the physician in his big warm heart like a son. Silently, he hoped for a further development of the events, as his loving soul had longed for them in secrecy.

This day marked the first foundation stone for this. The home was there now and the first thing that belonged in it was a woman. His brother Carl August's eyes were wide open when Philipp, just after the procession (as he called his dear guests) came down from the Sternberg, making their way to the Rhine through Rindern at one of the large gates. This gate was wreathed and decorated with flags and opened wide. People dressed in traditional costumes formed a guard of honor and then were led to the coffee table on the terrace where a huge birthday cake with forty-three burning candles and a small flag "Vivat Gertrud" was displayed.

A place was reserved for the birthday girl at the side of the dear old physician, opposite her Betty, led by Carl August. The Kleve and the Düsseldorf youth took turns in colorful rows. Philipp himself was the host who served his guests, supported by Veronika and Katharina, their niece, briefly introduced as Vron and Trine. The foreman did not start his duties until the evening, when the May punch was due.

As was to be expected, Gertrud and Betty had quickly made friends with their mutual relations in the Dutch neighboring kingdom. With the confidentiality thus gained between the family mothers of the same age, Philipp had given Betty a sign to observe silence at the first opportunity when, of course, one brother accused the other of having the privilege of confirmed bachelorhood and as quite inadmissible for a manor house. Putting a finger to her lips, Betty gave a signal to observe silence.

"What do you want," cried Philipp to his brother, "I am the son of a Lucanus. Uncle Fritz, the much older bachelor, still runs Quaritz in Silesia, even without a wife. Where, by the way, as Brother Heinrich writes, things are supposed to be much more fun, as in earlier years. You see, there was the uncle and there is now Brother Heinrich himself and our brother Ernst in Hecklingen, all splendid farmers and all unmarried."

"Oh, what enemies of women they are!" thundered Carl August, "don't stand for it, you women there!", appealing to Betty and his Gertrude, "make sure we have a wedding here at the same time as the harvest festival!"

At this point, of course, the whole farm was inspected, which the children had long since considered their prerogative. At the end, they guessed at a princely sum that the purchase of such an impeccable property must have cost.

"Brother Heinrich, who probably sold his last estate recently, invested the proceeds in you?" Carl August researched with interest but Philipp could not help responding without particular satisfaction, "Brother Heinrich doesn't know a single thing about my house purchase yet — you can be the first to write to him about it."

However, he did not reveal the price, the ridiculous price for which the Doctor had been able to get him the farm estate Endhuisen, albeit in a rather desolate state, and was only pleased to see how the curious ones were increasing their price estimates.

Then just at the right time the foreman rolled in the cask with the May punch, and a steaming ham of downright Westphalian proportions aroused the delight of the two housewives.

"I'm absolutely flabbergasted!" said Mrs Gertrud.

"And in addition on top of that new potatoes and cucumber salad." cried Betty enthusiastically.

"This housewarming party is worthy of reciting a poem by Goethe. But unfortunately for his friends in the Rhineland, he is now almost lost since he became a minister in Weimarsch and is involved in road construction and sewerage plans. Fritz is really angry with him, and his friend Merk, who is just like his father and doesn't know what to think of this latest poet's whim as a prince's favorite. He must have driven him crazy at the Weimar court, and those who have called on him are said to be afraid for the soul of the young prince.

"If you let sparkling wine ferment, it will become clear," the physician said calmly, and raised his glass.

"Let's drink to the welfare of Madame Justice Councillor, three cheers for our beloved birthday girl," and roaring with deep male voices and the soprano of the boys and girls, each singing a round of an old German song, followed by the festively decorated room being lit with pitch torches in the corners and a wreath lit by candles above the table.

Finally the children were showing signs of tiredness and it was time for the sandman. Gertrud reminded them that it was time to leave. Betty was lucky today and didn't have to walk very far.

A young moon was shining in the sky as the old physician and the brotherly family walked home through the streets of Kleve.

"Philipp is a hell of a guy," said his brother, not a little proud of him, "I'm just wondering who he's going to bring home as a wife—I heard the other day in the chamber that they've already applied for the title of Privy Councillor because of his eminent work performance."

"Just be patient!" replied the physician, after shaking hands, no less proud of his protégé.

"He's made it to a privy estate so now we need to see him as a privy councillor. You can be sure that the privy 'councillor-ess' won't be missing for long."

And indeed, so it was! Already little more than eight days later, in the first days of the Rose Moon, when the small Cupid sitting on a dolphin decorated the third fountain terrace of the amphitheater and the delicate garlands of roses that surrounded the water pool were in full bloom, Madame Goddard from Rotterdam moved into the fountain house as a spa guest, accompanied by her lovely daughter Kathleen. Nobody was more pleased about this enrichment of the spa roster than the wellness physician Dr. Schütte. Madame Goddard had already been coming here from the time when she still was at the same age as her daughter.

The doctor's lady friend, became one of the very first visitors to his spa and since then no Christmas had gone by that he had not regularly spent time with Mynheer Goddard and his family in Rotterdam. The old Kleve residents whispered to each other that Dr. Schütte, because of the beautiful Madame Goddard, previously Miss Kroustere, might have remained a single man for a long time. (Dr. Schütte had lost his wife and a son after nine years of marriage.)

Anyway, they were good friends, all of them. Mr Goddard, who as usual arrived for the follow-up treatment that summer, and the physician had even become bosom friends and for the little daughter Kathleen he was the dear uncle Willem. Philipp, who in that first summer of 1777 was stingy with every hour so he could spend time on agriculture at his new farm, was now to devote himself to the two ladies Goddard at the request of his old friend, the physician and had a really hard time meeting the many demands placed upon him.

However, he was still too much of a newcomer to Kleve that the many trips the physician made for the ladies would not have attracted him to take Sundays or late afternoons off. Especially the boat trips on the Kermisdahl were an experience for Philipp. He, who was born with so much romance in his blood, enjoyed the quiet gliding between the two of them along the riverside streets, behind which the courtyards with the beautiful parks and country houses rose. Among them the beautifully structured roofs, gables and towers of the Schwanenburg Castle, were by far the most impressive.

The young creature at his side, however, studied far more than the scenic charms but rather the pleasant features of the man's head next to her. She had to wake up the often absent-minded person from his reveries, of whom Uncle Willem always told her only the most favorable and praiseworthy things. This was always most effectively accomplished by addressing him in Dutch and thus forcing him to translate her speech.

„Wat vind' ik wonder, waak ik ga?
Waar ik het oog maar neder sla?
Ook in het stof, en mulle zand,
Daar zie ik uwe rechterhand.
Daar zie ik kracht en hoog beleid,
Dat my nooit Mensch en heeft gezeid:
Een Bloem, een Gras, het minste kruyd,
Dat reop uw' groote wonders uyt:
Dat doet ons reizen met den geest,
Waar dood noch helle werd gevreest.[91]

There was many a sweet smile, teasing giggles and often involuntarily loud laughter from her mother, when Philipp took pleasure in studying the most wonderful and impossible things from the words that sounded so unutterably flat and unpronounceable to his ears.

That evening, maiden Kathleen pouted at him because he had really overdone it. She scribbled her verses on a page from her notebook and gave him the punishment of bringing her a translation of them when they met again.

Philipp found the task cruel but took the leaf and said that it was not his fault that the Tower of Babel had caused this deplorable confusion of languages.

The dear old physician had now chosen Castle Moyland as his destination for the next trip. Philipp looked forward with joyful anticipation to the days when he would see the place his great king had owned, and where he had even first met Voltaire. His young companion wore a white muslin dress that day, tastefully decorated with black velvet ribbons. Philipp immediately noticed that it was the Prussian colors in which she had dressed today, and complimented her on this delicate attention to the King of Prussia.

He would bring her a small gift for the trip out, whether it was a bouquet of flowers, a bag of sugar candy or some refreshing fruit but today he presented her with a wonderful, half-blossoming water lily as a reminder of her recent trip out on the water. Wrapped around its stem, she discovered a piece of paper with writing on it that read:

What wonders me, where I am going,
I doubt mine eye, what is it showing?
In plainest cloth, in softest sand,
Showing me doth God's right hand,
There great power and glory see,
How no one ever reaches thee,
In flower and grass, in every weed,
Do God's great miracles succeed,
And our spirits walketh tall,
Where death and hell come to all,
Wonderful price I think it is,
O Child of Man but you are this.

"Well, has the pupil done right by his teacher and is she reconciled with him again," Philipp asked faithfully, trying to examine her red-hot little face under the broad straw hat.

"But the last line is not in my poem," she said embarrassedly.

"No," he said confident of victory, "nor did you forbid me to add in German what the Dutch poet had apparently forgotten".

When Mrs. Godard then wanted to see the German work, her little daughter knew how to put her off with an "Afterwards, Mama". The journey to Moyland went via Ledburg monastery and church, which had formerly been a Catholic convent and its collegiate church, the burial place of many a count's family.

Charlemagne is said to have built the church when he was tired of worldly commerce, turning to spiritual contemplation and performing his daily devotion here for a while. Today Bedburg was a monastery for Protestant young eligible maidens of noble families, who could of course marry from here. The royal house of Moyland (moy is the Dutch word for beautiful) was bought as a knight's seat of the Barons van Spaen[92] by the Elector Friedrich of Brandenburg[93], later to become the first King of Prussia in 1695. The castle has a considerable treasure of portraits on its two floors and was particularly worth seeing because of its life-size ceiling paintings depicting the nations of all parts of the world in their various costumes.

At the front entrance, the world in all its vanity is depicted in the picture. Opposite is the castle church, where the service for the reformed congregation is held. Wonderful oak trees and shady avenues adorn the pretty park belonging to the house.

Philipp could imagine that his King did not value this property too much and had it sold as unsuitable for his needs as King in 1776. He stood for a long time pondering at the window of the hall that had been described to him as the one in which the first meeting with Voltaire had taken place in 1740. The beautiful Kathleen, who had long since been informed by the physician of the veneration which Philipp attached to his commander from Silesia, honored his silent contemplation and waited calmly until he found his way back to the rest of society.

In the nearby inn, "The Schwan" they took a cup of tea and as the day was still before them, it was decided to drive to Calcar, which is not too far away, in order to visit the famous carved altars of Calcar in the St. Nicolai-Parochial church there. The most important one is the high altar, 7,25m high and 4,08m wide, made in 1498-1500 by different masters. The paintings of the wings were made by Jan van Calcar[94] in 1505-1508. The entire work contains 208 carved and 216 painted figures.

When Philipp heard the name Calcar, he immediately remembered the magnificent work of art of Jan van Calcar, which he had already admired in the Cathedral of Xanten during his journey through the Harz Mountains. At the same time, however, he had even more precious admiration for this city than the birthplace of his General von Seydlitz in 1721, a figure from his wartime years, to whom he held the highest veneration next to the King. He was an excellent cavalry general, after whom the King later named the Seydlitz cuirassier to which Philipp's own von Rochov's cuirassier regiment in Halberstadt belonged. Because of his intrepidness on the Glogau Bridge whilst a sergeant, he had already been noticed by the King who was so proud of him that he had him promoted from sergeant to cavalry master.

There were also other anecdotes from his short life that had survived and were of course faithfully preserved in Philipp's memory. The town of Calcar got its name from a branch of the Rhine and the brook The Leye, which are spread around an area, shaped like a spur, forming an island. Four beautiful gates and a very splendid large square market with a pretty town hall are the main decoration of the secular buildings, while of course the churches, as in all the Catholic cities of the Lower Rhine, are of a size, extent and magnificence out of proportion to the number of inhabitants.

Philipp rejoiced when he learned that in addition to the magnificent Parochial Church, which had a main pastor and ten chaplains or vicars in charge of their offices as well as three large monastic settlements and their places of worship, Calcar also had a Reformed church. Strangely enough, which is not the case with catholic cathedrals, the church was kept locked except for the times of church services.

Even before Philipp had found the sexton in the little house opposite, who approached with his bunch of keys and took the lead to his treasures from there on, a group of young maidens was waiting outside the church door, and now joined the physician's group. Indeed, every one of the fifteen altars was almost second to none in the quality of its carvings. In the dark oak wood, which almost approached black, the parables were masterfully depicted on one altar and the miracles on the other. Then again, the saints or the whole life story of the holy men and women in warm and well-proportioned figures with characteristic heads and lively features were masterfully presented and brought to life in tasteful altar capitals.

Despite the outstanding amount of carvings, painting had not been neglected. As certainly as the artists came from a carving school in Calcar, of which Jan had been the director, so certainly the 276 paintings in the wings of the altars were all painted by his own hand. The sexton knew how to tell the most amusing stories about this artist and showed that in the picture where the Hebrews were searching for manna in the desert, a baker from Calcar was shown in the middle of the picture. When the painter was feeling unwell and he had taken some bread from her shop, the baker ran after him scolding him, not hesitating to take the bread from him again. Jan swore revenge to her in his hunger and now immortalized the fiend in the Hebrew's picture, as having not taken part in the blessing of heavenly manna.

The drive home over the Montaberg, with a fresh and wonderful panoramic view over the Rhine valley with all its towns grouped around Kleve, was extremely enjoyable. Mrs. Goddard for her part now prompted the young Seydlitz Cavalier in the carriage to recite a Dutch hymn of praise, especially since he, for his part, had challenged her pride in her language somewhat strongly.

The group of young girls had laughed together in a visibly amused manner while listening to the sexton's stories about the painter-joker Jan. Enjoying the sexton's witty remarks in a language of which Philipp did not understand a single syllable but into which the sexton suddenly tuned in vividly by addressing himself exclusively to the funny and loud group, Philipp said to the maiden Kathleen, "How much of an advantage you now have as a Dutch woman and can understand everything, whereas I, as an ignorant schoolboy, want to learn and cannot."

"But they are not speaking in our language, it's just an ordinary Calcar Platt dialect! I can understand it because it's German but not actually Dutch," replied the beautiful young lady, this time visibly indignant, which the observing mother had not failed to notice.

In this way she showed him, the German horseman who once again had put his foot in the wrong stirrup, her noble Dutch language in its full beauty and Philipp immediately translated every line.

> *S Gvoget self kan nict mer syigen itsts singt en springt hier on de Tuygen*

The birds themselves can't keep quiet now they sing here and jump upon the branches

> *Om dat het nut en niezen Dag met een Vreugd aenschoewen mag*

Because again a new beautiful day with our joy to gaze at them.

> *Het leert uns met sein Quinkeleeren He jeder mal den Scheppen eeren*

With their chirping they teach us to honor the Creator at all times

> *Eb hertlig zym verhengt int Licht van zym heylotralen Aangesicht*

Heartiness alone helps us into the light of his bright shining face.

"So Miss Kathleen please have mercy on the poor ignorant me again," he added pleadingly and of course this put not only the lady but also her mother in the most conciliatory mood. That evening they parted on all sides with the highest contentment. The physician believed to be on the best way to gently cure his confirmed bachelor Philipp with the beautiful Kathleen. Mama Goddard saw the German officer making the most amazing progress in the Dutch language, which was of the utmost importance to Mr Goddard, her husband.

Miss Kathleen placed Philipp's water lily in a glass of flowers in her small room and showered his handwriting with the most tender kisses. Philipp was once again happy to have got to know so much of what was worth seeing in his new home, so that he did not have to regret his purchase of the estate here. Especially since, on his return home, Mamsell Trine announced to him, beaming with joy, "Our sir can rejoice — the sow from the Schenkenschanz has given birth to twelve piglets."

It had always been the wish of the physician that Philipp would one day invite the Goddard ladies to his farm and organize a small rustic celebration for them there. However, this had been postponed until Mr. Goddard had appeared for the follow-up treatment in Kleve.

Now July was already coming to an end and the harvest work began, binding the lawyer and farmer more strongly to his work on the land than before. They were now hoping for the arrival of the Dutch husband in the first days of August and Philipp now thought of decorating the threshing floor with harvest wreaths and getting his foreman to bring some of his friends together for a country-dance. The Goddards from the spa house, the physician of course and his friends from the Stechbahn were to meet in front of the manor house for coffee under the lime tree.

It had to be a somewhat premature harvest festival due to the imminent departure of the Dutch guests. The day was set for Sunday August 10, because Mr. Goddard was to arrive on Friday or Saturday. Dr. Schütte was just as busy with the preparations as Philipp and the aunt of Mamsell Trine, the old Vron was also there again. The pipers, who played for the dance afterwards, welcomed the guests with some cheerful waltzes at the gate and Philipp had thrown himself into the costume of a Dutch farmer to demonstrate the simple rusticity of his hospitality. He was no less astonished and equally astounded than were those of his guests who had already gathered under the linden tree. They had appeared in splendid summer dresses when Madame Goddard entered at the side of a rather youthful husband. Behind her, at the side of the much-loved doctor, was Kathleen, in the splendid costume of a rich peasant woman from the island of Marche.

During the all-round greeting, Mrs Goddard had to introduce her younger companion as a substitute for her husband, since the latter would have been prevented from carrying out his intentions if he had had to commission the first proxy to escort his lady on her journey home. Mr Engelbrecht, an extraordinarily skilful son of a merchant, with good manners, knew immediately how to introduce himself in his representative role in the most advantageous way. Philipp was touched in the most pleasant way. Instead of finding a stiff Rotterdam merchant, whose high demands on social luxury he knew from the occasional remarks of his ladies, he found a kind and helpful partner in Mr. Engelbrecht. He had long been known to him as a friend of the house and was one who had made himself at home in the courtyard and stables.

Even the young nephews from the Stechbahn knew the new guest to be a great acquisition and soon there was an exuberant, infectious cheerfulness among uncle Philipp's younger and older guests. The only one on whom her physician patron noticed a somewhat artificial cheerfulness was Kathleen, who was wearing her Mark[95] national costume. Not even her mother noticed her.

Every time she looked at her daughter, her motherly pride was gratified, because she found that her child was now a real beauty in the circle and all eyes were upon her. When the dance of the country folk, which was very amusing due to the wooden blocks they used to accentuate the rhythm from time to time, turned into a funny waltz at the end, Philipp approached the beautiful 'Margrave peasant woman' and asked her for a dance.

"Would you like to take a stiff-legged, shot-up cavalryman for a round dance?" He had, as it were, apologized that it had to be the first dance. Rather stiff, like a four-legged one compared to his servants, he turned his radiant dancer in circles. As if on command, however, Mr Engelbrecht replaced him right after the first round and, as was customary in the country, the young nephews of the house danced with the maids in the meantime and the tall sprouting daughter Sophie tried her best to get into the right step with the foreman.

Meanwhile, Philipp prepared the dinner table, which immediately transformed the dance floor into a dining room by setting the tables that only needed to be pushed in. At the top of the table, according to rank and dignity, sat the invited guests and since only cold food was served with refreshing drinks, Vron and Trine sat at the table forming the transition to the locals, who of course could not be deprived of their hospitality. Strangely enough, Philipp was not as stiff-legged as he was as a dancer and the moment when the host of Endhuisen and Mr Engelbrecht from Rotterdam ceremoniously drank schnapps together became the crowning glory of the festival.

Early in the morning, however, the harvest carts had to drive back into the field and the delightfully successful celebration had to end before midnight. The old physician and the Justice Councillor took each other by the arm for mutual safety, the two older ladies, Mrs. Goddard and the Justice Councillor's wife followed. Mr Engelbrecht with the beautiful Kathleen were the last as the animated company headed through the main street of Rindern towards the nearby spa and spring houses of Bad Kleve.

"Philipp understands," said Carl August on the way home to his wife Gertrud, "Wasn't that another lovely day today! And how splendid he has his subordinates on board—just like his squadron as a cuirassier used to be, I'm sure."

"Yes," said Gertrud, "he really understands it brilliantly, better than good old Schütte obviously does with his acquisition of a 'lady privy councillor'. But perhaps because at the chamber you haven't yet come forth with the 'Privy Councillor'. What's the problem?"

"I think one wants to see first," said Carl August, "whether his passion for agriculture doesn't distract too much from the enthusiasm for work in the chamber. One still needs his fantastic manpower up there too much and lets the hope of the Privy Councillor post continue for a while — the Prussian state understands that like no one else.

Philipp, for his part, was also fully satisfied with the small celebration, for in Mr Engelbrecht he had met a young man whose fresh, natural manner, combined with what seemed to him to be solid knowledge of his commercial vocation and social skills, appealing to him immensely. He also thought he had noticed that the beautiful Kathleen Goddard was probably the attraction for him in Kleve, for whose sake he had not reluctantly taken over the accompanying of the ladies to Holland. It was not that Mr Engelbrecht had put it on display, on the contrary, he had strictly avoided to be anything more than polite to his boss's wife and to show noble reserve towards his beautiful daughter. But Philipp instinctively felt that it was just because he himself did not appear as a rival to the beautiful Dutch woman, Mr Engelbrecht had also locked him into his heart.

Whether Mama Goddard would agree to this, he could not answer. He did not know to what extent Mr Engelbrecht was a preferred or acceptable son-in-law for her. He himself regretted it very much when his new young friend visited him the next morning to catch up on his inaugural visit since the party, as it were, to hear that Mr Goddard wished his ladies to return home without further delay and therefore Mr Engelbrecht thought he should pay him his farewell visit at the same time.

Philipp then found it only natural to accompany Mr Engelbrecht back to the ladies' hotel to say goodbye to them. Whatever flowers his garden had left over after the lavish feast, he quickly cut them and tied them neatly into two beautiful bouquets. He also met the physician at the spa house, who had just heard about the ladies' quick departure. "This time you must also bring your young friend for Christmas" was the warm invitation that Mrs. Goddard had already extended to the physician and now repeated personally to Philipp during his farewell visit. Since the beautiful Kathleen and Mr Engelbrecht also joined in with the heartiest words, Philipp could not help but accept the invitation with the warmest expressions of thanks.

A lot could happen during the long gap between the height of summer and the depth of winter. At first he was far too interested in his agriculture and devoted all the time he had left from his official work to it. It had been a very pleasant performance of duty towards the physician, to whom he owed so much gratitude, so that he had been allowed to be somebody for his friends and had been able to prove himself worthy for them. The Dutch, however, did not interest him any further. On the whole, he had no sympathy for that nation—they were mostly *peperzaks*[96] who had become rich and who had no great sympathy for the ideals of life.

He saw the doctor only a little during the summer who had a lot of spa guests and he himself had his hands full. In the bottom of his heart he was not at all sad that he had no more social obligations and that he could again devote himself with all his strength to his governmental business and in his leisure hours to the harvest and all the duties of agriculture which so richly impacted on him in the fall. He noticed with quiet joy that his life here was becoming more and more captivating and fulfilling and at the same time it lifted his self-confidence extraordinarily when he noticed in the Domain Chamber that his superiors had already honored him with exceptional tasks of trust and that his brother Carl August also often praised his enthusiasm and ability to work.

This was already echoed in the letters of his Glogau brother Heinrich and he himself felt deeply happy that here in Kleve he seemed to meet the expectations placed upon him. So the fall, this time a particularly golden and abundant one, flowed by and no one rejoiced with it more than Mamsell Trine and her Aunt Vrohn in the rich harvest blessing, since so much of the abundance of the estate's blessing also ended up in the kitchen and pantry of the good physician.

Back in the Stechbahn, Getrud appreciated the abundance of Endhuisen, and even though her brother-in-law from Glogau sang the old song again and again in his letters, "I hope to hear soon about a marriage of Brother Philipp," she was quietly surprised how the former lieutenant was still able to run an estate without a country woman at his side, organizing it so profitably. She thought it would be best to let him quietly do as he saw fit and now a visit to the Goddard's was in the offing for him.

The rich merchant's house in Rotterdam would not deny him his daughter and a far greater purchase of property in addition—so much she believed she had already heard from her mother's admiration for the Prussian battle hero. While Gertrud was indulging in such silent deliberations over her sewing basket of children's clothes, which in turn had to be put in order for an offspring, Philipp was sitting at home over a letter which the good Dr. Schütte had handed over to him when he had just met him at the spa house, accompanying him a little way.

"It will probably be a repeat of the invitation for Christmas," said the physician, "and it will soon be time, my friend, for you to prepare yourself to travel with me to Rotterdam—just make sure you get the necessary leave from the government in time," he added as a precaution.

Now Philipp deciphered the foreign manuscript, which correctly, as the physician had suspected, contained a second invitation from Mefrow Goddard. A letter from Kathleen was also enclosed and with great amusement he read the following warlike outpouring of the young Dutch woman's heart, "On our return journey we heard the reveille sounding early in Wesel and after coffee we walked to the Berlin gate to visit the same. It is indeed a very precious gate, decorated with many splendid pictures and at the same time solid and well deserving of attention. In the meantime the guards had been changed and the men on guard duty found themselves in front of their officers' quarters, beating more than 60 drums. On seeing them we remembered the old German heroes and how they were commonly depicted. We found a great resemblance between the two, in view of their great stature, manner and the clothing appropriate to their status.

"When we watched their exercises, it was just like watching everything being operated by a machine. In terms of skill and particularly dexterous loading of the rifle, few troops, let alone older ones, would be able to match the Prussian troops, much less surpass them. It is the most carefully selected personnel, their bodies well formed and their limbs flawless. They walk around constantly in green clothes and wavy, powdered hair. They have the finest rifles. Also a strict discipline and code of war is maintained among them.

"With all due respect to His Majesty, the gloriously reigning Prussian monarch Frederick the Other, who, by his bravery, heroic deeds, leading battalions and victories, has earned himself immortal fame throughout the world and who demands order, strict discipline and the most precise subordination from every soldier in his army, at the same time, His Majesty always looks upon a man who is called upon and trained to be a righteous soldier, rather than a man who is only outwardly dressed as one. However, all violent acts amongst them are seriously prohibited, whereas if His Majesty were to use gold to procure from abroad, he would get plenty of men.

"The great skill and swift firing of the Prussians surpass all other nations. It has been calculated that the Prussians fired five times before the Austrians loaded twice. As you can see, Lieutenant, I remembered what I heard from all around me and wrote it in my heart. I hope you enjoy it."

Philipp had to smile to himself involuntarily when he read this charmingly naive chatter of the Dutch lady. It would seem that the physician had betrayed his admiration for his King to her and had thus enthused her for 'Frederick the Other', as he was apparently called in Holland.

He folded the little letter and put it with the ones she had once given him to translate on the river trip on the Kermisdal. When at Christmas the physician went to Rotterdam for his usual Christmas visit, there was something else for Philipp to do and that was to find a gift. He was able to give the Doctor a pretty piece of gold-woven hand made spun yarn of the finest kind from the monasteries around Kleve, with hand made lace as wide as a hand for two headscarves, as the Dutch women were wont to wear them over their genuine thin gold bonnets in their country. They were to be taken in a parcel together as a present.

"Please tell Miss Kathleen that it would be a special pleasure for me if she would soon be using her shawl as Mrs Engelbrecht," he had written to Madame Goddard with a few lines of congratulations for both ladies. He was delighted with all his heart when, on New Year's Day 1778 — which as in France and Belgium is also the main holiday in Holland of the twelve holy nights — received a fine printed engagement announcement from his young friend Engelbrecht with the words, "Kathleen Goddard Jan Engelbrecht engaged Rotterdam New Years Day 1778". In the course of late autumn he had received many a small reminder, even once a whole box of tea and coffee for the household of Endhuisen.

Especially it had been the poor Dr. Schütte, stripped of his plans, when he came home from his Rotterdam trip, who obviously lamented that it was not Philipp but the Rotterdam merchant who was to marry the beautiful Kathleen Goddard. Philipp, however, knew how to make it clear to him that he could not use a lady of fashion for his life on the estate and that he would have to make do with his Mamsell Trine in its running for the time being.

On the other hand, which is why he had decided not to travel to Rotterdam, he had the opportunity to expand even further and to acquire a few more plots of land for his agriculture that winter. This winter of 1778 was quite a rainy one and on some days Philipp stared at the barometer before he went to the office. It seemed that the barometer would not lift at all and when he came home, his first trip was down to the Rhine to see how high it was.

The Spoygraben, as the main arm was called on which Kleve lays and which, together with the Kermisdahl below Rindern, pours its water into the main Rhine, was swelling massively. The Rhine itself was receiving so much water from Switzerland and on the way from its tributaries on the journey from the Alps to here in the nearby Netherlands that it almost looked as if the sea was coming from Holland to unite here with the mighty stream coming down from the mountains. He did not fail to warn the inhabitants down in the village, as much as he was able to, to rescue their possessions in time. Even in the manor house he was already working to have empty storerooms prepared in the upper town, so that he could offer help to the people.

So he soon became the personality from whom one can find advice and help and one would never leave his threshold without receiving such. After a few nights of hard work to clear out entire huts, he also had to realize that his newly acquired land had been washed away by the swollen floods and that in spring, at any rate, he would be staring at it, bare of all the arable land to cultivate and for the most part almost completely destroyed. These were the ugly disadvantages of this area that the doctor had told him about two years ago before he bought his house. He felt guilty that he had not consulted his old friend and advisor about his agreement to the purchase of the additional land, since the latter had been staying with his Rotterdam friends at the time.

After spring had happily passed and summer had made up for the devastation of winter as best it could, except for his land that had floated away, the Catholic part of the population made pilgrimages to the famous image "Holy Mary, Full of Grace" in Kevelaer[97], which was not far away. One day the doctor suggested going but to attend such a pilgrimage, not as a devout pilgrim but as a spectator. Philipp gladly accepted the suggestion and they took advantage of Corpus Christi Day and soon drove with Philipp's own carriage down the streets via Goch to the place of pilgrimage. It is of great importance not only to the Catholics of the Rhineland but also to the Dutch in Westphalia bordering on to it.

It was a strange spectacle that was presented to the visitors here. All the streets of the small town, the large tree-lined square, the chapel built over the image and a church next to it that is the main attraction, all converge towards this central point. On one side of the town, however, there is an avenue at one end of which the Crucifixion on Golgotha is depicted in larger-than-life figures and which, as the so-called Way of the Cross with its stations of suffering, is also of particular importance in the processions. Kevelaer's history of origins as a place of pilgrimage is based on one event. A little picture of the Blessed Mother that a pilgrim from Echternach, near Trier, had brought with him and placed in his prayer book that he showed to various friends and acquaintances at home and also to his clergyman, who, at the request of some of his friends, lent it to them to show it to poor sick people.

Soon the word spread that it had a miraculous effect and that the sick people who looked at it and worshipped it had become healthy. Now the owner demanded it back but since he did not succeed in getting it, he turned to the clergyman and he again passed it on to his authorities, because as a miraculous image, it should be given special consideration by the church as something worthy of veneration.

This led to the decision of the spiritual authorities to make the picture accessible to the public and to build a chapel where it could be venerated from inside and outside. So it happened that for decades, even a century, the picture has been the great attraction for all those who are burdened with infirmities to free themselves from their suffering by invoking its miraculous power.

For the great feast day of Corpus Christi, a particularly solemn procession and pilgrimage were planned at the same time. Thus the place was teeming with pilgrims who came with their clergymen carrying flags along the way. The streets were lined with wonderfully richly decorated altars at every corner and every house almost at every window and deep into the corridors decorated with carpets, candles and figures of saints.

Philipp had never seen anything like this before and it seemed strange to him as a simple Reformed man. He was little accustomed to church decoration and seeing the church celebration moved to the streets. He had much too much tolerance in his heart to view this kind of worship of God in anything other than reverence. As sunny and laughing as the sky had favored the celebration at first, thick raindrops coming out of a black thundercloud soon mixed into it. Now everyone in the first row was trying to save the altars and to put their hands to work to take care of the treasures of the church.

Philipp proved to be not the last one to be helpful in this and in the process, near the Chapel of Grace, he bumped into the middle of a procession of nuns, who, with their dresses piled high, were helping the choirboys to recover relics under the protection of the church roof. He clashed somewhat clumsily into a nun in a hurry and, while apologizing, her treasures slipped out of her hands and he now bent down to collect them into the lap of her skirt.

At one point he involuntarily looked under the wings of her bonnet and, as if moved by thunder, stood there for a moment and stared at the young woman's features. He involuntarily exclaimed "Maria!" but like the wind, the young nun was up and vanished into the crowd.

It took Philipp a moment to compose himself and then to find his companion Dr. Schütte, who in turn was also looking for him, quietly waiting nearby under a front door until the tangle around the chapel had come loose and Philipp was visible to him from afar. The actual procession came to an end with the thunderstorm shower and the pious crowds inside the Chapel of Grace, the church where the celebration was now progressing, were dispersing. The physician advised against staying longer there after a refreshing drink in an inn, while Philipp would have loved to try to see the young nun again.

But the doctor urged to go home and when he noticed Philipp's anxiety to stay longer, he simply asked him the reason for his wish. Philipp could not hold back any longer and replied that he thought he had seen a familiar face in a young nun and would like to be able to make sure.

"But, dear friend," replied the physician almost amused, "that could keep us going for days on end with this deluge of pilgrims. And then it is impossible for you to look under the bonnet of every one of these Beguines[98] — that would be downright offensive.

So Philipp had to surrender but he did not do so without asking the innkeeper if it was possible to find out which orders had made a pilgrimage here.

"I would like to inquire with the ecclesiastical authorities whether such a thing is recorded," the latter replied politely, and by leaving his address, Philipp gave him a fairly precise indication of the type of costume worn by the particular category of sisters.

"It seems to me that the sisters of Mount Zion were in Kleve," replied the innkeeper, "but, as I said, I will inquire.

Satisfied, Philipp steered his carriage home and knew exactly what he had to do in the next few days. In the evening after the thunderstorm had subsided, a rather hazy, damp veil had settled over the whole landscape and the journey home was less pleasant than the journey there. This was especially so since Philipp often sat there quietly and introspectively and the physician, who in his cheerful tipsy mood would have allowed himself a joke here and there, encountered a somewhat thoughtful comrade who did not seem to be like the Philipp he knew.

The next days were quite cloudy and rainy and the Rhine began to swell again, filling Philipp with much anxious concern about the harvest, which was already in full swing. Then one evening Trine came running to Aunt Vron and said, "The sir does not please me, he also says that he is not feeling well and has had tea made at the pharmacy."

Whereupon the physician had nothing more urgent to do than to hurry down to his friend's house Endhuisen and there to look after the patient. He immediately detected a high fever and prescribed a night vigil for Trine. He feared that it was typhoid fever, which prevailed a lot in the swampy neighborhood and which would not leave his friend's body without causing harm.

Just as the shrewd doctor suspected, so it came. After the second night, during which the patient fantasized a lot, a replacement had to be found for Trine, who was already heavily burdened with household chores. The practical Vron suggested sending to Mount Zion and asking for the help of a nurse, although they heard that the nurses were already under great strain due to the sudden epidemic in the area.

So the physician himself drove up to the monastery, which was located at the end of the Stechbahn and which had already provided him with help several times. On the way, he informed the Justice Councillor and urgently advised against visiting the patient, if only because of the danger of infection. However, he asked him to report the illness of the poor patient to the government. This was done dutifully and the convent sent, in the absence of sisters who were already busy, a young novice who willingly promised to assist the doctor in the care of his patient in Endhuisen.

Soon the sister, who did not wear any religious attire as she was only allowed to be dressed thus at high feasts, stood at the patient's bedside and proved to be a wonderful strength in her attentiveness, even in the face of Trine who was a little put out. She helped her everywhere, even occasionally with the farming where the management by the landowner was missing.

Gradually Philipp's consciousness began to return but as he watched the young novice at his bedside, he wondered how the physician had brought Maria here. "Maria?" replied the physician, "I don't know anyone of that name in the house."

"Yes, but the young demoiselle he had observed a few times from his bed was the demoiselle Maria Jacobs?"

The physician was silent and thought only that the patient was probably talking in a fever again. However, since during the next few days of recovery, the sick person always addressed the novice with Demoiselle Maria, he calmly implied that the novice accepted her name without contradiction, even though she had presented herself as Ottilie Baumann and that this was her name. The sick man apparently confused her with an acquaintance and the nurse then confessed that she had already been addressed as "Maria" by a gentleman during the pilgrimage in Kevelaer but that she had had to hurry away in the rain without thanks for his help and without explanation. She thought she might have the same gentleman before her but could not say for certain. The sick man had always been so patient and friendly in an exemplary manner and of course she did not care what name he called her by.

When the sick man began to recover and began to talk to his nurse, he asked her all kinds of questions to which she could not give him an answer and always said that she neither knew Emmerich nor had she ever been to the Harz mountains, nor had she ever grown up as a Mennonite, but as a Catholic. She had grown up with her parents on the island of Büderich, which is close to Wesel. Her parents had been country people and her mother had always had the wish to have a daughter in the monastery. So she decided, at first with a heavy heart but then at the request of the deceased, to try her service in the monastery and had already grown to love it, so that she resolved to consecrate herself to it.

Philipp now had to be satisfied that she was telling the truth. He was also quietly convinced, when he observed her intelligent actions and conduct, that he had a rarely practical farmer as a nurse and began to admire the future sister more and more in his heart, even to grow fond of her who simply asked to be named Ottilie when she was called.

Autumn was already approaching and the convent asked when the novice would return to her ministry and whether she would be dispensable at Endhuisen. However, since there was no housekeeper on the estate and Philipp did not yet feel able to look after things in the stable and barn, often needing supervision to ensure that he did not overtax himself, the physician asked again and again that the novice Ottilie remain at Endhuisen for a while.

Meanwhile, the Justice Councillor had been given leave of absence from the government until after Christmas for the recuperation of the convalescent. It went on into October and Philipp decided to take a yardmaster to help him in the spring. For the time being he did not know how he could live the lonely winter without Ottilie, she had become indispensable to his household and perhaps even more indispensable to his heart.

Then one morning a carriage drove into the yard. A pastor and a little girl of about three years of age got out of it and asked to speak to the lieutenant. When he was granted this permission, he asked at the same time to be able to leave the child in the care of Ottilie, who had opened the door for him, for as long as possible. Philipp, who had been kept as far away as possible from the still strange visitor, apologized, and after a short greeting, he offered his guest a chair, seating himself down opposite him.

By introducing himself as a Mennonite pastor, the guest sympathized with him since he had heard that the lieutenant had been ill. Now the pastor apologized, as he expressed himself, for his special mission. First of all, he took out of his wallet a small parcel that he unfolded and in the contents of which Philipp, to his boundless astonishment, recognized the necklace with the cross with which he had venerated Maria in Questenberg three years before.

"You mustn't be upset," said the clergyman, "when I bring you the legacy of a dear deceased member of my congregation who entrusted this to me, with the request that I bring it to you personally. Maria Jacobs slumbered gently, suffering from the same affliction as so many in the area, and was already halfway to recovery but her fragile constitution was not able to withstand a relapse. She has asked you to forgive her many times over if she has caused you pain and suffering, because she felt that she could not cope with a more eventful life after Questenberg at the side of a higher official and landowner.

"Even on the journey, when I picked her up from Questenberg, she confessed this to me and at the same time admitted to me that she must have concluded from your entire behavior that you did not share her Mennonite faith in the same conception of marriage and that you probably expected her to be disloyal to her mother's faith in order to do justice to yours.

"Therefore, however, she should never have asked to accompany you and leave her relatives for your sake. This only became clear to her after her departure from Questenberg. Half shy and half ashamed, she immediately looked back on the day on the Maiden's Meadow as a beautiful dream but with a sad awakening. She was very distressed for her own sake and for the disappointment she had to cause you but as she had already always been a very determined child, she could not be moved to abandon her decision. She asked me to take her to a more distant friend living on the other side of the border with Holland and to go to the Volga without her. I fulfilled her wish and when I came back to my home on the other side of the Rhine I visited her too and unfortunately I found her so frail that all I could do was fulfil her last wishes.

"She filled her life by raising a Mennonite orphan[99], which I now want to take care of, since she left her considerable fortune to her. The little girl she called Philippine Jacobs is out with her nurse and it is time for me to leave."

Philipp, who had listened with great composure to all this communication from the pastor, asked to be allowed to see the little girl and requested, spontaneously, whether he would not allow him to keep Maria's foster child and to be allowed to educate her from her legacy. The pastor was quite touched by this offer and agreed on the condition that if the little girl would be willing, which was his only concern, he would leave her behind for a fortnight as a trial.

Philipp asked his nurse to bring the little girl in. Ottilie, who was a real woman had immediately developed a great affection for the child and with whom the little girl seemed to have felt visibly comfortable, brought her into the room holding her hand. Phillip looked up at a charming child's face with blond hair and large dark eyes that looked up at the novice Ottilie with great affection and intimacy.

Philipp, whose noble heart immediately found the right words, asked the little one, holding her between his knees, "Would you like to stay with us, little Philippine?" The little girl looked at the pastor and when he showed his approval, she nodded her head as if she wanted to, if only the others wanted her.

Then, they shared lunch together, to which Philipp invited the pastor, whose coachman he had taken care of outside. Afterwards, the pastor set off agreeing to ask again in fourteen days and then to bring the papers of the little girl, assuming that she had settled in and Philipp had not decided to do anything to the contrary. He had already brought her few belongings of clothes with him, as he was originally intending to take her to friends of his.

When the pastor had left, Ottilie had cleared the table and bedded the tired little one next door for the night, the first thing Philipp did was to ask Ottilie to dedicate her afternoon to him completely and to escort him under the lime tree outside into the garden. Before that, Philipp had locked the chain with the cross away as a motherly memento for the little one. Now, however, he told Ottilie in the garden where and under what circumstances he had met Maria. When Ottilie had listened to him calmly and had only occasionally asked whether it did not upset the lieutenant too much, she listened attentively to him. On the contrary, it relieved his heart this day, for he still had something on his mind that had to be removed and from which Ottilie alone could free him.

Then the young woman looked down blushing, when Philipp convincingly made it clear to Ottilie that he must now have a mother for the child at his estate. He asked her if she could decide to become that mother and stay with him as his wife instead of entering the convent. The first thing Ottilie replied was, "But Sir, that could not be, Sir is Protestant and I am Catholic, I cannot change my faith."

"I wasn't asking you to do that, dear Ottilie. If you have nothing against me as a Protestant, each of us can remain what we are."

"But our Priest would never allow this to be a mixed marriage," and the tormented woman sobbed and continued, "O Lord, do not lead me into temptation, it cannot be!"

In Kleve there were four special congregations of different faiths—Catholics, Reformed, Lutherans, and Jews. The former were significantly in the majority, only that the Brandenburg House of Regents professed the Augsburg Confession to which the families of officials and a larger number of the most respected families largely belonged to. The main priest of the Catholic parish, an ex-Jesuit, was known for his intolerance and the principle of the sole legitimacy of his church was so firmly rooted in him that as a priest he never agreed to bless a mixed marriage.

Marriages between the two branches of Protestant culture had no such concerns. They had never had the least adverse effect on domestic, marital, or parental harmony. The Kleve Catholics, however, were particularly strict. Now, of course, it was precisely the sisterhoods that were under the influence of the head priest. The Handmaids of Christ, as they called themselves in the orders were concerned with nursing the sick and spent more time among families. They were particularly inculcated with the idea of apostasy as the greatest mortal sin.

Poor Ottilie, in whose heart a warm reverence had long since sprouted for her patient but which she did not dare to admit as love, was now not spared the bitterest struggles within herself. Strangely enough, she always found her greatest comfort and her special peace of mind when she was preoccupied with the little Philippine Mennonite child. The quiet simplicity of the child, who had grown up pure and unspoiled in the simple Mennonite community, gave her peace for her inner struggles and doubts. The child prayed her little children's prayers every evening and already out of consideration for Philipp, she did not dare to teach the young soul the prayers and intercessions of the Virgin Mary, who had such great importance in her cult. Instead she quietly folded her hands together with her.

Philipp was not the man to allow himself to be diverted by religious confession from his heart inclination yet a second time. He pondered and pondered how he could now persuade Ottilie to change her strict views after all. During the Mennonite pastor's visit he had gained clarity about his own feelings that Maria's strange behavior had very gently and gradually detached his heart from her. Now fate had given him back his full freedom for a new engagement. No! This could not again go unheard, simply because of the other's faith.

When the dear old physician came in the evening and found his patient dejected and upset, Philipp could not help but openly let him in on his heartache. The good, caring friend had himself recognized the patient's affection for his nurse and now heard why his earlier intentions with the beautiful Kathleen had found no response. At first he himself did not know a right way out for the removal of the religious difficulties, as he knew how the so-called Almighty of the Catholic Church of Kleve had spoken in a similar case.

"If the bride were to marry a heretic, it would be no different than if she were to lie in bed with the devil himself." But he wisely kept this from the patient and left him with the assurance that he would find some help for him, if only to lift the spirits of his convalescent.

The next morning, Philipp received the following handwritten letter from him through old Vron, "Dear friend, that it didn't occur to me yesterday! Did not the English on the other side of the Channel on the forgotten border between themselves and Scotland have a solution in Gretna Green? We also have one and very close by—a marriage El Dorado on the Lower Rhine. The old church books of the Reformed community of Hörstgen are still kept at the mayor's office in Kamp, a village in the Lower Rhine region visited by summer visitors. The old books tell a strange story. In the 16th century, the Barons of Mylendonk, whose ancestral seat is located on the Nier near Mönchengladbach, took over from the Barons of Blotdonk the free independent territory of Hörstgen, to which the house Fronenbruch, located between Hörstgen and Jevelen, also belonged. The dominion included the present mayor's office of Hörstgen and the Lords of Myllendonk[100] introduced the Reformation there. Even today, most of the inhabitants are Protestant. By inheritance the imperial baronial rule later came to the Lords of Krusebeck. They are the owners of a permanent, quite lucrative, but also strange source of income, whose yield was recently estimated at two hundred Reichstaler per year.

"As rulers of an imperially free minute country, the Lords of Myllendonk and also their successors to Fronenbruch have the right of marital consent and the right to grant dispensation in delicate marital matters, of which they make use to such an extensive degree that men and women from near and far, for whom obstacles of the heart have been placed in their way, make pilgrimages to Hörstgen. For several centuries Hörstgen couples from the most diverse social classes were married, sometimes by consensus, sometimes by dispensation of national sovereignty. The Counts of Moers often tried to present the jurisdiction of the Lords of Hörstgen as unjustified, and Kurköln denied the same, the glory of Hörstgen 'unfaithful to the fiefdom of Moers' and their actions were an encroachment on the rights of foreign territories, especially those of the neighboring Cologne Archbishopric.

"When and how the sovereign marriage law of Hörstgen was created is not known. The oldest message contained in the marriage register is from 1687, where it says, *'den 21 Martig Lyk on vers soek van myn Heer op het huyo Fronenbrok gedrouwet Hermen Ligrevoet mit der Maeght Helina'*. A special proclamation was made at Ankysheel that day.

"By the way, the courts of various places recognized the marriages entered into in Hörstgen as valid, in particular Kurköln was also forced to recognize the marriages contracted in Hörstgen as valid, according to canon law, although the marriages performed, especially since they were mostly of Catholic origin, were called illicit, they were thus recognized as valid. An old family tradition can tell of some highly romantic weddings, namely of members of neighboring aristocratic families who entered into holy matrimony at night and in the fog at Hörstgen with the participation of the local rulers. Interesting messages from those of Mylendonk containing numerous names from Duisburg and also Krefeld appear in these old documents as marriages.

"You see, dear friend, from this note, which I copied for you from an old volume about Moers in my library, that you need not despair. Good luck with your nurse! Best wishes from your old body and soul Physician Schütte."

When Philipp read the advice of the splendid doctor, which even to him seemed a bit romantic, he was very doubtful that Ottilie would let herself be married by a reformed priest in Hörstgen, even if she and any possible successors of her marriage union could remain and become Catholic. He wanted to ask his Catholic chaplain here in Hörstgen, whom he had already met several times during the flood disaster as a very calm and considerate young man, whether he would be willing to present this marriage ceremony in his church. It should at least be possible to find out whether he was a blind follower of the Almighty in Kleve, or a man with his own church opinion.

His first expedition out of his home after his illness at noon of that day led Philipp to the small house where the chaplain lived. How cheerfully and joyfully he left the same one hour later. The very accommodating young pastor was not at all averse to a Catholic blessing of a mixed marriage here in his parish in Rindern, if the husband would commit himself in writing not to influence his wife ecclesiastically and to have any children baptized Catholic. Philipp was quite relieved when chaplain Müller even, joyfully, agreed to win Ottilie as mistress of Endhuisen for the congregation, which greatly satisfied Philipp.

He calmly left Ottilie some more time for reflection and asked that only the priest influence her. He did not want to come back to the subject with her at first. When the Mennonite pastor returned after a fortnight and the little Philippine had long since become an Endhuisen accessory, everyone knew who Uncle Philipp or Aunt Ottilie were busy with and the little girl was already playing with dog and chickens in the stable and barn. It was soon decided that the little girl would now always stay with Uncle Philipp.

When the morning finally came and there was no longer any reason to leave the novice at Endhuisen, the monastery demanded her back, and Philipp had to ask Ottilie to look for a kind of tutor for the child, since the Mamsell Trine could no longer be burdened. When Philipp sent for her, she was told that she still had so much to sort out and had gone up to the convent early, coming back to say goodbye that evening.

Philipp waited silently and when she came it was just as the Angelus bells[101] rang in the evening. She knocked modestly at Philipp's door this time and when she humbly stepped up to him to explain her absence and to ask his forgiveness for her quick decision in the morning, she thanked the master for all his kindness and hospitality. Philipp, in turn, declared that he was the one who should thank her and ask her to accept a special gift for the church. She gratefully took it and asked if she might give it to the monastery, whereupon, of course, he gave her complete freedom of disposal over the money.

When he wistfully reached out his hand to bid her farewell, it was Ottilie who held his hand firmly in hers and, with a very emotional voice but looking up at him openly, asked him whether she should not come every morning and evening to care for little Philippine and return to him completely before the master had to return to office after Christmas. She had terminated her contract with the monastery on December 1, as she realized that the child would have to have a foster mother.

"Isn't it true, dear Ottilie, you have understood that I need a woman," whereupon she blushed but gratefully bowed her head in affirmation and squeezed his hand affirmatively. So, at the beginning of December 1778, a young housewife moved into Endhuisen, and all those who had come to hold Ottilie in such high esteem in the village, especially the physician, Vron and Trine had their special joy as participants in the silent celebration. Since the celebration took place according to the Catholic rite,

Philipp had not even let his family in on it and asked his friend to keep the marriage secret up in Kleve.

His family had only come to the estate for festive occasions anyway and the times weren't right for celebrations. The country was seething with activity because the revolution had begun to cast its shadow over the border. One Christmas day Philipp went up to the Stechbahn, where he had not been for so long, to report in good health and found everyone happy to see him again.

From New Year's Day onwards, his office also began to demand his familiarization again. It was a joy to see how it worked once more. It was a silent bliss for his heart, which had been lonely for so long, when he came home and Ottilie and the little one were already coming to meet him. His young housewife knew how to make his home more comfortable and harmonious than he had ever dreamed of.

He had the good fortune to increase his property more and more through good acquisitions and since he had found in Peter Olsendorf a hard-working and employable steward, no complaints about him could be heard. On the contrary, the government was extremely satisfied with his achievements and the Justice Councillor always knew only the best to report to his brother Heinrich in Glogau about his youngest brother.

In the spring of 1780, when the storks again moved to their nests on the chimneys of the villages, Mr. Stork Adebar also returned to the matrimonial bedroom in Endhuisen and put a little daughter in the cradle, so that soon the little Philippine, who slowly called Philipp and Ottilie her parents father and mother, received a little sister, who was born on May 16, 1780. On March 16, the Catholic priest Müller baptized her Wilhelmina, with the steward Olsendorf and a citizen of Rindern, Mrs. Anna Wantner, a close friend of Ottilie's, as godparents.

Philipp wrote in the baptismal booklet that he started with the following words, "May the Almighty God, for the sake of his dear Son, Lord and Saviour Jesus Christ, grant his grace and mercy upon her."

Two years later, in 1782, likewise in the month when the storks returned, Mr. Adebar brought another little daughter into the house who was baptized by Pastor Müller on the same day as her arrival, in the name of Carolina Louise. The godparents were the husband of Mrs. Wanter and the niece of Pastor Müller, Miss Agneta Nauland.

Ottilie had taken a lively interest in her young married happiness. In the evenings, when she belonged exclusively to her Philipp, she heard about his parents' house in Hecklingen, about his splendid mother, who had warmed him from an early age so completely for agriculture. And yet his mother liked it so much when he joined the Halberstadt regiment away from the university, where his father had sent him to study law, to fight for his King — against whom Catholic France had allied itself with Catholic Austria and the Russian Catholic throne.

Ottilie began to be as enthusiastic about the great King Frederick as the faithful man was. When many a customer came from across the border from France, which caused him the greatest displeasure, she showed them respect. How dutifully he fulfilled his duties in the chamber and how well he did. And how splendidly he cared for his wife and child. All his subordinates in the administration were devoted to him. She found that if one only acted nobly and well towards one's neighbor, practiced patience and cultivated the virtues, as his King and he did, many a Catholic could take the Protestant as an example.

In the fall of 1782, to Philipp's delight, an opportunity finally arose in the vicinity of Minden in Westphalia to acquire a domain that he was able to purchase with his already so richly increased means. He went there to view the castle and district of Hausberge and the Rothenhof outlying estate, because in his experience the very low location of Endhuisen seemed to him to pose a threat to the health of himself and his family. Although he considered himself to be in relatively good health, he knew that he still had to fight with the aftermath of his serious illness and without strong doses of quinine, which the doctor prescribed, it did not go well. Close to the cattle, down at the lock of the canal, the body of Johanna Sebus was found later in 1809 during the great flood when the floodwater had risen unusually that year and she, the neighbor and children were overwhelmed by the flood. A total of twenty-two people died.

Minden had already pleased him exceptionally well on the journey here to the Rhine eight years before and he searched among his books for the writings that he had just purchased about the property on the hill there to read it to Ottilie in the evening. Even the little girl Philippine was already sharpening her ears, knowing that her parents might want to move there. An inquisitive, spirited little girl loves nothing more than the prospect of a big new change that her parents had always wanted.

At the Stechbahn, where already the second son Carl had completed his legal clerkship and was trying hard to compensate for his older brother Gerhard with his parents and siblings. He had died three years earlier in Glogau of a hot fever within a few days. Of the other ten children, the youngest son Max was already seven years old and the older sons Christian and August as well as Wilhelm already attended universities and gave their parents a lot of pleasure, especially August, who proved to be extremely talented.

Since the most respected families of Kleve had joined together to form a "society", which in the meantime enjoyed a great reputation among the higher officials of Kleve that had many children, the adolescent youth of Brother August and his wife Gertrud had now found a welcome form of companionship. For the older members of Kleve society it created a source of debate and recreation, while for the young people it became the shining mirror in which they could examine and polish off their manners. The diversity of the official and business relationships of the members of the society compelled them to show consideration for one another, which was beneficial for their later life and conducive to frank modesty.

During the new years he had been working in the government in Kleve, Philipp had never decided to join this society. From the outset he had felt too young for the older family fathers of the Sethes, Berneth, Fock, Rappard, Jacobi, Reimann, Grohmann and, whatever his brother's neighbors and friends were called, and too old for the youth of the dance hall. He had had more than enough to do with his landowner's concerns, truly sufficient a pastime and stimulation.

Two years ago the Halberstadt monastery senior, Canon Arnold Kopstadt, had already moved his residence to Kleve and married a native of Clermont. His wife's family was in turn friends with Jacobis from Düsseldorf, and since Philipp's last visit to these people, circumstances, as well as his own, had brought about a profound change. The once so fervently close friendship between the Goethe friend and himself had not been cultivated any further.

Once he had met Kopstadt himself at his brother's house and they had used this occasion to celebrate the happy festival week in Halberstadt with the memories of his relatives Lucanus and the old kindly father Gleim, a happy resurrection. Gleim, so the Canon knew to tell, had even one day had the pleasure to receive the Weimar minister Goethe in his home and to introduce him into his circles of friendship. However, the collector of celebrities would like to have succeeded in winning the author of Götz and Werther over to the idea of having himself painted for his picture gallery.

For some time now a new light had risen in the heaven of poets in Friedrich Schiller, to whom no proper relationship had yet been established in Halberstadt or anywhere else in the Prussia of the great King. As a Swabian by birth in Stuttgart, educated at the Karlsschule, the stormy effervescent man had rebelled against the existing conditions of the princely houses, such as the electoral house in Hesse, through his first two dramas, "The Robbers" and "Intrigue and Love". He knew how to portray them clearly in his works, which had also been performed in Mannheim. This had provided the young, unusual talent with few patrons, and people were still waiting to see what would happen to him. The awakening youth, even in Kleve, had already devoured every new appearance that penetrated from the new star of poetry into the general public and, in their own desire for freedom, cheered his frank and spirited works. Even Lessing was said not to have denied the Swabian rival the testimony of genius.

Subsequently, Philipp, in his highly inflammatory sense of poetry and history, had been able to procure the first Schiller dramas and read the work to his Ottilie. Both recognized the high standpoint of the young world stormer and since then followed his work with sincere admiration.

The farewell from the fraternal circle was taken by all his people with sincere joy. Unfortunately, Philipp's appointment to Privy Councillor and the achievement of his often expressed wish to lease a larger domain was accompanied by heartfelt regret, for the youngest brother, brother-in-law and uncle had been appreciated and loved over the years. The saddest of all, however, was the old physician and the divorce from him was not only difficult for Philipp but also for his wife Ottilie and little Philippine. Only the promise to spend each Pentecost on the domain sweetened the bitter pill of being separated.

The steward and Trine formed the retinue that moved with him to his new home as he was now the tenant general of the Prussian administration of Hausberge and the domain Rothenhof in the Principality of Minden. He left the city that he had entered alone and he thought, counting the seven-member company of which he and his house now constituted, that he was now grateful for the rich blessing and full happiness that he had found here on the Lower Rhine.

Now he was to move a good piece towards his one time home and the Porta Westfalica was shining towards him as the connecting gate to this and his old youthful years.

IX

Rothenhof

Once the final decision had been made, Philipp Wilhelm finally concluded the lease of the domain in the spring of 1783 and Ottilie was ready to move in with her household. While the Government Justice Councillor and Physician expressed great regret about the unalterable decision made in Endhuisen, Philipp Wilhelm, who at the same time had to resign from his office there, was transferred to the government in Minden with the title of a Royal Prussian Privy Councillor.

Now everything was there that one could wish for and they moved into their new home with a sense of well-being. On the following morning, Ottilie thought she should now also offer a gift to her husband and solemnly declared to Philipp Wilhelm that she herself wished that they would all be Protestant there in those Protestant parts of Westphalia and that their marriage would be similarly blessed and all their children baptized accordingly. Nobody welcomed this more gladly and joyfully than Philipp Wilhelm himself. The first action on July 7, 1783 in the new home was that these new tenants of the royal Rothenhof estate together with Madame Ottilie were accepted and entered into the church register and in the community of the Protestant church of Holzhausen, in whose parish the Rothenhof estate was located.

Now a new life began on the Rothenhof and after Philipp Wilhelm had familiarized himself there, another little daughter was born to him in 1784 on April 22. He entered her in his baptismal book as Francisca Albertina, after she had been baptized by the Lutheran preacher of Holzhausen, Baumann, on April 26, at the town office. The godparents were the Military and Domain Councillor Albertus Meyer and the wife of the Chief Forester of Plathen.

He entered a prayer in his baptismal book:

God, Almighty and Merciful Father of all human children, for this child too I ask in the name of your dear Son for compassion and fatherly grace and mercy. Amen. Rothenhof, April 26, 1784.

On July 26, 1785 a boy named Friedeman Ludwig Alexander was baptized, born on July 23. The godparents were:

1) The Privy Councillor Military and Domain Councillor Baron von Schellersheim

2) The Frey Fräulein von Massow

3) The Captain, now forest clerk von Horn, of Hausberge

4) And the sister-in-law, wife of Justice Councillor Sack of Kleve, née Nordmann

And so it follows from the baptismal booklet that in 1786 another son, Carl Simon Benjamin, saw the light of day on the Rothenhof. The father records that his dear brother, Justice Councillor Carl August Sack of Kleve and his dear brother, Justice Councillor Simon Heinrich Sack of Glogau in Silesia, were the godparents, who were represented by the official legal adviser Ahland and the second legal adviser Müller. The third godmother was Demoiselle Friederica Sack from Bernburg.

A fourth son, August Ferdinand Heinrich, followed in 1790 on March 16. Godparents were August von Dentecom, Councillor for Military and Domain Affairs at the High Prussian Chamber of Military and Domain Affairs in Minden, as well as Carl August Sack of Kleve, Second

Councillor for Justice, in whose place again Philipp's legal adviser Müller, and third godparent Simon Heinrich Sack of Groß-Glogau in Silesia, represented by the legal adviser Ahland, are listed.

Preacher Baumann in Holzhausen again administered the sacrament of baptism on March 2. This child was later entered by his father's hand: "According to a letter from the Cavalry Captain von Cornberg, dated Schmolensk, August 21, 1812, my son died upon the bed of honor after a fierce action against the Russians on August 19, 1812 as a result of a shot in the abdomen and right side".

In the year 1791, April 19, Philipp Wilhelm records that his tenderly beloved wife Ottilie Baumann, née Baumann, gave birth to a daughter who received the sacrament of holy baptism on the blessed Easter day of April 25 from the current preacher in Holzhausen, Barkhausen, on the Rothenhof premises and was given the name Ottilie Adolphina Charlotta. With her — as Wilhelm Philipp noted — the godparents were:

1) The wife of Salt Inspector von Basfus née von Nersen

2) My dear brother the Legal Director Johann Adolf Sack of Glogau in Schlesien, represented by the lawyer Müller of Haus Berga.

For not only were more children born to the parents in the next few years but the household was also enlarged by employing farming apprentices on a subsistence basis, in order to be able to survive under difficult political conditions after the terrible French Revolution spread to Westphalia and caused great inflation.

In the year 1792 on March 18, after the beloved wife of the Privy Councillor had given birth to a daughter, who died immediately after the birth and was buried the following day in the churchyard of Holzhausen, the year 1793 was blessed on February 21 with the birth of a safe and sound son, who was baptized on the 24th of the same month by the current Lutheran preacher of Holzhausen, also at the administration building, receiving the name Friedrich August George Philipp. His godparents were:

1) Mr Friedrich Johann von Lucanus of Groß-Glogau, Royal Administrative Government Councillor, represented by Ahland of Hausberge, Judicial Officer

2) The Military and Domain Councillor Joh. August Sack of Kleve (the later Royal President of Pomerania) represented by the pensioner Koppe by the judicial officer Müller of Hausberge and Candidate George Linn of Weyer in County Katzenellenbogen.

"God give this child grace and blessing" — the father wrote at that time as a prayer, adding seventeen years later in the margin: "N.B. May 17, 1810, died in action in Kassel".

In the year 1794 on October 12, Sunday, his beloved wife gave birth to a well-formed son, who on the Friday of the 17th was given the name Wilhelm Eduard Hieronimo Maximilian by the preacher Barckhausen. Because of the weakness of this child, they had to hurry with the holy baptism and the father wrote that he himself had represented the position of baptismal witness.

Still in his sixty-third year of life, his beloved wife presented him on October 24 with a young daughter, who was baptized on October 30 at Rothenhof by the preacher

Barckhausen and received the name Ulrike Dorothea Sophie. The godparents were:

1) Colonel and Commander of the von Byonsche Curassier Regiment, which is garrisoned at Aschersleben, Baron von Frohreich.

2) The Colonel Baron von Oheim, hereditary, feudal and judicial lord of Holtzhausen, Ensen and several villages.

3) Baroness von Bandemer, wife of the country huntsman

4) The Captain's wife Baroness von Wuthenow, whose husband at the time as Chief Provincial Carriage Inspector was located in Hausberge's quarters.

"To you almighty creator of all creatures and saviour of the world and God the Holy Spirit, I commend this child to your gracious care."

Thus the pious father concluded this line about his children, adding on an extra sheet of paper:

My eldest daughter Philippine Antoinette, born March 10, 1775, is married to Ernst Johann Conrad Schultz, Royal Judge and tenant general of the Baron von Klenck's estate of Langreder near Hannover.

Marriage contracted on July 17, 1794 children born

1) One daughter Ernestine born April 15, 1795

2) Eduard Wilhelm born October 15, 1796

Schultze died December 24, 1798.

From all these personal entries it is clear that Philipp Wilhelm felt quite differently in his element in Westphalia and even close to the Porta Westfalica where eight years ago he had seen it as a historical battlefield of the Germanic tribes against the Romans—a more congenial point of contact with his Peaceful Old Prussia than in the borderlands of the Lower Rhine.

Now that his wife and all his children formed a unified Protestant family, he announced his marriage and the adoption of the little Philippine Antoinette not only to his brother in Kleve but also to his Silesian brothers, including Simon Heinrich of Glogau who had always urged himto marry. They all congratulated him heartily.

From the enumeration of the godparents of his Westphalian children it can be seen that every single one of his brothers joyfully took over the role as godparent and the protestant nobility of Minden did the same. A lively social intercourse with the higher civil servants of Minden began immediately after the move to Rothenhof.

Ottilie proved to be an excellent mother and a prudent and organized housewife because in the next decade, raising twelve children and taking care of her husband's farm was no small task. She enjoyed great esteem in the whole Minden area and her Philipp Wilhelm regularly drove himself in the first half of the last decade of the 18th century from the Rothenhof to Minden in a carriage drawn by four horses. As a privy councillor and general leaseholder of the district of Hausberge and the domain of the Rothenhof, being a former cuirassier officer he also had a great passion for horses, proving to be an excellent horse breeder. Thus at home he knew that he was an eminently talented and energetic representative of all interests.

In spite of all her rigor, however, there was no lack of cheerfulness that the home so inviting to a larger circle. At its centre was Ottilie, with her cheerful, fresh mind and her tender reverence for her beloved husband, whose depth of heart and goodness she knew best. With wisdom and femininity she mastered the intercourse in the neighboring circles. She also felt at home in this area that her husband had missed for so long and loved so much, growing from year to year in making the house a place of the most beautiful hospitality through diligence, order and thrift.

She knew her way around the stables as well as she knew how to cradle her children. In the big garden as well as in the rooms of the long house, busy as a bee, she remained slim and elastic and carried her child blessing as God's gift of existence, healthy and without complaint, flourishing vigorously.

The eldest child of the house, Philippine, had now blossomed into a virgin and possessed a lovely, modest nature with admirable circumspection, helpful and caring everywhere.

On October 24, 1796 our German sixty-two-year-old warrior notes in his own hand that his last little daughter Ulrike was born. After having married off his daughter Philippine at the age of 19 to the Royal Judge and tenant general of the Baron von Klenk estates in Langreder near Hanover and having already been awarded two grandchildren by her, the Rothenhof was struck by the cruel fate which had long since affected the Lower Rhine during the time of the French directorate and which now spread to Westphalia.

At the end of the year 1794 his son-in-law Schultz had died on December 27, and his widowed daughter with her two small children returned to the family home. Prussia and Austria after the French Revolution wanted to restore order but had no luck with this and in 1705 Prussia made peace with France and withdrew its troops.

During the retreat the army of von Möllendorf moved into the former principality of Minden and the artillery under General von Möller established its base in Hausberge. Prussia had committed itself to France to neutrality, the establishment of a demarcation line for the protection of Northern Germany and to keep a force of 25,000 men under arms. Obligation fell on the area around Minden, chosen right at the Porta because of the ferry over the Weser there—the ideal gathering place for the troops and their baggage and for the princely and other high rulers of the enemy. This burden lasted no less than 5½ years until November 1801.

In the intervening period, the marriage of the two daughters, who had grown up in the meantime, took place at the Rothenhof on December 10, 1797. On September 14, 1797, the 17-year-old Wilhelmine was married to Major Friedrich Heinrich von Festow, who was stationed in Aschersleben, and on September 14, 1798, the daughter Caroline Luise was married to Lieutenant Ludwig Sigismund Anton von Roeder, heir, feudal lord and bailiff on Hoym and Harzgerode.

In the case of the daughter Wilhelmine the following information was added:

> Married in 1797 to Major Friedrich Hans von Flotow. From this marriage was born:
>
> 1) Friederike Wilhelmine Philippine Ottilie Margarete Sophie von Flotow born June 14, 1798.

In the case of the daughter Caroline Louise married on September 14, 1798 to Lieutenant Ludwig Sigismund Anton von Roeder, Hereditary, Feudal and Court Lord of Hoymb and Harzgerode. From this marriage was born:
1) Ottilie Valeska Louise von Roeder, born January 31, 1801

In 1791, the brother Simon Heinrich was in Glogau like his great King, the great Frederick five years earlier, suffering from gout that fatally degenerated into dropsy in both of them. Apart from a legacy that Philipp and his wife received in taler, each of the twelve children received the same amount of money — the sons for studies, the daughters for dowry.

On March 17, 1807, at daybreak, Hausberge was suddenly completely surrounded by French soldiers. Many Prussians who did not want to enter French service were to be deported to France but the others were promised heaven on earth if they would only join the newly formed Westphalian battalion. From 418 of the district only three had reported. It was assumed that the others were hiding in the woods but in the whole district the French did not manage to get hold of a single one. They had to return to Minden without having achieved anything.

Finally the day of change of fate came. The Russian campaign brought it about when the burning of Moscow and the icy cold carried off the Napoleonic troops in the winter of 1812. The Russian-German legion was being formed and Boyen concluded the convention with the Russians, albeit without the consent of the King of Prussia. This made Alexander an ally of Prussia, based on his generalship. Napoleon himself hurried back to France—yes, one can say—fled, hiding his defeat to allow new troops to be raised for the spring. The King of Prussia issued the memorable decree that in April 1813, in spite of their poverty, enrapturing and thrilling the inhabitants of Prussia to make the greatest sacrifice to free themselves from the French yoke:

For Minden on the Weser

To the inhabitants of the former Prussian provinces ceded by the Peace of Tilsit.

It was not my free will or our guilt that tore my formerly so beloved and faithful subjects from our father's heart. The power of doom brought about the peace of Tilsit, which forcibly separated us. But even this and all the treaties concluded later with France, were broken by our enemies. They themselves, through their disloyalty, have rid us of our troublesome association with them, and God has prepared the way for the freedom of Germany through the victories of our mighty allies.

You too, from the moment my faithful people took up arms for me and for themselves and for you, are no longer bound by the forced oath that tied you to your ruler. To you, then, I address the same words that I spoke to my beloved people about the cause and purpose of the present war:

You now have the same demands on my love as I have on your devotion. Reunited with my people, you will share the same dangers, but also the same reward and the same glory.

I count on your devotion, the fatherland on your strength. Join your young men to my warriors who have recently proved themselves anew before the eyes of Prussian arms. Seize the sword, form your territorial army and your storm troop according to the example of your generous brothers, whom I call my subjects with righteous pride. Obey unconditionally the officials whom I will send you, to make known to you my orders and to direct your power — men who in former times lived and worked among you with trust and benefit.

Then, when you join in the fight for our common Fatherland, when, through your efforts, you have helped to establish your independence and prove that you are worthy of your ancestors and of the Prussian name, then the future will heal the wounds of the past, and we will find lost happiness in the consciousness of mutual faithfulness and of the unclouded enjoyment of freedom and peace.

Issued in Berlin, April 6, 1813 Friedrich Wilhelm.

To my people! April 7, 1815.

When, in the time of danger, I called my people to arms, to combat for the freedom and independence of the country, the whole mass of the youth, glowing with emulation, thronged round the standards, to bear, with joyful self-denial, unusual hardships, and resolved to brave death itself. Then the best strength of the people intrepidly joined the ranks of my brave soldiers, and my generals led with me into battle a host of heroes, who have shewn themselves worthy of the name of their fathers, and heirs of their glory. Thus we and our allies, attended by victory, conquered the capital of our enemy. Our banners waved in Paris — Napoleon abdicated his authority — liberty was restored to Germany, security to thrones, and to the world the hope of a durable peace.

This hope is vanished: we must again march to the combat. A perfidious conspiracy has brought back to France the man who for ten years together brought down upon the world unutterable miseries. The people, confounded, have not been able to oppose his armed adherents: though he himself, while still at the head of a considerable armed force, declared his abdication to be a voluntary sacrifice to the happiness and repose of France, he now regards this, like every other convention, as nothing; he is at the head of perjured soldiers, who desire to render war eternal; Europe is again threatened; it cannot suffer the man to remain on the throne of France, who loudly proclaimed universal empire to be the object of his continually renewed wars; who confounded all moral principle by his continued breach of faith; and who can, therefore, give the world no security for his peaceable intentions.

Again, therefore, arise to the combat! France itself wants our aid, and all Europe is allied with us. United with your ancient companions in victory, reinforced by the accession of new brethren in arms, you, brave Prussians, go to a just war, with me, with the princes of my family, with the generals who have led you to victory. The justice of the cause we defend will ensure us the victory.

I have ordered a general arming, according to my decree of September 3, 1814, which will be executed in all my dominions. The army will be completed; the volunteer companies of infantry be formed; and the militia called together. The youth of the chief classes of the citizens, from the age of twenty and upwards, are at liberty to join either the militia first called out, or the infantry corps of the regular army. Every young man who has completed his seventeenth year, may, if possessing the requisite bodily strength, join the army of his own choice. I publish a particular regulation on this subject. Concerning the formation of the single corps, and of the militia, a notice will appear in every province from the constituted authorities.

Thus united, with all Europe in arms, we again enter the lists against Napoleon Buonaparte and his adherents. Arise, then, with God for your support, for the repose of the world, for order, for morality, for your king and country.

(signed) Friedrich Wilhelm.

The constant conscription (regulations, harassment) had met with resistance from the stubborn spirit of the proverbial Westphalian *tete cares* (thick skulls). This was especially true for a farmer who had been severely tested, who was now to give up his last son and who made the small town of Hausberge the scene of an almost patriotic heroic deed. While the conscription commission was looking for the son and the father said he did not know where he was, the son was able to reach a hiding place in the rugged terrain of the Weser Mountains, where one after the other of the sons who had fallen victim to the military finally joined him. Here other young people could bring them the necessary food at their own risk of death.

Nor was the Commission able to find a young man in the Hausberge farms. Thereupon it was decided to occupy the small town with a dense military force that did not relent or soften its efforts, keeping a sharp scouting patrol occupied for months.

Despite all their efforts, they did not succeed in breaking the stubbornness of the Hausberge citizens. A mentally unbalanced shepherd finally became a traitor. The son had been present at his mother's funeral in Hausberge and the mother's death had been caused by an incident of self-defense against lewd attempts by members of the French quartering. When the peasant complained to the higher officer of the conscription commission on the day before the burial of the woman, the whole company of conscripts had marched out and disappeared, which the peasant was able to let his son know.

But when after a week the French all moved back into Hausberge and nothing happened to initiate an investigation against the culprit but rather the harassment of the farmer took on even sharper forms, the captain of the conscription commission, who had been the main culprit in the repeated harassment of the farmer's wife, succeeded in blackmailing the stupid shepherd into confessing that the son had been seen in the meantime.

The peasant was immediately arrested, the shepherd telling them where the young man was hiding in the rocks. While the dozens of boys were being taken away, tied up because they refused military service, the stubborn peasant was placed against the wall of the prison yard and mercilessly shot. His property was confiscated and the satisfied conscription commission moved away.

In the same year of 1810 the seventeen-year-old son of the Privy Councillor Sack, August, had to turn himself in on March 17 and had gone to Kassel to join the guard. His brother Ferdinand, three years older than him, was one of the first to be drafted into Jerome's service at the age of seventeen, immediately after the seizure of the city. As a lieutenant in the Westphalian Guard, he had already become familiar with the lively life at the Kassel court from his own experience and perspective. It was not without grave concern that the aged father now saw this second son, no matter how young, being dragged into the same moral quagmire. The only more conciliatory side he could win for this new sacrifice was that the square-built, tall young man had been found fit to be his own beloved old weapon-bearer, the cuirassier, and would now be called upon as an *avant-gardist* (volunteer, newcomer), initially with heavier duties of service. The cuirassier regiment was also part of the guard, so the brothers had both found a respectable employment.

During these years, the whole of Europe was surprised by the event whereby Napoleon had desired and received the hand of the daughter of the Emperor of Austria. Astonishment and displeasure at this humiliation filled every better mind. It seemed unthinkable that on the smoking battlefields of Aspern and Wagram the myrtles should blossom, that the German princess should share the purple that was tinged with the noblest blood of her people. Yet it was assured that the archduchess had already expressed great admiration for Napoleon during the campaign of 1809 and that she had willingly extended her hand to him.

Since Napoleon did not want to lose any time to fulfil — as it was said in the court language — the duties imposed upon him by Providence for the best of France for the continuation of the fourth dynasty, the engagement was publicly performed on February 12 and the marriage on April 2, 1810. The young empress combined with much grace a great soul, dignity and attitude in her conduct, zeal for duty and a desire to ennoble and delight everything that surrounded her.

The situation of Europe at that time gave the Emperor of Austria hope that by allowing Napoleon to marry, he would win Napoleon's favor in order to gain time, recover and be well equipped for battles that would later become inevitable. The Austrian cabinet was well aware that Napoleon valued a marriage that would flatter the French but that it would not change his policy against Austria. If he had previously striven to destroy it by war, he would in future seek to tie it up by treaty and subjugate it by participating in pernicious undertakings in the Roman manner. If it resisted his intentions, they would become enemies again until the purpose was achieved in another way.

It was perfectly clear in Vienna that the young empress was perhaps even destined to be an instrument to destroy the Austrian monarchy. However, they were determined to resist Napoleon's interference and to give the means of power out of their hands. The immediate consequence of the closer ties with France was the complete dissolution of the alliance with Russia, which had already weighed on mainland Europe since the Tilsiter Peace Treaty.

In the summer of 1810, Queen Luise had caught a cold on a trip to her father and died after just a few days. She passed away at the Castle of Hohenzieritz in her thirty-fifth year. Her death in full youth and beauty aroused the most vivid mourning everywhere, heightened to national feeling by the misfortune of her last years. The inhabitants of eastern Westphalia still had the best memories of her affable and amiable appearance from her visit there. Her loss was discussed in deep emotion in all circles of the population. It was well known that Napoleon had persecuted her with his bitter, unquenched hatred and had caused her the most outrageous insults. It was recalled how she had unsuccessfully tried to save the country of Magdeburg in Tilsit and the opinion was openly expressed that the grief over the suffering of the country had undermined her health for some time, now bringing about her untimely death.

How did it feel to see the King and his orphaned children so relentlessly persecuted by fate! In 1805, Prussia, in its own fettered helplessness, even had to watch calmly as

Austria was overthrown and all of Western and Southern Germany was enslaved by Napoleon. The reward for this had been that he had abused and constantly disregarded Prussian neutrality. By the time Prussia joined the alliance against France in November 1805, Napoleon was already completely in control of the situation and the Prussian envoy was so shamefully deceived by him that the King of Prussia had to approve the Schönbrunn Treaty *nolens volens*.

In the summer of 1806, Napoleon conducted his hostilities to humiliate Prussia to such an extent that Prussia mobilised and prepared for battle. Philipp's son Friedemann immediately enlisted among the academic youth but, since being a commoner he was denied an officer's career, his father sent him back to his studies.

In October the two armies clashed. The first battles at Schleiz, then the skirmish at Saalfeld on the 9th and 10th, in which the heroic Prince Louis Ferdinand of Prussia was killed, were already to the detriment of Prussia until on October 14, 1806, near Jena and Auerstädt—where Flotow's son-in-law had also fought—his army was completely defeated. This was followed by shameful capitulations of the strongest fortresses.

Frederick Wilhelm III was forced to flee to the eastern parts of his monarchy and contacted the Russians but fortune eluded him. After the bloody battles of Eylau and Friedland, he was forced to cede half of his land to Napoleon in the Peace of Tilsit on July 9, 1807. By the time Prussia joined the coalition in 1805, the von Lettow Regiment had left Minden and had to let the citizens take over the watch. As long as the mobilization lasted, the citizenry had to provide many services as escorts for the transport of recruits.

On November 8, troops of the French army of the north approached the Weser with four hundred Dutchmen who entered the city and, finding it completely bared of troops, experienced no resistance. Events were now multiplying like lightning. On November 14, the French Governor General Gobert, Commander Fourier and an Intendant Siccard arrived. On November 16, there was a procession to the cathedral where a *Te Deum* was sung. An illuminated procession was ordered for the evening.

The guards were manned jointly by the citizens and the Dutch soldiers. The citizen officers, who acted as orderlies, had to appear at the table of the Intendant. New passages of Bergisch and Dutch troops took place that were used to enclose Nienburg, to where Lettow's regiment had withdrawn. The nearby town of Hameln had already capitulated shamefully on November 20—its commander von Schöler took up residence in Minden and got no little amount of ear bashing from the washerwomen when he dared to show himself outside the gate near the laundry.

The capitulation of Nienburg soon followed at Hameln by the 25th. The prisoners of war from there were also taken to Minden to the Protestant church but the civil guards let every soldier who wanted to leave escape, so that only a few people were left the next morning. Minden had to pay 14,000 Taler war contribution because of this that had to be settled by December 3.

When Napoleon's coronation feast was celebrated on December 7, the civil servants and citizens had to attend the festivities in the cathedral—they also had to offer music by torchlight to the governor, the commander and the director in the evening.

At the beginning of the New Year a French National Guard was organized in Minden and in the course of January two companies of the Catholic Prince Primate, who were very popular with the citizens, took the place of the Bergish troops. On January 20, there was a parade on the large cathedral square with National Guardsmen and citizens standing in line. The city director Aschhoff was accused of doing nothing for the completion of the officer corps, even though he was appointed director of the National Guard. He had to take remedial action but when conscription for the Westphalian battalion was ordered on March 10, no recruits were found.

On March 29, the citizens were asked to hand over their weapons and on March 30 the prisoners of war were asked to turn themselves in. On April 9 the battalion of two hundred men formed in Minden marched to Münster but lost ninety-five on the way through desertion. The Prince Primate's company was replaced by the French on July 2, and eight days later the news of the conclusion of an armistice arrived, followed by the announcement of the peace of Tilsit on July 14.

Instead of rejoicing about it, an embarrassing uncertainty lay over Minden and the surrounding area. It was learned on July 24, that Minden was to fall to the newly established Kingdom of Westphalia and come under the rule of a Napoleonite. This news caused a terrible sensation among the citizens and had an especially horrifying effect among the Prussian officers and officials.

In July, Justice Councillor Müller was appointed as Mayor of Minden, von Bandemer as secretary of the municipal administration and forester Brüggemann as police commissioner. Minden got much French quartering because King Jerome wanted to stay in Nenndorf. On September 13 he also visited Minden, where Mayor Müller presented him with the keys of the city on a silver plate. The King was very pleased with the reception he received. Still on the Weser Bridge, he expressed the most lively pleasure as he departed.

Only he had noticed that the citizen companies still carried the Prussian eagle in their flags. He therefore gave orders to convert it into the French one but this was only carried out as far as painting over the head and neck a little. The cost of the King's four-hour stay had already amounted to 2138 Taler for the treasury.

The loosened ties with Russia had not only created a new situation in Austria. Napoleon, too, now decided to withdraw all influence from Russia in European affairs and let it serve only as an instrument of his monstrous plans. First he wanted to force Russia to wage a joint war against Turkey, then drive the Turks out of Europe, conquer Asia Minor and Persia and prepare everything for the advance to the East Indies in order to weaken England completely by its conquest and to rob it of its sources of supply.

The Russian emperor, however, very quickly recognized the situation and secretly began to prepare for an imminent war. In order to instill paralyzing fear everywhere, Napoleon, in an address to the merchant class, had boasted brazenly about his own power and insulted Russia. His remarks had gushed out, "I have 200 million in cash, I am an elephant, I will always wage war and will subjugate England in the next war."

On both sides armament continued on an ongoing basis. The army, which Emperor Alexander maintained in May 1812, consisted of more than one million—Napoleon's army, when it crossed the Niemen, is said to have possessed half a million warriors and an incredible force of men and animals. Prussia, through whose territory these armies were advancing, and with the reinforcements of Westphalia and Rhineland conscripts, had to decide in time on which side it would fight. The King and his statesmen prepared themselves for the decisive moment.

France was pulling troops together at the border, the State Chancellor von Hardenberg reported to the King that Prussia was threatened with ruin but Napoleon remained silent on all inquiries about the purpose of his measures and so the next winter passed in embarrassing uncertainty. Then Napoleon himself took up the negotiations and dictated his will to Prussia—the French army would march through Prussia and demand thirty million francs in food costs from Prussia on top of the twelve million francs of war contribution already remaining. The Prussian army was only allowed to be 42,000 men strong, 20,000 of whom were to join the French army and the rest were to be sent to fortresses. The King of Prussia was to go to Breslau, which remained neutral within a certain radius.

The moment of decision had now come. Surrounded by enemy troops one had to declare oneself for or against France without procrastinating. On March 5, the King signed Napoleon's treaties. The French armies now filled the whole of the former Prussian Kingdom and lived in abundance, abandoning the inhabitants to hunger and need. A war could not have been worse than this horrible passage of troops.

As in all countries under Napoleonic rule, old religious foundations, chapters, monasteries and the like were abolished in the Kingdom of Westphalia (in return, the immoral activity of the Tuilleries Palace[102], in all its vain outward appearances, vices and servile spirit, was transplanted to more than one of the Rhine capitals).

In Kassel, the court of Jerome Buonapartes, the "Merry King", soon became one of the most immoral of the modern age. A stay in this haze of bacchant lust caused the better feelings to suffocate even amongst the strong-willed. For the circles that had grown up in the orderly, thrifty and just Prussian administration, these incessant demands on the pleasure life and vanity of higher-ranking people meant a terrible ordeal.

New festivities were repeatedly ordered in Minden for Napoleon's victory at Wagram and the name day in honor of Jerome shortly afterwards. On the name day a *Te Deum* was to be celebrated in the cathedral that not even twenty-five citizens attended. So on May 5, 1812, another shooting tournament was decreed and those who did not appear were threatened with punishment.

The absence of a celebration at the birth of the King of Rome in 1807 had to be subsequently arranged by high command and on July 30 the conclusion of peace was celebrated with a church ceremony in the cathedral, a banquet, ball and illuminations. Similarly, Napoleon's birthday had to be celebrated again on August 8 and the marriage of the new King of Westphalia, Jerome, to Princess Katharina of Württemberg on August 16. The new King ordered that five bridal couples, which he provided with money, would be married on this his wedding day in the cathedral by the preacher Sanct Marien.

On January 1, 1808, a deputation of the citizen's representation led by the city director Aschoff had to attend the act of homage in Kassel. "The King's throne was draped with light blue cloth and trimmed with gold braid. When I took a closer look at them, I found that they were fake, which struck me distinctly," Philipp Aschoff later recounted. Otherwise there had been no celebrations at all and the deputies could return home immediately.

Relatively orderly conditions returned to the Minden area in 1808. The Chief Prefect of the Weser Departement was appointed in the Tax Councillor von Postel, a born and bred Minden citizen. As Sub-Prefect for the Arrondissement Minden the Military and Domain Councillor Backmeister, who was a particular friend of Philipp and godfather of his son Detloff, was appointed Tribunal President of the District President von Arnim[103].

A provisional commander was quickly sent from Kassel to Minden in mid-February, as the conquest met with great resistance in the area and could only be carried out with the utmost rigor. On March 16, 1809, Colonel d'Astery replaced the provisional military commander after the citizens had taken the oath of homage on March 1. The quartering of transient French and Westphalian troops kept the citizens under constant pressure to pay taxes and often they had to accompany conscripts and serve in the execution squads in the villages.

The bitterest thing for Philipp, the former co-victor of Rossbach and Leuthen, however, was the decree when Napoleon ordered him to vacate the Rothenhof, as all domains and state possessions in Westphalia were transferred to the power of the Emperor of the French in 1807 by the Tilsit peace treaty. In a touching decree, the King of Prussia had relieved the old, loyal officials of his government, his courts and other state institutions of their oath of allegiance to him and the old warrior from the Rothenhof wept searing tears when this terrible fate befell him too.

His wife Ottilie, however, the ever serene and composed heroic mother of twelve children, knew that even in this hour of the hardest trial she had to endure. She had good advice for her Rothenhof husband, who had been cruelly expelled from Prussian service and at the same time from the Rothenhof estate, which had been so rewardingly and satisfactorily elevated by her own long years of farming. Even before the date came when the house had to be vacated and the inventory of the establishment was to be given into the hands of the French officer to whom the domain was endowed, Philipp was persuaded to move to the so-called 'castle'. This was the old property of the former Lords von Berge, for which she had always had a special passion, since she had read to Philipp from a history booklet she had brought from Minden twenty years ago. Now, devastated by the quartering and abandoned by the house owner, the property would certainly be up for sale and so it received her special attention.

Once she had persuaded Philipp to take a look at the property with her, which he called an impossibly feasible new home, she found it in a miserably desolate condition. However, her practical sense immediately recognized that in time a comfortable retirement home would have to be created both for her husband and a home for her sons who were being educated in the higher colleges as well as for the youngest children still under her care. So it had to be found quickly. She believed that they would all benefit by being allowed to buy this desolate building with its overgrown castle garden that had been shunned by the demanding foreign soldiers.

There was also no one better for the community and the Minden authorities, still in the process of transformation, with their friend Backmeister at the head, than their Philipp, the twenty-year-old official administrator of the Hausberge municipal authority. It was self-evident that the old Prussian, at seventy-four years of age, did not want to resume his office in the service of the enemy. And she, who had learned to share every feeling and every thought with him and had always found her highest happiness in this, knew that all too well even before he dared to speak his mind.

She welcomed all the more the opportunity to create a cosy home for Philipp from the desolate castle and its stables were still spacious enough for Philipp's favorite horses and for the high carriage, which he still used to drive himself. As the diplomatic regent of the household, she knew how to put these advantages into perspective and soon won her Philipp for purchase and relocation to the old historical "Hus vom Berge". Even her husband's conciliatory teasing about the fact that the former noviciate was only interested so much because of the pious house of the religious masters, she let the joke blow over her, parrying it and emphasizing that he, Philipp himself, had taught her to love these masters first.

The history of the house, however, she had remembered well at the time and she often said to herself in silence that Philipp had won her heart through his noble tolerance with the little booklet that he himself had always had on his desk and from which she had once had to read to him during his illness. Where today the so-called castle stood, a spacious house with a strongly walled side wing and sufficient space in its two floors for the occasional rescue of all Philipp's children and grandchildren, there had been a fortress Sachsenburg one thousand years before. At the time of Charlemagne, the owner of this fortress was the Saxon Duke Wittekind[104], who had for so long resisted the attempts to convert him from paganism by Charlemagne.

Once the Franconian emperor finally succeeded in winning him for Christianity, his Wittekind's dynasty as the Lords of Berge, played an important role in history from then on. In time they became the reeves of the Minden bishops and had to represent them in all church and other legal matters.

Around 1349 a Wittekind was cathedral provost and from 1369–83 the same Lord of Berge was bishop of Minden. His brother Otto followed him in this dignity, another brother Gerhard was bishop of Hildesheim. The noble lords of Berge were also the owners of the Wedigenstein, which is called Wiburg, later Widegenborg already at the time of Pipin in 753 as part of a Saxon camp. The old Margaret Chapel, which was located above the Wedigenstein, was supposed to have been founded by a certain

Thatewief, who would have settled there with other Christian virgins.

With Bishop Otto, however, the dynasty of the Lords of Berge died out around 1398, after 700 years of flourishing in the castle. Otto bequeathed the whole dominion Hausberge with the Wedigenstein, to the monastery of Minden, under the condition that the bishop may use the castle for his residence but never sell it. Furthermore its owner was obliged to protect the fields and agricultural land belonging to the city of Minden against raids. In disputes between the bishop and the city, however, the castle was never allowed to be used as a base.

Thus at the end of the 14th century the castle Hausberge became a bulwark of the Minden monastery and at the same time Hausberge became the center of the small town, which had already settled around the castle as well as the surrounding Minden agricultural area, with its own legal customs and jurisdiction. Even in Philipp's time, the gallows and, in front of the Protestant church, the stake of shame where the smaller offenses had to be expiated, were still preserved. Often the castle had been the site of hot feuds in the following centuries and several times it was reduced to ashes and rebuilt.

During the Reformation, the priest Nicolaus Bildebeek (died in 1618) converted to the Reformation and the castle chapel as well as the church in the town joined the new faith after bloody battles for it. One of the Minden bishops, Christian of Brunswick and Lüneburg (from 1599-1633) had therefore dissolved the previous episcopal court in Kostede, later called "Rothenhof", and leased the land of this castle courtyard. The Margaret Chapel above the

Wedigenstein was assigned to the few Catholics who remained in the Hausberge area.

In addition to Wedigenstein, Kostede Castle and the three further castle estates belonging to Kammern were part of the Hausberge castle estate. The families of Weihe, Hartling, Frohnhorst, Vincke, Langen, Lettow and Hinderking were able to assert themselves as Protestants tenants and some of them have remained there until the present day. The villages of Nachen and Lerbeck, the Hainholz, a forest estate of 1685 acres, the Wittenhusener Bürgerfeld with Wittenhusen, the meadow behind the Weser and the whole ridge of the mountain up to the old Heerstrasse were also part of it. In order to preserve the old rights of the castle, a commission of councillors from Hausberge, with their mayor or, as they were still called at the time, the bailiff at the head of the commission, organized a border inspection patrol every few years to check the boundary stones and signs and to make sure that no border aberrations had crept in in the meantime.

Two days were needed for such an operation while the Commission had to be paid at the community's expense. Those days were real holidays for the participants. Ottilie remembered one of these events, because according to the custom, the magistrate had to invite to a festive meal and later Philipp had brought her the bill for the things eaten at such a feast for the items that were to be paid for by the community.

After visiting the Hausberge castle in the evening, she took out the old booklet and, together with her husband, delved into its prehistory once again. The invoice of September 1, 1795, which was placed in the booklet, fell into her hands and in the time now so hard pressed by the war and the enemy invasion, the opulence of those days seemed downright sinful and reprehensible to her. The following were recorded as having been eaten at the final banquet: half a calf, one ham, beef and mutton, one hare, nine partridges, eight pounds of carp, fifty eggs, four young chickens and the appropriate drinks for each course.

Of the original proud medieval castle (the Schalksburg[105]) there was nothing more than the mighty substructure that had been built over the centuries on the mountain crest plateau rising above the former moat. On this rock-solid cyclopean-like foundation, a very picturesque building with three gables, various oriels and a castle chapel with a small tower had once risen. In 1723 the last castle buildings were demolished due to dilapidation, the remains being used in 1779 for a Minden house construction and for the construction of the Weser bridge near Nienburg.

In 1720, the complex of houses around the castle, with its church and school, was granted city rights. Before that, it had only had a city constitution with a mayor and council. Only the baroque style of its construction indicated when the spacious house, now called the castle, was built on the imperishable foundations of the original castle. This placed little value on corridors in the interior and allowed the rooms behind them to spread out, mostly from a larger and a smaller living room accessible from these alone.

The pretty stairwell, with a small comfortable staircase set back in the middle, connected the floors to each other. At the top of the staircase, the main building was connected to a longer side wing, which also connected, without a corridor, a series of interlocking rooms facing the inner courtyard. This wing was immediately destined for the daughters of Ottilie's house, because here, during the visits of the married couples, the grandchildren would romp and frolic to their heart's content without disturbing their grandfather.

Its rooms filled the ground floor of the main house, next to which, right next to the front door, the kitchen and ironing room were also located to serve the doorbell. In the main house and on the main floor, the largest entrance room was the General Living Room, where meals were also shared at a large solid oak table that had been built immovably into the room by the carpenter.

Through this meeting room one entered the hall, the so-called good parlor of equal dimensions, where the spinet and the mother's bookcase found their place, next to the various plush sofa entertainment and games tables. From this room, but also accessible through a small wallpapered door from the front or living room, one reached Ottilie's boudoir, which from its sewing table oriel window seat offered a magnificent view over the Schlossbrück and castle moat, over the Weser mountains with the Jacobsberg in the foreground.

From there, one reached the marital bedroom, which was located above the kitchen and again had an exit to the stairwell. In the upper, attic floor, the sons slept in the same adjoining rooms, emanating from a common study room. The servants had their chambers in the wing occupied by the daughters, accessible alone from their floor by a small separate staircase.

Since Albertine, the fourth of the series of daughters, had already reached out her hand to a young master builder Gantzer in 1804, who had his employment and occupation in Minden, she had remained in constant contact with her parents' house and now, in the renovation of the dilapidated rooms, the beloved son-in-law had been able to render the most excellent services.

For the time being, only sixteen-year-old Adolfine and the youngest child, the eleven-year-old Ulrike, lived in the daughter's wing. Later, Adolfine married Fritz Plöger, an assistant judge, in July 1807, and their best friend and bridesmaid Louise Antoinette von Beesten joined the circle as a permanent guest.

Even if the confusion in the new Kingdom of Westphalia, inevitable after the Tilsiter Peace, spread beyond the borders as has been described in more detail above, the castle proved its original character as a fortress where peace and harmony prevailed. Ottilie had her hands full with the task of repairing the exterior of the property after the home furnishings had been completed and for this purpose all the hands of the young people had to help her. Additionally the sons and daughters were able to make the work in the yard and garden into a source of great pleasure.

During the reign of Frederick the Great, who would have liked to introduce silk production to his lands, an attempt was made to plant mulberry trees on the Schlossbrinke, the slope that rose quite steeply between the moat and the castle plateau. Even though the base of the moat was damp and swampy, it remained sunless, and higher up the slope was sunny but lacking in water.

Ottilie now planted this Brink area on a large scale, with the finest varieties of apples in the higher position and plums in the lower position. She also had a small terrace built under the beautiful old lime tree, which may always have been the favorite and pride of the former inhabitants, by means of a small wall which the sons naturally built widely around it. From here one could not only admire the Brink and the mountains and woods opposite, one also had a good view of the gate, the entrance to the farm and the house from here. Whenever the father drove in his team of four, one would jump up and help him to find the groom or even to water the animals and to unharness them. How much did Philipp always have to tell his own and how happy he could be that he had shaken off the burdens of office.

In such hours of quiet enjoyment he remembered, apart from the merits of his splendid wife Ottilie, also his brother Simon Heinrich, who had been resting in the peace of the grave for fifteen years. It was only thanks to the income constantly flowing in from Glogau from his family foundation that he was able to give his daughters all the means necessary for their social standing and to have his sons educated at external schools and universities.

The grave concern for the enslaved fatherland had to be kept from the old master of the house as far away as possible, which Ottilie had made a principle. Even when he himself was infected by his closest friends in Minden, his wife and children knew how to distract him from thinking too deeply and brooding through providing new literary publications.

After all, during all these years at the Rothenhof, the great new poet Friedrich Schiller had outshone all the other poets, even Lessing and Goethe. The great dramas he had completed were presented in the evenings with old and young people taking on roles in which they could take part in reading aloud. Then Philipp must have told about Halberstadt and Gleim and was glad when he heard through cousin Lucanus that the old Anacreon was still able to enjoy his temple of friendship.

The news from the distant outside world about the flight of the royal family after Tilsit weighed heavily among them but there were also some uplifting things to report. For example, one of the sons of his brother from Kleve, his nephew Johann August[106], who was named August for short, had become acquainted with Minister Stein during his career as a lawyer and mining magistrate in Wetter on the Ruhr. Stein had already been appointed by the King as Governor General of the lands between the Elbe and Oder rivers, after he had already been appointed President of the Immediate Commission, which had prepared and concluded the peace of Tilsit in Berlin.

Brother Carl August, who as an octogenarian in Münster — where he and his colleagues from the Royal Administration Government of Kleve had been transferred for more than a decade or would have had to flee — had long since taken his well-deserved retirement, after his excellent wife Gertrud had already been snatched from him by death in 1799. He had a loving nurse in his only remaining daughter, who was married to Judicial Councillor Sethe, who had also been transferred to Münster. At his advanced age he was able to enjoy with pride the significant successes of all five sons he had left and of his son-in-law.

Of his own brothers and sisters, only sister Friederike was still alive and she was in the Lucanus Ladies' Foundation in Halberstadt. Although she was already in her eighties, she still faithfully maintained the connection with the brothers in Westphalia.

In September and October 1808 many Spaniards came to Minden and Hausberge to be used as Napoleon's auxiliary troops against Sweden and England. However, since Napoleon's war with Spain broke out soon afterwards, the auxiliary troops left his army and were left to their fate disarmed. Many a chorus sounded from the lips of the sunburnt figures, who were sometimes a little light fingered on their way and who for the time being were unable to make it back over the Pyrenees.

On October 14 of the same year, the long feared strict execution of conscription was now also carried out in Minden and its surroundings. At the beginning of March 1809 a second one was ordered. The former Chief Prefect von Pestell was appointed to the Council of State. Philipp lost a valuable patron and friend in him. His son Friedemann was twenty-three years old, already a junior lawyer employed at the Minden court. Because he was already over the age of compulsory military service, 18-year-old Ferdinand visited the university in Halle and was enraptured by it.

The father now often brought disturbing news home with him when he had been to Minden or had heard what news had been brought from the Rhine. He was in constant contact with his brother Carl August in Kleve.

Through him, whose son August worked at the Kleve chamber in constant company with the chamber president Baron von Stein, they had already learned all sorts of unpleasant things about the defensive war waged by Prussia and Austria against the encroachment of the French revolutionary powers.

The King had been forced to withdraw his troops from France without having achieved anything and the other neighboring countries had also failed after weak attempts — von Dalberg, the Elector of Mainz, had capitulated to the Jacobins, and nothing more stood in the way of the French invasion of the left bank of the Rhine. The Military and Domain Chamber at Kleve — Philipp's old field of activity, in which his brother and nephew were still loyal officials — found it appropriate to relocate the files and cash holdings to the right side of the Rhine to Emmerich.

August, his nephew, it has been said, was constantly the connecting confidant between the chamber and its president, who resided in Hamm, Westphalia. The French invasion took place like an inevitable matter of course on the Rhine and the future lay heavy and dark over the Prussian fatherland.

The summer of the year 1794 began when a special event excited the inhabitants of the Rothenhof. Philippine, the father's darling and the mother's support and pride, was to leave the house forever and, according to German custom and practice, was now to follow a man of her choice as wife and housewife.

It had not been difficult for this just nineteen-year-old to say "yes" to an older widower with five children from two previous marriages. Already in autumn 1793 she had accepted the invitation of his second, young wife Leonore Hedemann, who had been snatched from him in the spring of 1794. She had been the daughter of this landowner's apprentice on the Rothenhof and Philippine and her had become close friends. Thus she had got to know their young married happiness at the side of the magnificent bailiff of Langreder.

When Leonore was expecting her second child, she had asked Philippine to take care of the other four children during the week and so Philippine hurried to her again to fulfill the request of the extremely tender and now almost frail young mother. Thus she witnessed this joyful event with the Schultze couple. At the same time, she had to experience the concern of the good father before the difficult hour for his young wife had come, because he already then feared to lose her.

The oldest son August from the first Schultze marriage already had a fourteen year old boy. He had won her whole heart by his chivalrous and caring nature, which he displayed towards all his brothers and sisters. In return, the serious and energetic student held strong feelings for her. Philippine, who was always helpful and capable, could no longer do without her friend, until finally her father at Rothenhof urged her to visit all of his family at home for Christmas.

There was great sorrow in the Schultze household and only the promise to come back next summer calmed the downcast spirits there. Philippine had provided for a strong second maid in the Schultze's house, because Leonore was recovering very slowly and often it seemed to Philippine as if her friend had become more frail after the birth of her second daughter. The happy mother, however, never complained but gave this new little child almost all the strength she had left with an almost exuberant tenderness. Philippine's departure seemed cruel to her.

"Father, make her swear that she will come back to us already in the spring," she had begged her husband, who feared the departure of the caring spirit of the household —Philippine, almost as much for the welfare of the whole house as his Leonore. However, Philippine had grown up in the strict breeding of the Rothenhof and knew no opposition and no pleading when he, her most beloved father, desired something. His wish had always been the command for everyone at the Rothenhof. Then, when she stood under the Christmas tree again as the eldest in the complete circle of all brothers and sisters and her parents in their hearty healthy and cheerful piety joined in the beautiful Christmas carols, her young heart swelled so full of happiness and bliss that she fell around her mother's neck with tears of joy in her eyes.

"Oh, Mother, what a wonderful place this is in your home!"

In the spring of the following year, when Philippine was surprised that she had not yet received a new invitation from Langreder and concluded that she was not needed there, the news suddenly reached the house that Mrs Leonore Schultze, née Hedemann, had died of galloping consumption on April 23. Philippine was beside herself in her grief. She reproached herself most bitterly for not having visited her friend again since Christmas, who had probably already been ill, by not having fulfilled the oath she had taken when she left.

When she put herself in the position of the five orphaned children, even Ottilie hardly knew how to free her from the most dismal ideas and distract her. It took strong rebukes from the father to tear his favorite daughter out of pathological thoughts and recurring self-reproaches. She wanted to go to the children and could not understand that she was not called to help now. Only when her mother introduced her to the fact that Schultze's sisters or Leonore's mother were now the ones called to do so and that it would be against all decency to allow her to travel to the house of a widower just for the sake of it, did she finally succeed in finding strength and consolation in the fulfillment of her domestic duties at home.

Then suddenly, at the beginning of July, the widowed bailiff Schultze appeared at the Rothenhof for a long conversation with her father. Philippine had not been told about the announced visit and had been sent away with an order to friends living far away.

When she came home later, she found out who had been there and for what purpose and that her father had granted the visitor permission to get the answer from her the next morning. To be allowed to become a mother to the poor orphaned children from now on filled Philippine's heart with such satisfaction and joy that she just the next morning, timidly sparing the widower any questions, stretched out her hand to him and, looking him firmly and calmly in the eye, said, "Yes, I do."

Schultze therefore urged only that she should allow him to immediately issue the dispensation of the banns, as any delay in her own firm determination would be an offense against the two youngest children. When she referred the bold suitor to her parents for all these questions of bridal law and manners, her father put the hands of the engaged couple into each other's hands and implored God's blessing down upon the couple with a short prayer.

"You will, dear son, to the best of your knowledge and belief, take matters into your own hands as a bailiff. If the difficulties are cleared up there, I, as bailiff of Hausberge, will have none here."

The consequence was that on July 17, the pastor married Ernst Johann Conrad Schultze from Klenkesch and Altensch, manager and general leaseholder of Langreder and Dessau to Mademoiselle Philippine Antoinette Sack, eldest daughter of the Prussian Privy Councillor and general leaseholder Mr Sack of Rothenhof, in the office of Hausberge near Minden in Westphalia, after obtaining dispensation because of the widower's half year of mourning.

The Rothenhof witnessed a quiet wedding ceremony that was the first of the Sack's house daughters in its rooms, the children of Langreder loudly cheering the new mother in her orphaned circle.

On October 12, 1794 Ottilie gave her husband the 6th son who was born so weak that Pastor Barkhausen had to perform an emergency baptism on him and the father alone was the godfather. He was christened Wilhelm Eduard Hieronimus Maximilian. Meanwhile the little world citizen strengthened himself increasingly in the presence of his proud mummy, which made his parents and siblings very happy.

On April 16, 1795, Philippine blessed her husband with a little daughter who took her father's name as Ernestine.

In the following year 1795 Prussia officially made peace with France and withdrew its troops completely into the interior. With the return march the von Möllendorf army moved into the former principality of Minden—the Rothenhof also got its share of quartering—two officers and a considerable portion from the 3500 strong troops.

From now on the horses of the regiment were the most dominant in the stables. General von Möller, however, was accommodated in Hausberge with the merchant Brodbecker, and Ottilie was particularly pleased that he had preferred the quarters in the small town, for in his special entourage there were, in addition to two chamber servants, a chef and a laundress.

At Fähranger, where the gallows had stood in former times, very close to the ferry across the Weser, the cannons and ammunition wagons had been installed. It was also the meeting place of passing troops and their baggage as well as of the hauling horses when princes and other high rulers were on their way to the greater Prussia beyond the Weser. The Porta Westfalica was once again the great gateway for the mobilized army.

One can imagine what this meant for the adolescent boys of the Rothenhof, who attended primary school in Hausberge but were then driven to Minden to attend secondary school. In the peace treaty Prussia had to commit itself not only to neutrality but also to the establishment of a protective demarcation line against northern Germany and thus had to keep a force of 25,000 men under arms in Westphalia alone. The fact that this resulted in a quite extraordinary burden for the inhabitants was not taken into account.

In the former brewery house at Hausberge, Philipp, as bailiff, had a large field hospital set up and felt again as in his grand youth, once again a military servant of his King. The extreme camp life in his hitherto so peaceful district, which had actually been imposed by the enemy of Prussia, became a barely tolerable burden for him over time—after all, this accommodation lasted no less than 5½ years until November 1801!

What he, the aging man, had to endure in silence and devotion in the form of increased burdens of office and everywhere perceptible reductions in salary and power in his territory was only possible for him through his firm belief in a wise and benevolent Providence.

When on October 24, 1796 in the evening between 9 and 10 o'clock a little daughter was born to him to complete the living dozen—just as he had known it at his parents' home in Hecklingen—he thankfully entered this event in his little baptismal book with the words:

"In my 63rd year my beloved wife Ottilie Baumann gave birth to a young daughter, who was baptized on Sunday, October 30, here at Rothenhof by preacher Barkhausen from Holtzhausen: Ulrike Dorothea Sophia. The godparents were:

1) Colonel and Commander of the highly eminent von Beyernschen Courassier Regiment, which is in garrison at Aschersleben, Baron von Frohreich
2) Colonel Baron von Oheimb, hereditary and judicial Lord of Holtzhausen, Ensen and several other places.
3) the wife of Royal Huntsman, Baroness von Baudemer

4) Wife of Cavalry Captain Baroness von Wutgenow, whose husband was a Provincial Chief Inspector of Transportation in Hausberge at the time.

"To you Almighty Creator of all creatures and to you Saviour of the world and to you Holy Spirit I entrust this child into your gracious care.

"Philipp Wilhelm Sack Privy Councillor and Leaseholder General of the Royal Prussian Administration Hausberge in the Principality of Minden".

In Langreder on October 5th, a young nephew who, like his youngest uncle at the Rothenhof, had received the name Eduard Wilhelm Schultze, had already preceded the little world citizen. The baptismal feast at the Rothenhof had once again been quite a joyful one. The circle of godparents had been considerably increased by the presence of neighbors and officers who were in quarters all around. Quite furtively, the adjutant of the first-mentioned godfather had managed to secure his place at the side of the now eldest daughter of the house, in whose big dark eyes he had already had the opportunity to sink his own blue eyes several times.

Captain von Flotow and his colonel were billeted on the Wedigenstein, the most beautiful estate all around, where a family called Felsen had settled. Since the sixteen-year-old daughter was a close friend of Minna Sack there and the parents also often met, the officers stationed on both estates were soon drawn into this friendly intercourse.

After the golden October, Minna had missed the otherwise so popular walks through the beautiful forests of the Porta Hills with her girlfriend in order to relieve her mother of more arduous duties in the house. After a mild November, which offered plenty of work in the garden and also favoured small visits, an early winter was to follow and the youth looked forward with longing to the pleasure of skating. There the friends could meet on the Weser without having to travel the rather long distance by land to Wedigenstein or Rothenhof. The Rothenhof was on the right side of the river, the Wedigenstein on the left and while the Wedigenstein and its park went right down to the water, the Weser made a bigger loop just in front of it, thus encircling the royal domain. This made it look like a peninsula on which the manor house, the Rothenhof estate, lay embedded in the middle of its fields and acres.

To walk to the river was not far from all sides and to cross it on the ice and to pick up her girlfriend was done in the shortest time. This was especially the case when a handsome, strong cuirassier officer practicing run archery on this side of the river used the opportuninty to escort the fiery-eyed demoiselle Sack across. And father Sack had also accepted his wife's understanding, allowed his two oldest daughters to attend the balls at the Minden Soiree that winter.

O you golden, blessed days of youth!

Even during the carnival, the father had the horses harnessed and drove the mother and her beautiful, youthful daughters there by themselves to introduce them to the dance hall. When the dance cards were quickly filled, he left the daughters in the care of their mother and drove his animals back to their home stable.

At midnight the servant brought the ladies home in the heavy carriage. Thus the winter months flew by for the two young budding girls in vain lust and joys and in spring they celebrated their engagement at the Rothenhof, because the brisk Captain von Flotow had meanwhile conquered 'fortress Minna' victoriously.

Unfortunately in April the regiment was changed and instead of the cuirassier squadrons of Bavaria the Fusileer battalion von Wedell came to the town of Hausberge for quartering. The bridal couple's abrupt farewell was mitigated by the fact that father Sack, who had grown very fond of his future son-in-law, gave him permission to take the bride home after the promotion that was probably not long in coming and after he had been discharged by the Regiment Adjutant.

In the following summer they had to procure the necessary furnishings for their home. Needle and thread diligently flowed at their favorite place, the park, which offered a far view as far as the city of Minden and which overshadowed the manor house on the north side with its wonderful old giant trees. The manor house was on the south side and was further framed in a semicircle by the stables, outbuildings and stables, allowing only one entrance in grand style on the east side to Vennebeck and in the middle a passage to the quite extensive garden area.

The Rothenhof was already an old and extensive farm estate, which has been recorded for centuries as outpost of the Domain Administration of Hausberge in the annals of the Principality of Minden. In 1725, then already in royal possession, the main residential building had been reduced to ashes and for a long time the authorities had been negotiating and pursuing attempts to punish the murderous arsonists. In a published and more detailed account of this matter kept in the Minden city archives it reads, "the one who can denounce the originator of this misfortune, whose name should not only be kept secret on request but also be given 20 Rthlr (rich man) as compensation and besides, when he is a contributory subject, should be granted freedom for one year."

The long document was signed, "Signatum Minden, on February 19, 1725 in place of and because of His Royal Majesty in Prussia". (Eight names of court officials follow).

The new building, which was erected after clearing away all the fire debris, was an elongated residential building with a high roof and a handsome so-called frontispiece rising above the front door, which, carried out towards the courtyard and garden, contained two spacious, high guest rooms. The ground floor had a hall in the middle, facing the garden, which had three corridors, to which the living room was attached on the left and the study room on the right.

Meals were also usually taken in the living room and only on special occasions in the hall. Next to the living room was the mother's small private room, to which the parental bedroom was attached. To the left after the court lay the boys' bedrooms — to the right of the front door the kitchen and the daughters' bedrooms. Upstairs, in the wide floor space, were the maids' chambers. The inspecting administrator, coachman and servants slept above the office in an adjoining house at the corner of the entrance, to which the beautiful exemplary stables were attached in a semicircle.

The house testified to its character as a model estate to everyone who entered the stately courtyard, for there was painstaking order and cleanliness there—there was no garbage permitted to be left laying around and it was always tidy.

The new regiment, which moved in spring 1797 and of which this time the colonel with his adjutant preferred the Rothenhof, (Mr Schussbacher on the Wedigenstein was a big industrialist and ran a glassworks) stayed again for another year—but the summer was often clouded for the family, apart from the bridal sorrows of Minna, which were actually only pleasures, because the news from Philippine from Langreder was by no means pleasant. In addition to the unavoidable health problems in a larger circle of children, there had been a noticeable decline in father Schultze's strength, something that was a serious threat to a man who was only fifty-two years old.

After the autumn manoeuvers, however, Captain von Flotow was able to announce his promotion to major and at the same time to inform that he was no longer regimental adjutant but had been appointed as a prospective adjutant of the Duke of Saxe-Weimar, remaining with the regiment and in the garrison of Aschersleben. This news caused a great deal of joy especially for the bride, especially since the new major asked the father to let the wedding take place in the late autumn before Christmas—he would then gladly postpone the holiday to which he was entitled.

Now it was time for all hands to the wheel, because everything was supposed to be ready when the sweetheart arrived. After a long back and forth, the parents had granted him the date of December 10 for the wedding. So the happy couple moved out as newlyweds to their new home in Saxony and it was not easy for the parents to have the seventeen-year-old daughter already placed in an independent circle of duties. The military occupation, however, had undoubtedly helped to achieve this. It had broadened the daughters' horizons and had given them social forms and a confidence in their appearance that was astonishing.

In nature they mostly followed their father who, as we know, was exceptionally tall (but Ottilie was also of stately stature) and so at least Minna and already Liese, the next following fifteen-year-old, seemed far more mature than their friends of the same age. They had learned to work in the management of the house and farm at an early age. Anyone who had grown up under Ottilie's care in the already large domestic circles which were now being replenished by apprentices was not afraid of any work and had a rich knowledge in this field.

The young warriors may well have observed and learned to appreciate this in silence, for even the exuberant Liese had whispered in the sister's ear when she said goodbye, "Don't cry, Minchen, watch out, I'll soon be with you in Saxony!"

The Langreder couple had regrettably had to give up their wedding party. Philippine wrote that now, in the colder season, her Ernst should not be subjected to a journey and she could not leave him under any circumstances. That her husband was already confined to bed and the doctor was concerned about the stomach ailment that had been dragging on for so long was something the distressed young woman had not wanted to admit in the wedding atmosphere at home.

However, it could not be concealed for long. A second doctor called from Hanover had probably consulted the family doctor for a long time but the remedies given since then did not help the patient's strength. When Philippine reported this to her home, the father was no longer able to stay there. He arrived in Langreder on the 22nd and was deeply shocked to see the poor, emaciated sick man — there was no thought of returning home for Christmas, let alone taking Ernst and Philippine and the whole group of children with him, as Ottilie had suggested. His poor, poor brave young daughter — oh how good that he was with her!

On Christmas Eve, when they had opened the door to the Christmas Room with the illuminated Christmas tree and the unsuspecting children, he soon fell into a deep sleep, smiling, from which he would not wake up again. Philippine had become a widow that Christmas Eve — the seven children of the Schultzes had been orphaned again.

With all the sad duties that now followed, her sturdy father stood beside her like a firm oak tree, to which she clung like storm-blown ivy. He knew how to relieve her of all her burdens and invited the relatives of the children from the previous marriages to the funeral. Before they left, he had agreed with them that they would share the care for the orphans.

Brothers had come from the first wife, who wanted to keep two sons with them in Hanover for the time being — the eldest was already at university, two of the sisters of the second wife's two daughters offered to take over the upbringing — the two youngest of course returned with Philippine to Hausberge on the Rothenhof. He also negotiated with the owner of the large estates leased by Schultze, who was a skilled and experienced tenant general of the Rothenhof. He had the books of the administrator presented to him—everything was in perfect order—the financial circumstances for the children and the widow were not brilliant but completely sufficient.

Father Sack arrived at Rothenhof at the end of January with Philippine and her two children. Ottilie could now testify to her grandmotherly love for them, which was not difficult for her, the consoling generous soul. When the violets stretched out their heads between the green leaves, Philippine wanted to return to their precious grave, where the other children of the father had promised to come at Easter. With the strengthening support of her parents' home, the grieving young woman had consolidated her strength and her father and mother could confidently let her return to her own home alone.

It was her own wish to keep her living arrangements there for the time being, as the lease had provided for this in order to secure her livelihood. Her parents had also promised to send her sister Albertine (called "Tinchen")—who had left school around Easter and was then confirmed—to Langreder at Whitsun for her amusement and for her further education in household and garden. Therefore Philippine could also look forward to the coming time with optimism.

She had already turned twenty-five in March and she felt young and strong and felt that she could no longer be a burden to her parents. It warmed her sore heart when the children hurried to greet her in Langreder on Maundy Thursday and the splendid maid who had been left behind stood with them at the front door as she alighted. As quiet and solemn as Good Friday was at the grave of the dear departed, and even though such a beautiful consecrated mood had lain over the Easter days, her heart became rebellious when the relatives of the other mothers demanded the children back.

It was the eldest of the three sons who had remained her darling at all times and who was now already nineteen years old and attending university in Göttingen who urged her to return his brothers to the male education of Uncle Drosten in Hannover. Finally, the young man used his last means of persuasion and told Philippine that his uncle had also let him read a letter in which his father had asked him to take care of his three nephews after his death. Then the agitated woman became silent and stood there for a long time, concerned, "So did father know that he had to leave us? And still has filled me with courage and confidence! O the great, the noble man!"

Then, after a while, "No! I didn't know that, of course you shall all go back to Uncle Droste. Just ask him that we may always meet again at Easter here at Father's tomb."

Then she lived quietly with her own two little ones and looked forward longingly to the feast of Pentecost, which was to bring her Tinchen from Rothenhof. "Turbulent times in which we live," the ageing privy councillor thought and now often said to his Ottilie. "if only we could get rid of the quartering! The new colonel is not as nice as Frohwein! And his adjutant is no Flotow!"

"But father, on the other hand the young relative of the Major, who always likes to come from Hausberge to visit us, is a splendid fellow! So fresh and stimulating and always cheerful and funny," said his wife Ottilie, "Our boys, they all adore him. Only yesterday he brought little Carl a new butterfly for his collection."

"So?" Got something! A butterfly? He's a man who likes to nibble on the flowers himself," the good old man growling into his stiff stand-up collar and withdrawing from the living room to his study.

In the corridor, however, he suddenly met the "butterfly" he'd just been talking about, who had come to ask the privy councillor for a brief talk, his heels clenched together, the helmet clasp in his hand and a little embarrassed. He quickly pulled himself together.

"Follow me, please." With this, the person addressed continued on his way with the lieutenant behind him.

"Well, what are you bringing me from that little town down there?" With this question the privy councillor opened the requested dialogue.

"Just a moment honorable, Privy Councillor, I bring nothing but myself and ask for the hand of your demoiselle daughter Caroline."

"But what's this? Are you serious, Lieutenant? Lina is only 16 years old."

"And I'm only 24, Mr. Privy Councillor. No one has ever regretted marrying young."

"But dear Mr von Roeder, you're only a second lieutenant, not even a first lieutenant, let alone a captain and I can't give my daughter dowry for her, I have too many children for that."

"Forgive me, Mr. Privy Councillor, I did not come here to ask for a dowry, I only asked for the hand of Demoiselle Caroline. I have no intention of becoming a first lieutenant or a captain. Let me explain. My eldest brother died in 1798 in France in the revolutionary army, my second brother lost his health during the war in France, then resigned as a captain and took over our father's Hoym estate in 1795. But now he can no longer cultivate it and wishes to hand over father's inheritance to me.

"However, I don't want to do this alone but only when I have a woman at my side. I also want to marry as an officer, so that my wife, if I die before her, will still receive a royal pension. The estate is large enough, if well managed, to feed us abundantly. I had always wanted to become a farmer as a boy but I had two older brothers, so, as was the custom, I had to become an officer like the second one. And Demoiselle loves the country, just as she told me."

"So so! Well, it seems to me you and my daughter have already reached an agreement."

"Yes, professor, it had to be, I couldn't ask the Privy Councillor before that."

"Well, yes, determined! But the privy councillor must first ask his wife, which is the custom here," the Privy Councillor evaded.

But the boy began to please him. "I have no fear of falling, may I fetch her here, Privy Councillor?"

"But young sir, you seem to be conspiring with my whole house! — have you apparently already come to terms with her?"

"Only half, Privy Councillor, I was supposed to bring her the other half's yes first! So may I, Privy Councillor?"

"Son of Hades! Man! For God's sake, yes!" Turning around to the left, the lieutenant was in the living room with one single bound.

Then he put his arms around Ottilie's neck, "He said 'yes'! Where is my little Lina? Lina—he said yes!"

Lina already had her arms around his neck. This all happened on May 5, 1798 and on September 9 of the same year little Lina was already Mrs von Roeder, future heiress and mistress of the Court of Hoym and Harzgerode. The engagement was celebrated in the Honeysuckle Bower[107] with May Punch, the wedding in the great hall of the Rothenhof. The wedding ceremony took place in the living room.

"Into my grandfather's homeland, where my father's cradle stood, I now return this my child," the father of the bride could say when he gave the speech in the great hall again in front of friends and neighbors.

Philippine had not come because she was in mourning. Mrs von Flotow had to nurse her first child, who had arrived in mid-June having to stay in Aschersleben. Instead there was another Mrs. Flotow at the wedding table, a sister of the bridegroom who had become the wife of the major in Aschersleben. Both brothers were happy to be joined here together as new relatives.

The bride was pleased to relate to everyone that Harzgerode, Hoym and Aschersleben were situated on the same high plateau of the Harz, which from the east is considered to be the Harz foreland with the beautiful ruins of Arnstein and can be reached by good highways from Stolberg and the southern Harz as well as from the Selketal (Alexisbad) and Ballenstedt.

It was not long before little Lina and Minchen were again in each other's arms and in the next decade had to take turns in admiring and dealing with their young offspring as mothers.

Now that the three oldest daughters were allowed to enjoy the privilege of keeping their parents on their toes at the Rothenhof for a while, the three older sons came to the fore in the next few years with their studies. The blessed foundation of the brother Heinrich in Glogau had not only allowed the daughters to secure a dowry for their respective household, it now enabled the Privy Councillor to have first the eldest son Friedemann, then Carl and Detlof continue their studies at universities. The former two chose jurisprudence, the latter the building trade as their life professions. Göttingen and Halle were the preferred universities of the particularly favored brothers — the second, because from there it was so easy to visit the sisters on the edge of the Harz Mountains. They especially enjoyed going to an estate for a visit!

Quartering along the so-called demarcation line was finally abolished in 1801 and the whole of Westphalia breathed a sigh of relief — not least the inhabitants of the Rothenhof. But the distress of recent years had also had its good sides. In order to cope with the traffic at the Porta, which had been greatly increased by the military, the shipping activity on the Weser had gradually increased by a significant amount. Furthermore, greater attention had been paid to the roads in the country, especially in the Principality of Minden.

Thus the son Detlof decided to turn his attention to the construction of roads, as the most promising area for fast career prospects. On the Rhine, the Peace of Basel[108] followed, then that of Luneville and now the sad situation had been created that the whole left side of the Rhine became French. Prussia was forced by France to compensate by the dissolution of German dioceses, abbeys and Catholic church estates and that of the former free imperial cities. This strongly influenced the conditions of Philipp's eldest brother, the Judicial Councillor Carl August.

He had buried his wife in 1799, after his son, the protégé and employee of the Chamber President von Stein, had married his childhood sweetheart in Kleve, after he had been appointed to the Ministry of Finance in Berlin as a Privy Financial Councillor. His son-in-law was transferred to Münster in Westphalia in 1803. The wife, his daughter, was a support for the widowed gentleman and so he took his leave and moved with the couple to their new destination.

In 1803 and 1804, Baron von Stein, who had in the meantime been appointed Minister of Finance, was given the task of secularizing the church estates of Westphalia and Hanover. For this purpose, the minister had asked his young friend Johann August Sack of Berlin to be his assistant. The latter, however, who in earlier years had already worked with his patron in Westphalian mining and in making the Ruhr navigable, was then replaced in this special field by his own brother Ernst, who now held the highest position in the Westphalian mining authority as mining director. In place of Baron von Stein, Baron von Vincke had taken over the position as Chamber President of Hamm and later as District President with seat in Minden.

Philipp had now been able to resume contact again with his relatives who had become dearer to his heart as a result of these new circumstances. Many a petition from the sons of Rothenhof went up to the older cousins, who had already reached influential positions, when the time came for them to find employment in the civil service of the province. Despite a certain formality and distance that had to be practiced in this intercourse, a deeper kinship and goodwill was expressed on the part of the Kleve cousins. Especially the Mining Councillor of Wetter on the Ruhr, cousin Ernst, made it his business to guide the young Rothenhof Detlof, even encouraging him to turn back to road construction. He himself now left the mining profession to climb higher as a government councillor.

However, in the autumn of 1806, in the midst of these hopeful efforts for peace, the terrifying news of the battles of Jena and Auerstädt, lost by Prussia, arrived. As a result, the areas on the left bank of the Elbe were suddenly open to French invasion, just as they had been before.

The unfortunate double battle had been fought on October 14, nevertheless Minden remained free from the enemy for several weeks. The fortress was completely cleared of Prussian troops, as the fortifications were not considered sufficient to withstand an enemy onslaught.

Thus, on November 9, the first divisions of the French army of the north moved in with four hundred Dutchmen, and Divisional General Gobert set up quarters in the governorate building. On the same day he issued an imperial proclamation that "the lands he had been appointed governor of would never again become the property of the Prussian princes who had ruled them before. Happy are the peoples who inhabit such, their fate will in future depend only on the best, the most respected and the most powerful sovereign on earth. Nations trust in the goodness and magnanimity of the insurmountable Napoleon—he has commanded me to create your happiness, and I will fulfil his will."

The Prussian officials, as far as they were compliant, remained in their positions for the time being and it seemed strange when, on November 13, under a decree of the Prussian Military and Domain Chamber and on November 23, under a decree of the Imperial-French and Royal-Italian Military and Domain Chamber, the same names were present.

The French occupation was celebrated on November 16 with a ceremony in the cathedral and a torchlit procession. Representatives of the nobility and clergy of all religions, a committee of citizens and all officials had to accompany the governor to the cathedral in the morning. Such festivities were repeated constantly. So on the first Sunday in December, Napoleon's Day, the day when the Emperor was crowned and the day of the Battle of the Three Emperors at Austerlitz, it was ordered "to celebrate with all the pomp and circumstance befitting such a festival."

No one of rank and position was allowed to exclude himself from church celebrations and evening balls without legitimate reasons. Hypocritically, Napoleon ordered that a French Westphalian regiment should be set up at the request of all Prussian soldiers, since these countries would never again become Prussian this side of the Elbe. The first appeal, which the magistrate of Minden had to issue and likewise the second appeal of general Gobert, who was already threatening with punishment, were in vain. No one came to report.

In March 1807, conscription was announced and, as there were still no recruits, execution was ordered. In Minden a battalion was violently put together on April 8, 1807. On the 9th it marched towards Münster but on the way ninety-five deserted. The civil authorities were held responsible for their recapture and threatened with the death penalty if they withheld information from the population.

In addition to this formation of troops, which Napoleon immediately used for his war campaigns, national guards were deployed in the catchment communities, which were militarily organized and whose supreme command was under the French General Gobert. The financial burden and all the usable material for these new formations as well as food and horse fodder for the never-ending troop movements, threatened the inhabitants with a shortage of their own. The city of Minden had to raise 14,000 Reichstaler by December third.

The extension of the Continental Blockade against England by Napoleon's decree from Berlin in November 1806 suddenly paralyzed the flourishing Weser navigation and caused trade and traffic to come to a standstill. All income vanished while needs and expenditure grew immeasurably.

Yet there was a testimony to great determination in these times of tormenting tribulation in that here was a father of six adolescent sons, of whom the two oldest were at the universities and the third in Berlin at the grammar school, also nurturing the desire to take up the subject of mining and to skip a semester in Halle.

It was at this point in time when a young man appeared in the person of Friedrich Ploeger, an assessor at the

Higher Regional Court in Minden, who in December 1806 asked the old Privy Councillor for the hand of his 15-year-old daughter Adolfine.

I only want to take her as my bride and be allowed to protect the beautiful girl here legally against attacks of the French officers — I will only take her home to Minden when we have peace again.

This was an offer that was gratefully accepted by the rather worried father, who himself had recognized the dangers that the French rule had also imposed on his entire territory and even on the Rothenhof with its French occupation.

"However, the engagement cannot be announced until her sixteenth birthday — until then, you two are secretly promised to each other apart from us parents."

Even if they had hoped to celebrate their engagement under the Christmas tree, the couple was already overjoyed with this yes-word from the father. For Adolfine, who possessed a particularly rich imagination, the certainty of now being firmly attached to her suitor was a curb on her easily aroused imagination and she felt herself to be twice as interesting, shrouded in the veil of mystery. Incidentally, the father had threatened to send her without mercy to a reformatory in Halle if he detected even the slightest approach by a French officer. This was the assurance he had also given the secret groom to pacify him.

The winter passed relatively quietly on the Rothenhof but the news from outside kept everyone in suspense and excitement. Berlin had already been abandoned by the King of Prussia, he and his ministers residing in Königsberg. The capital was a playground for French troops, which exploited and harassed the Mark Brandenburg as much as the Westphalia region here. Even though here the Governor von Vincke represented the Prussian government in an obviously devalued manner, the King, when he and his family left Berlin, had appointed the Privy Councillor Johann August Sack as Governor of the capital and of the whole province on Stein's advice. As was later learned, this brave man and exemplary official reported the events to Königsberg every day in regular reports, so that the King remained informed of everything.

Son Detlof had been allowed to attend the Royal Prussian Academy of Architecture thanks to the application written by his cousin at the time and because of his good conduct, qualified for the University of Halle there in September 1806. After he had completed four semesters there, he came as mining apprentice for work experience under his cousin and Royal Mining Director Ernst Sack. Ernst Sack showed him warm affection. He was employed in Wetter on the Ruhr.

In the meantime Napoleon had driven the unhappy King of Prussia to the furthest corner of his empire by marching troops even as far as Königsberg. However, Friedrich Ploeger, now appointed to the Military Council, was able to take the old Privy Councillor at the Rothenhof at his word and in April, on Adolfine's birthday, the engagement was announced.

By the time May was approaching, a ceasefire had already been agreed and negotiations with the Immediate Peace Enforcement Commission had begun. At that time the two peace commissioners on the Prussian side were Baron vom Stein and the minister Count Schulenburg-

Kehnert. There a new confidence developed with the Privy Councillor, who was always sympathetic towards Stein. At the baptismal celebration of his second granddaughter Gantzer in Minden he voluntarily gave the Minden bridal couple permission to arrange the wedding in the summer.

The trousseau was ready, peace was in progress, what were they waiting for? A suitable apartment could be found in time for St. John's day and the wedding was also fixed for that day. There he had gathered them all around him once again. Also the daughters and sons-in-law from the Harz mountains had come and each of them brought along their eldest daughter. Together with Philippine's two children and the two-year-old Ottilie, Mrs Gantzer, who had advanced to become the wife of the Government Councillor, brought her five grandchildren. Thus the young generation were already well represented.

There was already a much larger crowd. It was a wonderful Sunday, and the student sons Friedemann, Carl and Detlof had provided for a fun at the wedding-eve party with a little rhyme:

Rothenhof has already rid itself of Pini,
Mine, Lina and Tin' and Fi.
Only left is little Rieke
All there's left now to flee.
Rieke, Rieke in five years,
You too will shed your tears.
Your turn to jump joy's quarry
As jump today – Fritz and Fi!

On the 7th of July the lamentable peace was made in Tilsit with the terrible sacrifices that were imposed on the King of Prussia, including the separation of the province of Westphalia from his kingdom forever and its annexation to France. This peace marked the peak of Napoleon's power. From the Pyrenees to the borders of Russia his will was law and only for the love of the Russian Tsar had he not completely wiped Prussia off the map of Europe, which had been his intention after the victorious battles of Eylau and Friedland. Thanks to this skilful granting of his petition, a personal friendship bond was formed in Tilsit with the ruler of Eastern Europe.

Napoleon had not possessed such moral power in his own country since his coronation as he did at that time. After all, their emperor now had the princes he had defeated at his own beck and call, he created principalities and occupied them according to his own liking. Thus he created a new kingdom of Westphalia. It consisted of Hesse-Kassel's states, in which he had expropriated the Elector, then of the districts of Paderborn, Münster, Minden, which had been taken from the Prussians, further from Brunswick, Fulda as well as part of the Electorate of Hanover.

As King over this new kingdom he appointed his brother Hieronimus (Jerome Bonaparte). He had originally intended him for the marine sector and had sent him to North America. Napoleon did not recognize his marriage with Miss Paterson there, he simply had it revoked by his council of state, despite the papal objection. This brother had nurtured hopes of becoming King of Poland after the Battle of Warsaw but these hopes were not fulfilled. In return he received the Westphalian royal crown and had to make a princess of Württemberg his queen.[109]

At the Congress of Vienna (1814–15), which redrew the map of Europe following Napoleon's defeat, Prussia acquired rich new territories, including the coal-rich Ruhr.

Jerome's expensive habits brought him the contempt of Napoleon. His court had expenses comparable to those of Napoleon's court (which supervised a much larger and more important empire), and Napoleon refused to support Jerome financially.

In 1812 Jerome was given command of a corps in the Grande Armée, which marched towards Minsk. Jerome insisted on travelling in state and so Napoleon rebuked Jerome by ordering him to leave his court and his luxurious furnishings behind.

As the news of the dissolution of the Kingdom of Westphalia and Jerome's removal as King became known, there was rejoicing in Hausberge. Philipp Wilhelm was only able to take pleasure in this for a short time as he had become very frail. He passed away in the bosom of his dear Ottilie on December 22, 1813 at the age of 79. As we know, in his old age the Sack couple had bought the so-called "castle" in Hausberge near Minden. The graves of the couple are still to be found in its garden.

Philipp Wilhelm could never have imagined that he would become the father of many generations whose members would often display the same courage and strength to lead useful lives.

He left behind six sons and six married daughters, whose descendants are generally known as "the Rothenhofers" to this day. During the wars of 1813-1815 five sons were officers in the army, two of them fell in Russia and one was seriously wounded. As the recorded genealogy shows, he has produced the most numerous offspring amongst all his siblings.

The Rothenhof Legacy

The many children of Philipp and Ottilie were strongly influenced and motivated by their active and influential parents. In their turn, they were able to pass this spirit of adventure and ability to their children. As Philipp's brother had constructed a unique foundation endowed with considerable funds, university education, dowry's and standing in society were almost guaranteed.

The following is a little of what had happened to the descendants of our subject up until 1900. The story continues to this day, as a registry of descendants and the family magazine, *The Taube* produced in Germany and *The Dove* produced in Texas together with the *Silver Book* published from time to time, bond the family together and motivates to the highest achievements and care for the fellow man and the world we live in. The book "These are the Generations in two volumes" by Flora von Roeder continues the stories of the descendants of the Rothenhof family who emigrated to Texas up to the present day.

Philippine Antoinette Sack, the eldest daughter, 19 years old, married in 1794 the High Count and General Tenant of the Baron von Klencker estates, Ernst Johann Conrad Schulz of Langreder near Hannover. After she had given her husband two children, a daughter and a son, she lost him on Christmas Eve of 1798 after only 4 years of marriage.

As a young widow she moved back to her native Hausberge near Minden and lived there until her death in 1853. Her daughter married the later President of the Supreme

Court. From her, who raised eleven children herself, come the families Zernial, Grubitz, Vogelfang, von Lanzenauer, Lene, Kirberg, Rothert, Wex, Walbaum, Stallmann, Wegener, Lücker, Hahn, Biermann and Schreyer. Her three youngest daughters, some of whom were great-grandmothers, were still alive in 1900. Eduard Schulz, the son of Philippine, was a theologian and lived as pastor of Mühlheim on the Rhine. His only daughter, married to Superintendent Bick of Solingen, died childless after a short marriage in her twenty-ninth year.

Wilhelmina Luise Sack, the second daughter of the Rothenhof, married in 1797, barely seventeen years old, Friedrich Heinrich von Flotow, major in the Cuirassier Regiment of Byer zu Aschersleben[110]. Von Flotow was at the same time an inspection adjutant of the Duke of Saxe-Weimar and as such took part in the campaign in the Champagne in 1792 and in the battles near Jena and Auerstätt in 1806. Sent by his Duke to Blücher he was captured near Lübeck but released on his word of honor. After the freedom wars he took his leave and then lived several years on the estate of a cousin in Walzengarde in Mecklenburg-Schwerin until he bought himself a small property on the Warnow in Gehlsdorf near Rostock (in 1900 it had become a refuge house for neglected children). After the death of his wife, which he lost in 1816 at the age of thirty-five years with the birth of her seventh child, he moved to Rostock and died there in December 1828. He lies buried at the side of his wife in Toitenwinkel (Gehlsdorf belonged to this parish). Of the three daughters of the von Flotow couple, one daughter died at the age of nine years and the youngest, Luise, remained unmarried, while the oldest,

The Rothenhof Legacy

Ottilie, married the Procurator of the Higher Court Johann Joachim Valentin Beselin of Rostock. Of his five sons, the eldest, Rudolph who had trained as a farmer founded his home in Sweden, which he had got to know on a journey in 1848 and found particularly promising for agricultural purposes. Herewith a strong circle from the foundation's family tree was permanently transplanted to Scandinavia. Rudolph's seven children have all remained there and have partly married locals, whereby the Swedish families Schjöler and von Braun joined the foundation. The other four sons of the High Court Procurator Beselin have mostly remained resident in Rostock. One of their daughters (daughter of Richard Beselin) is married to the bank director Victor Koch in Hamburg. Another (daughter of Berthold) with Dr. med. Wolfs of Berlin, a son of the poet Julius Wolff[111], another (daughter of Johann Beselin) with the pastor Heyn of Stralsund[112]. The only married daughter of the High Court Procurator Beselin was married to the Royal Privy Councillor Scharenberg, that humorous old gentleman, well known from the first days of the family, who lost his faithful partner a few months before his golden wedding anniversary in 1893 and followed her in death in November 1899. The male successors of the von Flotow couple are the present Chief Forester von Flotow, member of the family council and Baron Gerschau von Flotow, a Russian state councillor and chamberlain of Jacobstad in Kurland. The sister of the Chief Forester, Clara von Flotow, was married in her first marriage to the early deceased corvette captain Edwin Schelle, of whose three sons the eldest, Alexander, as an outstandingly capable officer entitled to the best hopes but died at the young age of twenty-nine. The second was a second lieutenant at sea with the landing party of S.M.S. "Swallow" and took part in the storm on Buschiri's[113] camp (East Africa), being the first to reach the enemy entrenchments, where he met his heroic death. A beautiful obelisk decorates his grave at Bagamayo in Tanzania. The third son, Felix Schelle, is first lieutenant in Inf. Reg. No. 16 at Cologne on the Rhine.

Caroline Luise Sack, the third daughter of the Rothenhof, was married in the autumn of 1798, like her sister Wilhelmine at the age of 16, to Baron Lieutenant Anton Ludwig Sigismund von Röder, Hereditary and Court Lord of Hoym and Harzgerode[114] and an acquaintance of the philosopher and theologian Schleiermacher. Sigismund had been in Prussian service with his four brothers and had taken part in the French Revolutionary Wars. His sister was married to a brother of Major von Flotow, mentioned above. While two of his older brothers had died in the battles of 1793 and his last brother had to retire in 1795 as a captain for health reasons, Anton Ludwig Sigismund had taken over his father's estate immediately after his marriage and the first of his sixteen children were born there. However, the rural seclusion of Anhalt did not appeal to his and his wife's lively temperaments. The couple soon moved to Paderborn and bought the Marienmünster monastery estate near Höxter in Westphalia in 1820. In 1827 the paternal estate Hoym was changed in its title from lands with feudal tenure to complete ownership and Anton Ludwig Sigismund sold it to the widow of his brother Victor, whose grandson Victor Eduard von Röder still resides on Hoym today (1900). In 1834, a friend (Mr Ernst) drew attention to the great agricultural advantages of the newly developed land of Texas in North America. Anton Ludwig Sigismud von Röder sold his abbey property, whose economic yields could not be raised to any level under the oppressive conditions of the impoverished fatherland anyway and decided to emigrate to America with his entire family, which by then was already mostly adult. Friends and relatives of the same age joined the enterprising youth, so that the traveling party consisted of the following members: Anton Ludwig Sigismund von Röder and Caroline, his wife, their son Rudolph, their son Otto with wife Pauline née von Donop and sister Antoinette von Donop, who later became Rudolph von Röder's wife—furthermore the sons Wilhelm, Ludwig, Albrecht and Joachim von Röder, the daughters Valesca, Luise and Rosalie and the husband of the latter. Also Robert Kleberg, a junior lawyer at the Higher Regional Court of Bredenborn, and his brother Ludwig Kleberg, who later married Luise von Röder.

Four of the newlyweds, the brothers Ludwig, Albrecht and Joachim with their sister Valesca, accompanied by an old servant and provided with a rich supply of building materials, clothing and equipment, saddlery etc., had travelled ahead of the larger company. The others boarded the steamer "Congress" on September 30, 1834, where they met several like-minded passengers, mostly from Oldenburg. After a sixty-day journey they landed in New Orleans. Here they heard bad news about the wild Texas conditions but decided to follow the other travellers. After eight days of sailing in a coastal schooner, they were shipwrecked at Galveston Island. All the passengers were rescued and as the captain and crew seized the next opportunity to escape, the suspicion that the passengers were the victims of an American scam to send the old, unseaworthy ship on one more trip to collect the high insurance money seemed well-founded. The poor cheated people had no other choice than to build a big tent out of the sails and masts of the wrecked ship and to settle down on the uninhabited island as well as possible. The jungle offered birds and red deer in abundance and while the male part of the company was responsible for hunting, the women had to take care of the tent and the meals. Three days after the shipwreck, the steamer "Ocean" noticed the hoisted flag of distress.

Since its captain only wanted to take a few of the castaways with him, Robert Kleberg[115] and Rudolph von Röder decided to go to Brazoria and rent a ship to catch up with the others. On their arrival in Brazoria, however, no vessel could be obtained. Having hiked on foot to St. Felipe, they were asked to pay a thousand dollars for the journey by the sole owner of one, which sum exceeded their means. In St. Felipe, however, they heard for the first time details of their predecessors, who they decided to seek out. They found them, fourteen miles from St. Felipe, in wretched huts, abandoned to misery and distress. Valesca and Joachim von Röder had already died.

Finally they managed to rent a ship to Felipe for three voyages at the price of one hundred dollars. Four weeks after his departure, Robert Kleberg returned with it to Galveston Island, where he found all those left behind in good health. The next day he reembarked with his wife, parents-in-law and his sister-in-law Caroline von Röder and after a stormy crossing they reached Harrisburg where a house was rented and the women and children were accommodated. An unusually severe winter caused six more journeys there and back and the winter of 1835 had already set in before the last passenger was transferred from Galveston Island to Harrisburg.

The male members of the family had meanwhile started to build wooden houses and cultivate the land at the river branch near St. Felipe. In September 1835 they were able to collect their wives and children from Harrisburg, while they left their treasures, including the old family pictures, books, instruments etc. in the house they had rented there.

While the courageous settlers had already had to endure much adversity, the worst came when in the spring of 1836 the Mexican dictator Santa Anna set out to subdue the what was to become the young Republic of Texas and, covering the country with war, threatened the settlement of the von Röders. Harrisburg had already fallen into the hands of the conqueror and the valuables left behind by the von Röder family there had become a sacrifice to the flames.

The situation became more and more desolate from day to day and under a mighty oak tree, with Anton Ludwig Sigismund von Röder holding the floor, a war council was held on whether to defend Texas' independence or to flee to the older states of North America. It was decided to fight for the new fatherland and after Albrecht and Ludwig von Röder, the former already unfit for battle, had returned from the battlefields of San Antonio de Bexar, Robert Kleberg, Ludwig and Otto von Röder were ordered to go along as warriors. The others, with their livestock of horses and cattle, were to try to gain the border of Texas and wait for the decision to return.

A few days later, the historic battle of San Jacinto took place, in which Santa Anna was defeated. Kleberg and Ludwig von Röder distinguished themselves in an outstanding manner. In the wake of General Rusk, Kleberg took part in the action to pursue the defeated Mexicans to their border.

In the meantime the remaining family members had finally found their way back to Galveston Island that had already granted them a place of refuge before. This time they had built their own vessel, on which they brought their belongings over. They had been guided by the thought of making their home there if the war ended unfavorably, not knowing that the islands were the fundamental property of the government. After their warriors had returned to them unharmed as victors, they only stayed on the island until the ladies and children, who were mostly ill due to poor nutrition, had to some extent recovered. Mrs. Pauline von Röder née von Donop died there giving birth to a son and was buried under the "three solitary trees". In October 1836, the others managed to reach the mainland and, having gained experience and insight, they decided to settle in the provinces of Austin and Dewitt.

Here, too, the severely tested colonists had to endure many fights and privations, failures, attacks by natives and threats by snakes before they could call a safe home their own. However, after the difficult beginnings came a better time, when the wilderness turned into fertile land and Texas developed into a great free republic, where commerce, progress and culture were established and where the past struggles sometimes seemed like a fairy tale to the survivors.

Robert Kleberg died at the age of 85 in 1888 and his name is indelibly linked to the history of Texas—as the hero of San Jacinto and he will always be remembered as the wise judge of Austin and Dewitt County,. His brave wife is still alive, who as a young mother with the baby at her breast on horseback, escaped from San Felipe back to Galveston Island. Rosalie Kleberg née von Röder is now in her 88th year and is full of intellectual vitality. Among her seven children she proudly counts her son Rudolph Kleberg[116], who as a member of the White House in Washington is a mainstay of the Republican representation of the country, taking the fatherland of his parents as a model and striving to promote and uphold German culture in Texas.

The younger generations are also a source of joy for Rosalie. Her two great-granddaughters Rosa and Lily Hohfeld graduated from California State University in May 1899. During their four years of study, they consistently maintained first place in all subjects and were subsequently awarded the Gold Prize Medal. Never before, during the 30th anniversary of the Californian University, has a student had a similar success. Also the same favorable news about her brother Wesley N. Hohfeld[117], now studying for three years at the same university, can be reported. He, devoting himself to jurisprudence, is also at the top in all subjects.

When in the course of time the conditions in Texas improved and Robert Kleberg became Land-Commissioner of Texas, several members of the Rothenhof branch decided to emigrate there, so that a group of over four hundred people from the Rothenhof tribe represents the Hofrath Sack family on the other side of the ocean. The foundation members Sack, von Röder, Plöger, Kleberg, Ernst, Eckhardt, Langhammer, Engelking etc. married into each other so often later that it requires a very special study of the family tree lists to unravel the intricate ramifications, the further clarification of which would lead too far here.

Franziska Albertine Sack, the fourth daughter of the Rothenhof, married in 1804, at the age of 20, the foreman Johann Friedrich Gantzer of Wesel, born on June 14, 1775, who worked under Napoleon's regiment during the troublesome years of the time. In 1806, Gantzer was transferred to Paderborn in the Kingdom of Westphalia as a building inspector and later, under the Prussian government, to Minden as a construction councillor.

When he celebrated his fiftieth anniversary of service on June 30, 1846, now appointed a Privy Government Councillor, the celebration was arranged by the Government Collegium, the Domain Chambers, the ecclesiastical and municipal dignitaries of the province and the representatives of the construction trades, into a great homage celebration with a procession and gifts of honor. It was attended by the entire city. In 1855 the Gantzer couple celebrated their golden wedding anniversary and then moved away from Minden to Bad Oeynhausen, where one of their married daughters lived on a larger estate, the outhouse having been extended for her parents. Here Albertine died in 1857 and one year later her husband died in the 83rd year of his life. Six daughters had blossomed out of the

Gantzer's marriage (two sons had died early), three of whom were married to the lawyers Vinke, Höpker and Richter and the youngest to Captain Brée.

When the daughter Ferdinande, who was married to Councillor of Justice Höpker, died in 1837 after barely four years of marriage, with her husband succeeding her in death in 1845, the nine-year-old son Albert Höpker was brought up by his grandparents. The daughter Emma, married to the Government Councillor Richter, had also returned to her parents' house after the death of her husband in February 1837, together with her two-year-old daughter Marie Richter, later wife of the President of the Regional Court Eduard Sack. The Gantzer's house in Minden thus formed a favored meeting point for the growing family of grandchildren and their numerous Westphalian cousins. The grandmother, richly endowed with energy and spirit, was a genius in the financial field and knew how to meet the most extensive requirements with limited means. Through a grandson of her daughter Bertha, who married von Vinke and whose eldest son Friedrich had already been married to Mathilde Princess von Sayn-Wittgenstein in her first childless marriage, a German royal house has recently entered into a relationship with the Hofrath Sack Foundation entitled to inherit. The son Itel-Jobst, born in 1899, who was the result of the marriage between Lieutenant Friedrich von Vinke and Sybille Princess of Hesse (a distant cousin and sister-in-law of the German Emperor), forms the connecting link in this regard.

Friedemann Ludwig Alexander Sack, born in 1785, the eldest of the six sons of Rothenhof, had taken part in the wars of liberation in 1813 and 1815 like his two younger brothers and, after he had been resident as a bailiff in Oldenburg in 1822, he held the same position in Adenburg near Höxter until his emigration to America in the early 1840's. He married Luise Antoinette von Beesten, the surviving bride of his brother who died near Smolensk in 1812. Of his descendants, all of whom went with him to America, no further news has reached Europe since 1846, when Friedemann died over there—all efforts to find out have been unsuccessful to date[118].

Carl Simon Benjamin Sack, the next of the Rothenhof family, was born on December 7, 1786. His godparents were the Criminal Councillor Carl August Sack of Kleve, the Court Councillor Simon Heinrich Sack of Glogau, and his aunt, the demoiselle Friederike Sack. He received his legal training in Jena and Helmstädt and was employed in 1809 as a notary public in Meissen in the then Kingdom of Westphalia. On December 11, 1811 he married the seventeen-year-old daughter of Pastor Erdsiek of Minden[119] when he was twenty-five—his "Lottchen", with whom he lived in the happiest marriage for fifty-one years and who gave him twelve children. During the times of war he stood helpfully by his aging parents and after the re-establishment of Prussian rule he was appointed as Assessor and later Councilor at the District and City Court of Vlotho on the Weser, where his house with the beautiful mountain garden was a much-visited friendly meeting place of the large Westphalian family until 1849. In the latter year he found a new home in Bielefeld, where he died on December 14, 1884 as District Court Councillor. His wife followed him on January 7, 1885 after her 90th birthday, faithfully nurtured by her daughter Emma, who still lives in Bielefeld today (1900) as a 77-year-old canoness.

The eldest son of Carl Simon Benjamin, Philipp Sack, had married a cousin from another branch of the Rothenhof family. Already as a trainee and at the same time as his younger brother Ferdinand, who had studied medicine, he had followed his Sack relatives to Texas, where both brothers died after a short time in 1844. Philipp's only surviving daughter of three children has remained in Texas with her numerous family. Her sons have mostly devoted themselves to banking and hold positions of respect in Alice. Of the other three sons of Carl Simon Benjamin, Albert was Mayor of Herford, where he died in 1875. The next was Eduard Sack, who is well known in the family as the chairman of the provisional family council and has moved his residence back to his native Bielefeld since the beginning of this year. The youngest son is the Privy Government and Trade Councilor Rudolf Sack of Königsberg in Prussia, and is the current (1900) publisher of the family magazine, the *Taube*. Through the daughters of the Bielefeld branch, the Delius, Ritschl, Poggenpohl and Schneider families were added to the foundation and, in further succession, the families of Wendt, von Düffel, Steeger, Boetzelen, Dahlhaus, Dieckmann, Hünke, Bertelsmann and Kling. In the same branch, ten male bearers of the Sack name are currently alive, two of whom belong to the first, seven to the second and one to the third generation.

Detlof Friedrick Otto Sack, born in 1788 as the third son of the Rothenhof family, dedicated himself to the subject of mining after graduating from the Joachimthal Gymnasium[120] in Berlin. During foreign rule he was assigned to his cousin, the mining director Sack in Essen and Bochum.

After the wars of liberation, during which he had joined the ranks of the Russian-German legion as a volunteer light infantryman, he switched to the building trade as an inspector of road building and in 1817 married Sophie Trippler, who gave him four sons and three daughters. In his position he had his residence in Essen on the Ruhr, where he and his family were always able to keep in touch with his youngest brother Eduard who lived in Düsseldorf.

Detlof's eldest son was the Privy Councillor of Justice Otto Sack of Essen on the Ruhr, who has recently died as a member of the provisional family council. His next son died as director of mines in Sprockhövel and of the two others who devoted themselves to the rank of officer, Carl died in 1893 as Lieutenant Colonel of Minden, Eduard already in 1866 as Captain. Detlof's eldest daughter Ottilie married in 1845 to Dr. Budde, the senior teacher at the cadet school in Bensberg. Ottilie's only grown up sister Elise, married the General Practitioner Bitkow and four sons from this marriage, a third daughter of Detlof had died in 1844 at the age of five. In this branch of the Rothenhof family there are four male representatives of the name Sack among the living, two of them in the second and two in the third generation.

August Ferdinand Heinrich Sack. No information has been preserved about the fourth son of Rothenhof who participated in the Russian campaign as a first lieutenant in the Royal Westphalian Chevau-légers Regiment, other than a note from his father in the baptismal book kept on his children, which reads at the relevant place, "According to a letter from the cavalry captain von Cornberg, dated Smolensk August 21, 1812, this my son died in a fierce action against the Russians on August 19, 1812 by a shot in the abdomen and right side, dying upon the bed of honor."

Ottilie Adolphine Charlotte Sack, the fifth daughter of the Rothenhof married, at the age of seventeen, the Higher Regional Court Councillor Friedrich Plöger in Minden, later in Paderborn, to whom she gave six children. Her eldest daughter Ottilie married her cousin Theodor von Röder in 1831, who was the senior border controller at Höxter and died there in 1834, even before his parents emigrated in the same year. Theodore Plöger, Adolphine's second daughter, had married her cousin, Philipp Sack, a junior high court clerk from the Carl Simon Benjamin branch above. She too became a widow after only a short marriage, and Emilie Plöger, Adolphine's fourth daughter, who had married Potthof, an assistant high court clerk, lost him after barely a year of marriage.

The latter two widows later moved to America, where they soon remarried, namely Theodore with her cousin Otto von Röder, Emilie with a German immigrant named Schumann. The desire to emigrate took over more and more of the Rothenhof family circles and their brothers Ferdinand and Carl had already moved to Texas in 1844. The eldest widowed daughter Ottilie married in second marriage the Judicial Councillor of Rabenau of Iserlohn and was the only one of all Adolphine's children who remained in the fatherland. Auguste, a fourth daughter (third eldest), had also chosen America in 1844 with her husband, a young German lawyer Sarrazin. After the death of her husband, Adolphine was left alone and decided to go to America herself to get to know the new home of her children. It was no small thing for the woman, who was used to a German civil servant's life with its regulated domestic conditions, to start the ocean voyage, which at that time did not offer the comfort of today, and to venture into the primitive Texas conditions with all its hardships.

After a round trip visiting her local loved ones, Mrs. Adolphine also liked to return to her home town, and after first living in Essen for a few years, where the Rabenau Counselor of Justice had meanwhile settled as a lawyer in community with this family, she chose for her permanent residence the local Hausberge, where at the same time so many of the relatives were resident. Her lively spirit, however, did not allow her to enjoy the peace and quiet she had chosen for herself. The longing for her children soon presented her with a rosier view of faraway America than her home country and so she underwent — well over sixty years old — a second trip to Texas with all the privations that entailed. Here she spent a rather long old age, living alternately with her son Ferdinand and her daughter Emilie, until she died in the autumn of 1878 at the age of 87. Her grandson is the Privy and Senior Government Councillor Carl von Rabenau of Magdeburg. His sister, the widow of the District Court Councillor von Rodenberg, who has been widowed since 1892, lives in Berlin, while a younger brother von Rabenau is considered a practical member of the family council. Rabenau died early.

The Rothenhof Legacy

The numerous descendants of the five Plöger's children who settled in America are characterized, like those of the von Röder family, by a strong sense of solidarity. In their circles they cultivate a warm reverence for the German way of life and, whenever the opportunity arises, maintain family relations with their old home country with zeal and devotion.

Philipp Friedrich August Georg Sack, the fifth son of Rothenhof, born there in 1793, was a lieutenant in the second Westphalian cuirassier regiment under Napoleon and is said to have died there in the battle of Borodino on the Moskva after capturing a Russian flag. His body was not found however. He was declared dead by the Higher Regional Court in Paderborn on October 22, 1821.

Eduard Willhelm Hieronimus Maximilian Sack, the youngest of the Rothenhof sons, born on October 12, 1794, after having temporarily served as studiosus juris with the Gard du Corps in Kassel in 1813, was prompted to report to General Chernychev upon his arrival there on September 28, 1813 to join the Russian-German Legion. On January 3, 1814, he and his brother Detlof joined Ravensberg's Light Cavalry Detachment, where he was elected Senior Infantryman, procuring his equipment at his own expense and remaining mostly in Westphalian garrisons until the dissolution of the Corps in June 1814. On Napoleon's return from Elba, following the call for volunteers, he left his studies in Halle once again and in April 1815 set out from Minden on the march route, via Aachen, Liège to Charlesroy, where he was assigned to the first Westphalian Uhlan regiment as a lieutenant. Wounded in the foot in the Battle of Ligny during an attack on the Carrée, he returned home incapacitated via Antwerp and was first received and cared for by his cousin Sethe in Düsseldorf. After he then resumed his legal studies at Göttingen, he received his first civil service appointment as an auditor on March 15 of the same year. Appointed as an assessor in 1818, he was appointed to the Regional Court of Kleve in December 1820, after he had married Dorothea Ficker, the daughter of the famous doctor Privy Councillor Dr. Ficker of Paderborn[121], on his 25th birthday. Soon afterwards he was appointed Royal State Procurator of Düsseldorf and as a cofounder of the Rhine-Westphalia Prison Society, he made great contributions to the improvement of the prison system. In 1826, he was appointed to the position of Government Councillor and Legal Advisor at the Provincial Tax Directorate in Cologne, where his thorough knowledge of French law, which was only occasionally cultivated at the time, was very much appreciated. With his lively interest in all public welfare matters, he soon became one of the most eager initiators for the resumption of the cathedral construction and the opening of St. Gereons in Cologne is mainly due to his tireless work, in which he had a special interest as the owner of the so-called Provostry of St. Gereon. After the death of his first wife in 1832, he left his official career and took over the stamp duty administration in Koblenz and in 1834 the one in Düsseldorf. Here too, in addition to his official duties, he devoted himself to the city, church, school, art and other public affairs and, with clear judgment and a clairvoyant mind predicting future things, he drafted a brotherhood order in 1841 that was intended to prevent the social revolution he had prophesied. He also presented this to the King.

In 1864, on the occasion of his fiftieth anniversary of service, he was appointed Privy Councillor. In the autumn of 1866 he succumbed to the prevailing epidemic in his 72nd year of life. His second wife was a stepdaughter of Professor von Fichte[122], son of the philosopher famous for his "Speeches to the German nation". Eduard Sack was the father of twenty-three children, of which eighteen have reached an advanced age.

Despite his many-sided occupations, he devoted himself with admirable zeal and sacrificial love to his household and the education of his children. As a great warm-hearted philanthropist, he also supported many fellow men with advice and action, pursuing not insignificant private ventures. His eldest son from his first marriage was Dr. Wilhelm Sack, the editor of the first *Silver Book* of the Sack Family Foundation.

His youngest son from his second marriage is the Imperial Vice-Admiral Hans Sack of Berlin. Through its numerous other sons and daughters, who with few exceptions have all found their sphere of activity abroad, this branch of the family has a very international character, since among the sons and daughters-in-law those of American, English, Spanish, French and Greek origin are represented.

Caroline Sack in particular, who remained unmarried for a long time, had a rich and eventful life. With a great love for children, she began her teaching career at a boarding school in Neuwied, stopped over in Berlin on a trip to Russia, staying there until 1850. She soon went on an art trip through France, Belgium and England with American friends and then held a teaching position at the Higher School for Daughters in Lennep for nine years. In 1864 she went to England as a private teacher and when her pupil there died, she took over the position as a missionary teacher at the Seminary of the British Schools in Syria for five years. After three years she had to travel Europe for the mission to win contributions and friends for the work of love in Beirut. One year after her return she had to leave her sphere of activity there due to illness, finding a new sphere of activity in Constantinople (Istanbul), on the Asian and European shores alternately, teaching in schools and private homes.

Her return to Germany was connected with further longer stays in France and Switzerland. After a short break with her relatives from the Rhine, she began a journey to America in 1839, which took her first to Texas to visit her siblings there. Turning north, her destination was Sioux City, where she visited a young orphaned niece. Here she found a new home in 1886 at the side of an older husband, the Swiss born Theophile Heggi, whom she lost again after seven years of marriage. Then she spent several years at the home of her nephew Dr. Albert Fuchs, staying in Loyal. A year ago, she exchanged Loyal for Des Moines in the state of Iowa, where she is now seventy-five years old and strives to spend her old age in a women's home with unimpaired mental activity and useful literary work. Apart from Caroline Sack in this branch, several female representatives, especially from the younger generation, have dedicated themselves to a larger sphere of activity, among them the first female doctor from the family, Dr. med. Adele Fuchs from Sioux City, and Lilia de Casis, Adjunct Professor at the University of Austin.

Ulrike Dorothea Sophie Sack, the sixth daughter and the youngest child from Rothenhof, grew up in Hausberge like all her siblings and married Albert Wittich, who was then captain of the Genie-Corps[123] in Jülich, when she was 23. Wittich had taken part in the wars of liberation as a lieutenant and took part in the most important battles of Blücher[124]. Five children were born to the couple in Jülich, among them four daughters and one son. After his promotion to major and his transfer to the engineering corps in Minden, Wittich took his leave and moved with his family to Hausberge where he died in 1844. As the children grew up, the residence was moved to the more sociable Münster and the property in Hausberge was sold. Ulrike and her brother Eduard, as the closest siblings in age, had been intimately connected from early on and both had an extremely lively temperament and a great ideal world view in common. As a proof of her warm human love and devotion, it can be assumed for Ulrike that when her brother Eduard became a widower in 1832, she immediately agreed to take his six daughters, the oldest of which was twelve years old and the youngest a few weeks old. The children stayed with her until her brother entered into a second marriage three years later. When Ulrike's daughters got married, she lived mostly in their places of residence, as she did in her last years in Bad Oeynhausen. Finally she moved back to Hausberge, where she died in 1877 at the age of 82 and is buried at her husband's side. Right up to her late age, she knew how to maintain her mental activity and physical freshness. In the face of everyday life, she often was an original and, because of the vividness of her imagination and her drastic creative powers, an artist. She lost her youngest daughter when she was only 18 years old. The two oldest married Prussian officers — Ottilie to the Captain, later Lieutenant General von Riedel, Therese to the Captain, later Lieutenant Colonel Lehmann. Their third daughter Charlotte, married Dr. med. Büttner, and moved with him to America, as did their son Gustav Wittich, who took his leave as a Prussian lieutenant and died childless on the other side. Ottilie von Riedel, who is 81 years old, is today the senior of the Rothenhof branch. Her daughters Ulrike and Jertha are ladies-in-waiting, the former currently to the Queen of Württemberg, the latter to the Schwarzburg-Rudolstadt court, while Hedwig, the youngest, lives partly as a nun at Menigsen and partly with her mother at Rudolstadt. All of von Riedel's sons and grandsons became Prussian officers. Through the marriages of Therese Wittich's daughters, married Lehmann, the names Selig, Schwartz and Ranzow were added to the family. Therese's only son is a major in the Feld-Art.-Regt. No. 6 of Breslau. Charlotte Büttner's two daughters married in St. Louis, America, where her 78-year-old mother is still practicing her profession as a caring grandmother.

Notes

On the following pages the reader will find additional explanatory notes.

The information has been extracted from wikipedia.org or wikipedia.de and translated into English unless otherwise stated. For more detailed information, the reader may find it useful to read the full articles online as these notes make no claim to being exhaustive but are intended as a quick reference for the reader.

1   The family has a whole array of famous persons.

Johann Heinrich Lucanus (1752-1828) was one of the cofounders of the Halberstadt "Literary Society" in 1785 and published "Gemeinnützige Unterhaltungen" (Charitable Conversations) in the weekly journal of the society. (changing titles 1785-1810), in continuations "Beyträge zur Geschichte des Fürstenthums Halberstadt" (Lectures on the History of the Principality of Halberstadt). Some books were also dedicated to the history of Halberstadt. Lucanus was government assistant councillor in Halberstadt and in 1797 he succeeded Gleim as secretary of the cathedral chapter. He spent the last years of his life in Silesia. (https://st.-museum-digital.de/index.php?t=objekt&oges=842 – translated)

Friedrich Gottfried Hermann Lucanus (December 3, 1793 in Halberstadt–May 23, 1872) was a German pharmacist, art lover and restorer.

He wrote the chronicle about the village of Schachdorf Ströbeck and its chess tradition. Already his ancestors had written down the history of Halberstadt (Lucanus Library from 1556 to 1732). In 1828 he founded the Halberstadt Art Society with the help of Werner Friedrich Julius Stephan von Spiegel. In 1839 he experimented with the photographic process daguerreotype.

Lucanus' son was the lawyer and politician Hermann von Lucanus.

Hermann Karl Friedrich Lucanus, since 1888 von Lucanus, (May 24, 1831 in Halberstadt–August 3, 1908 in Potsdam) was a German lawyer, Prussian State Councillor and head of the Privy Civil Cabinet of Kaiser Wilhelm II.

He studied law in Heidelberg, Göttingen and Berlin. Since 1853 he was a member of the Corps Vandalia Heidelberg.

In 1854 he became an auscultator, thus a Prussian civil servant, and in 1859 an assessor and "assistant worker" in the

Prussian Ministry of Culture in Berlin. In 1866 he was appointed Government Councillor, in 1871 Privy Government Councillor, in 1878 Ministerial Director and in 1881 Undersecretary of State in the Prussian Ministry of Education and Cultural Affairs. In 1886 he became Crown Privy Councillor with the title of Excellency, in 1888 Privy Cabinet Councillor and Head of the Privy Civil Cabinet of the Emperor and King. From 1897 he served as a member of the Council of State. He was a friend of Adolf von Harnack and supported his theological views, which were almost revolutionary by standards at the time (in his "Textbook of Dogma History").

Lucanus was also Capitular of the Merseburg Cathedral Monastery.

2   Court chaplaincy refers to the totality of the ecclesiastical ministers at a princely court.

In the Middle Ages, the court clergyman was called upon both for spiritual care (capellanus, chaplain at the court chapel) and – due to his education – for clerical work (cancellarius, chancellor at the court chancellery). Initially he did not live at court, but as a deputy of a monastery or abbey in the area of the territorial ruler. He was provided with material by means of grants and not by the court. In some cases the court clergyman accompanied the ruler on journeys and in wars.

With the development of the professional notary in the late Middle Ages, the clergyman increasingly concentrated on the political sphere as well. He appeared as an advisor to princes and kings. In addition, he exerted considerable cultural influence at court, for example as the author of court texts in the vernacular. These include the authors of Lucidarius, Heinrich von Veldeke or Herbort von Fritzlar.

When Hofburg chapels were transformed into Hofgemeinden in the 15th century, a differentiation of offices took place. In Vienna, for example, the court chaplain was joined by the court priest, the court preacher or the almsman in a celebration of the pagan festival on the summer solstice. Another legend tells that the origin of this festival can be traced back to the lost and found daughter of the knight Knaut on Questenberg.

5. The Battle of Rossbach took place on November 5, 1757 during the Third Silesian War (1756–1763, part of the Seven Years' War) near the village of Rossbach (Roßbach), in the Electorate of Saxony. It is sometimes called the Battle of, or at, Reichardtswerben, after a different nearby town. In this 90-minute battle, Frederick the Great, king of Prussia, defeated an Allied army composed of French forces augmented by a contingent of the Reichsarmee (Imperial Army) of the Holy Roman Empire. The French and Imperial army included almost 42,000 men, opposing a considerably smaller Prussian force of 22,000. Despite overwhelming odds, Frederick employed rapid movement, a flanking maneuver and oblique order to achieve complete surprise.

The Battle of Rossbach marked a turning point in the Seven Years' War, not only for its stunning Prussian victory, but because France refused to send troops against Prussia again and Britain, noting Prussia's military success, increased its financial support for Frederick. Following the battle, Frederick immediately left Rossbach and marched for 13 days to the outskirts of Breslau. There he met the Austrian army at the Battle of Leuthen; he employed similar tactics to again defeat an army considerably larger than his own.

Rossbach is considered one of Frederick's greatest strategic masterpieces. He crippled an enemy army twice the size of the Prussian force while suffering negligible casualties. His artillery also played a critical role in the victory, based on its ability to reposition itself rapidly responding to changing circumstances on the battlefield. Finally, his cavalry contributed decisively to the outcome of the battle, justifying his investment of resources into its training during the eight-year interim between the conclusion of the War of Austrian Succession and the outbreak of the Seven Years' War.

6   At the Battle of Leuthen, fought on December 5, 1757, Frederick the Great's Prussian army used maneuver and terrain to decisively defeat a larger Austrian force commanded by Prince Charles of Lorraine and Count Leopold Joseph von Daun. The victory ensured Prussia control of Silesia during the Third Silesian War (part of the Seven Years' War).

The battle was fought at the Silesian town of Leuthen, 10 kilometers (6 mi) northwest of Breslau (Wrocław), now Lutynia in present-day Poland. By exploiting the training of his troops and his superior knowledge of the terrain, Frederick created a diversion at one end of the battlefield, and moved most of his small army behind a series of low hillocks. The surprise attack in oblique order on the unsuspecting Austrian flank baffled Prince Charles; the Prince took several hours to realize that the main action was to his left, and not to his right. Within seven hours, the Prussians destroyed the Austrian force, erasing any advantage the Austrians had gained throughout the campaigning in the preceding summer and autumn. Within 48 hours, Frederick had laid siege to Breslau, which resulted in that city's surrender on 19–20 December.

7   The Mennonites are members of certain Christian groups belonging to the church communities of Anabaptist denominations named after Menno Simons (1496–1561) of Friesland (which today is a province of the Netherlands). Through his writings, Simons articulated and formalized the teachings of earlier Swiss founders. The early teachings of the Mennonites were founded on the belief in both the mission and ministry of Jesus, which the original Anabaptist followers held to with great conviction despite persecution by the various Roman Catholic and Protestant states. An early set of Mennonite beliefs was codified in the Dor-

drecht Confession of Faith in 1632, but the various groups do not hold to a common confession or creed. Rather than fight, the majority of these followers survived by fleeing to neighboring states where ruling families were tolerant of their belief in believer's baptism. Over the years, Mennonites have become known as one of the historic peace churches because of their commitment to pacifism.

The Dordrecht Confession of Faith is a statement of religious beliefs adopted by Dutch Mennonite leaders at a meeting in Dordrecht, the Netherlands, on April 21, 1632. Its 18 articles emphasize belief in salvation through Jesus Christ, baptism, nonviolence (non-resistance), withdrawing from, or shunning those who are excommunicated from the Church, feet washing ("a washing of the saints' feet") and avoidance of taking oaths.

It was an influential part of the Radical Reformation and remains an important religious document to many modern Anabaptist groups such as the Amish. In 1725, Jacob Gottschalk, a Mennonite bishop, met with sixteen other ministers from southeastern Pennsylvania and adopted the Confession. They also wrote the following endorsement, which Gottschalk was the first to sign:

"We the hereunder written Servants of the Word of God, and Elders in the Congregation of the People, called Mennonites, in the Province of Pennsylvania, do acknowledge, and herewith make known, that we do own the foregoing Confession, Appendix, and Menno's Excusation, to be according to our Opinion; and also, have took the same to be wholly ours. In Testimony whereof, and that we believe that same to be good, we have here unto Subscribed our Names."

8 Menno Simons (1496–January 31, 1561) was a Roman Catholic priest from the Friesland region of the Low Countries who became an influential Anabaptist religious leader. Simons was a contemporary of the Protestant Reformers

and it is from his name that his followers became known as Mennonites.

9 Siegfried Sack (Siegfriedus Saccus) (March 27, 1527 in Nordhausen-September 2, 1596 in Magdeburg) was the first Protestant cathedral preacher in Magdeburg.

Siegfried Sack was baptized by Lorenz Süße according to the Lutheran rite. His father was Thomas Sack, the cutler, alderman and mayor of Nordhausen from 1522. Johann Sack (1523-1592) was the older brother of Siegfried, who also became mayor of Nordhausen from 1581.

After attending the Nordhausen high school, he went to the University of Wittenberg together with his brother in 1546. Siegfried studied theology and received his master's degree in 1554 and his doctorate in theology on May 29, 1570. Afterwards he was rector of the school in Magdeburg and then preacher at Magdeburg Cathedral. Siegfried Sack was regarded as an esteemed theologian and writer. Many of his funeral sermons have appeared in print.

10 An Irminsul (Old Saxon 'great pillar') was a sacred pillar-like object attested as playing an important role in the Germanic paganism of the Saxons. Medieval sources describe how an Irminsul was destroyed by Charlemagne during the Saxon Wars. Sacred trees and sacred groves were widely venerated by the Germanic peoples (including Donar's Oak), and the oldest chronicle describing an Irminsul refers to it as a tree trunk erected in the open air.

11 The Cimbri were an ancient tribe. They are generally believed to have been a Germanic tribe originating in Jutland, but Celtic influences have also been suggested.

Together with the Teutones and the Ambrones, they fought the Roman Republic between 113 and 101 BC. The Cimbri were initially successful, particularly at the Battle of Arausio, in which a large Roman army was routed, after which they raided large areas in Gaul and Hispania. In 101 BC, during an attempted invasion of Italy, the Cimbri were decisively defeated by Gaius Marius and their king, Boiorix, was killed. Some of the surviving captives are reported to have been among the rebelling gladiators in the Third Servile War.

12 The Teutons are generally classified as a Germanic tribe. Some historians have suggested a Celtic origin for the Teutones. It has been suggested that their name is Celtic, though this is controversial. Certain ancient writers classify the Teutones as Celts. This might be explained by the fact that writers of the time did not clearly distinguish between Celtic and Germanic peoples. The early traveller of the 4th century BC, Pytheas, mentions the Teutones as inhabitants of the northern ocean coasts along with the Gutones. Strabo (64 or 63 BC–c. AD 24) and Marcus Velleius Paterculus (c. 19 BC–c. AD 31), moreover, classify them as Germanic peoples. According to a map by Ptolemy, they originally lived in Jutland, which is in agreement with Pomponius Mela, who placed them in Scandinavia, implying that they may have originally inhabited both regions previously. The Danish district of Thy claims to be their homeland.

13 The name Suebi refers to a Germanic tribal group that once lived in the northeast of Germania magna on the Baltic Sea up to the German low mountain ranges. In Roman sources the Baltic Sea was named after the Suebi as "Mare Suebicum". The ancient geographer Claudius Ptolemy (* around 100, † around 175) localized in his geography Hyphegesis at the place of today's Swine and Oder the river Syebos. Thus the tribal name Suebi can be interpreted as "Oder people" or the river name Suevus as "Suebian river", matching the original settlement area.

14 From about 500 B.C.–A.D. 400, several Celtic tribes, the most important of them named the Helvetians settled in Switzerland.
(http://history-switzerland.geschichte-schweiz.ch/history-celtic-helvetians-switzerland.html)

15 Augustus (Imperator Caesar Divi filius Augustus; September 23, 63 BC– August 19, AD 14) was a Roman statesman and military leader who became the first emperor of the Roman Empire, reigning from 27 BC until his death in AD 14. His status as the founder of the Roman Principate has consolidated an enduring legacy as one of the most effective and controversial leaders in human history. The reign of Augustus initiated an era of relative peace known as the Pax Romana. The Roman world was largely free from large-scale conflict for more than two centuries, despite continuous wars of imperial expansion on the Empire's frontiers and the year-long civil war known as the "Year of the Four Emperors" over the imperial succession.

16 The Kyffhäuser, sometimes also referred to as Kyffhäusergebirge, is a hill range in Central Germany, located on the border of the state of Thuringia with Saxony-Anhalt, southeast of the Harz mountains. It reaches its highest point at the Kulpenberg with an elevation of 473.4 metres (1,553 ft). The range is the site of medieval Kyffhausen Castle (Reichsburg Kyffhausen) and the 19th century Kyffhäuser Monument; it has significance in German traditional mythology as the legendary resting place of Emperor Frederick Barbarossa.

17 The Charudes or Harudes were a Germanic group first mentioned by Julius Caesar as one of the tribes who had followed Ariovistus across the Rhine. While Tacitus' Germania makes no mention of them, Ptolemy's Geographia locates the Charudes on the east coast of the Cimbrian peninsula. Their name suggests that they may have at one point settled in east jutland and founded the city of Charudes (Arus or nowadays Aarhus).

18 Arminius (German: Hermann; 18/17 BC–AD 21) was a chieftain of the Germanic Cherusci tribe who is best known for commanding an alliance of Germanic tribes at the Battle of the Teutoburg Forest in AD 9, in which three Roman le-

gions were destroyed. His victory at Teutoburg Forest would precipitate the Roman Empire's permanent strategic withdrawal from Magna Germania, and made a major contribution to the eventual fall of the Western Roman Empire several centuries later. Modern historians have regarded Arminius' victory as Rome's greatest defeat. As it prevented the Romanization of the Germanic peoples, it has also been considered one of the most decisive battles in history and a turning point in world history.

Born a prince of the Cherusci tribe, Arminius was made a hostage of the Roman Empire as a child. Raised in Rome, he was drafted into the Roman military at an early age, during which he was granted Roman citizenship and became a Roman knight. After serving with distinction in the Great Illyrian Revolt, he was sent to Germania to aid the local governor Publius Quinctilius Varus in completing the Roman conquest of the Germanic tribes. While in this capacity, Arminius secretly plotted a Germanic revolt against Roman rule, which culminated in the ambush and destruction of three Roman legions in the Teutoburg Forest.

In the aftermath of the battle, Arminius fought retaliatory invasions by the Roman general Germanicus in the battles of Pontes Longi, Idistaviso, and the Angrivarian Wall, and deposed a rival, the Marcomanni king Maroboduus. Germanic nobles, afraid of Arminius' growing power, assassinated him in AD 21. He was remembered in Germanic legends for generations afterwards. The Roman historian Tacitus designated Arminius as the liberator of the Germanic tribes and commended him for having fought the Roman Empire to a standstill at the peak of its power.

During the unification of Germany in the 19th century, Arminius was hailed by German nationalists as a symbol of German unity and freedom. Following World War II, however, Arminius was omitted from German textbooks due to his association with militaristic nationalism, and many modern Germans are unaware of his story; the 2,000th anniversary of his victory at the Teutoburg Forest was only lightly commemorated in Germany.

19 *Polterabend* is a German wedding custom in which, on the night before the wedding, the guests break porcelain to bring luck to the couple's marriage. The belief in the effectiveness of this custom is expressed by the old adage: "Shards bring luck" (German: *Scherben bringen Glück*). The expression is derived from a time when the word "shard" referred to the unbroken clay pots of pottery makers, and not just the broken pieces. It was said that a full jar was a lucky thing to have, therefore the expression "shards bring luck".

The word *Polterabend* comes from German verb *poltern* (making a lot of noise) + noun Abend (evening). It is not the same as a bachelor party (*Junggesellenabschiedsfeier*), which have become common in Germany. At a Polterabend, the couple celebrates together with their friends, breaking porcelain to good luck in their new companionship, according to the superstition, whereas at a bachelor party the bride and the groom go out separately with their friends to celebrate the last day of their so-called freedom.

The *Polterabend* normally takes place in front of the house of the bride (or that of her parents), although exceptions are made for space considerations, for example. The couple generally announces the occasion but does not specifically send out individual invitations. Word spreads via word of mouth, and those with a desire to show up may do so. Many couples use this as a way of including people whom they are not able to invite to the wedding itself. Something to eat and/or drink is arranged (either provided for or requested of the guests). Often guests will bring their gifts to the *Polterabend*.

The actual high point of the custom is the throwing onto the ground of porcelain that has been brought by guests.

However, stoneware, flowerpots or ceramics such as tiles, sinks and toilet bowls are also happily thrown items. Metal objects such as tin cans and bottle tops are brought along to the festivities. Glass is not broken because for some glass symbolises happiness. Mirrors should not be broken due to the old superstition that breaking a mirror will bring seven years of bad luck, in addition to the good things—or the lack thereof—in the breaker's and/or breakee's past. The couple must thereafter take care of cleaning up the pile of shards. This is supposed to make the couple aware that they will have to suffer together through difficult conditions and situations in life.

20 The elder brother of the philosopher Friedrich Heinrich Jacobi, Johann Georg was born at Pempelfort near Düsseldorf. He studied theology at Göttingen and jurisprudence at Helmstedt, and in 1766 was appointed professor of philosophy in Halle. That year he made the acquaintance of J. W. L. Gleim, who, attracted by the young poets *Poetische Versuche* (1764), became his friend. A lively literary correspondence ensued between Gleim in Halberstadt and Jacobi in Halle. In order to have Jacobi near him, Gleim succeeded in procuring for him a prebendal stall at the cathedral of Halberstadt in 1769, and here Jacobi issued a number of anacreontic lyrics and sonnets that were not at all appreciated by the intellectuals of his time. Herder called Jacobi's anacreontic poetry tasteless nonsense, Goethe criticized the jingling verses as only impressing women, and Lichtenberg ridiculed Jacobi as a *doctorem jubilatum*.

From 1774 to 1776, Gleim and Jacobi edited Iris, to which Goethe, Heinse, Lenz, and Sophie La Roche were contributors. In 1784, Emperor Joseph II appointed Jacobi as professor of belles lettres at the university of Freiburg, the first Protestant professor of that institution. The city's Catholic population and the teaching staff considered this a provocation, but Joseph was known for his erratic acts of forced Enlightenment.

Freiburg's educated ladies appreciated the new professor for fine arts and science particularly during afternoon tea circles. At times more female admirers than students followed his lectures at the university. In 1791 the opposition of his male Catholic colleagues eventually vanished. They elected him as the first Protestant rector of the university. This happened again in 1803 during Napoleonic domination of the Breisgau when Jacobi's excellent knowledge of French helped to overcome differences with the authorities.

Following Napoleon's defeat Freiburg and the Breisgau were not restored to the Habsburgs but remained under the rule of the Grand Duchy of Baden. To make this acceptable to the local populace, Jacobi said of the grand dukes, who were descendants of the old Zaehringen dynasty, "Now the two coat of arms during hundreds of years separated become one again and the Duke's kindness will not only unite the territories but marry the souls of the good citizens alike."

When Jacobi died in 1814, an enormous crowd of dignitaries, students and citizens attended his funeral.

21 Friedrich Heinrich Jacobi (January 25, 1743–March 10, 1819) was an influential German philosopher, literary figure, and socialite.

He is notable for popularizing nihilism, a term coined by Obereit in 1787, and promoting it as the prime fault of Enlightenment thought particularly in the philosophical systems of Baruch Spinoza, Immanuel Kant, Johann Fichte and Friedrich Schelling.

Jacobi advocated *Glaube* (variously translated as "faith" or "belief") and revelation instead of speculative reason. In this sense, Jacobi can be seen to have anticipated present-day writers who criticize secular philosophy as relativistic and dangerous for religious faith.

In his time, he was also well known among literary circles for his critique of the Sturm and Drang movement, and implicitly close associate and intimate partner of Johann Wolfgang von Goethe, and his visions of atomized individualism. His literary projects were devoted to the reconciliation of Enlightenment individualism with social obligation.

He was the younger brother of poet Johann Georg Jacobi and the father of the great psychiatrist Maximilian Jacobi.

22 Gottfried of Strasbourg († around 1215), German poet and epicist

23 The Golden Meadow ("Goldene Aue in German") is a valley in eastern Germany, in the states Thuringia and Saxony-Anhalt. It is situated between the towns Nordhausen in the west, and Sangerhausen in the east. It is bordered by the mountain ranges Harz in the north, and Windleite and Kyffhäuser in the south. The river Helme flows through the Goldene Aue.

24 At the Battle of Leuthen, fought on December 5, 1757, Frederick the Great's Prussian army used maneuver and terrain to decisively defeat a larger Austrian force commanded by Prince Charles of Lorraine and Count Leopold Joseph von Daun. The victory ensured Prussia control of Silesia during the Third Silesian War (part of the Seven Years' War).

The battle was fought at the Silesian town of Leuthen, 10 kilometers (6 mi) northwest of Breslau (Wrocław), now Lutynia in present-day Poland. By exploiting the training of his troops and his superior knowledge of the terrain, Frederick created a diversion at one end of the battlefield, and moved most of his small army behind a series of low hillocks. The surprise attack in oblique order on the unsuspecting Austrian flank baffled Prince Charles; the Prince took several hours to realize that the main action was to his left, and not to his right. Within seven hours, the Prussians destroyed the Austrian force, erasing any advantage the

Austrians had gained throughout the campaigning in the preceding summer and autumn. Within 48 hours, Frederick had laid siege to Breslau, which resulted in that city's surrender on December 19–20.

Leuthen was the last battle at which Prince Charles commanded the Austrian Army, before his sister-in-law, Empress Maria Theresa, appointed him as governor of the Habsburg Netherlands and placed Leopold Joseph von Daun in command of the army. The battle also established beyond doubt Frederick's military reputation in European circles; it was arguably his greatest tactical victory. After Rossbach (November 5), the French had refused to participate further in Austria's war with Prussia; and after Leuthen (December 5), Austria could not continue it by herself.

25 Now Mohrenstraße, used to be called Topfgasse (Pottery Lane). Glogau itself had a flourishing pottery trade in the late Middle Ages

26 "The old Emperor Friedrich Barbarossa has been transferred by a spell, i.e. a supernatural secret power, to an underground castle on the Kyffhausen hill in Thuringia. Here he sits sleeping on an ivory chair and rests his head on a marble table. His red beard, similar to yellow flax when alive, glows like embers of fire and has grown through the table, almost around it. At times the emperor moves his blond head, raises his heavy eyelids halfway and winks or blinks his eyes. By such' dreamlike winking of his eyes he waves in long periods — of 100 years — to a dwarf, hardly the size of a boy, to go up and see whether the ravens, the images of discord and unhappiness, still fly and croak around the mountain. If this is the case, the emperor closes his eyes with a sigh, sleeps and dreams for another hundred years. Only when the beard has grown all the way around the round marble table and a mighty eagle soars up in proud flight, circles the mountain and frightens away the

swarm of ravens, only then will the emperor awaken with his equally enchanted faithful."

27 Emperor Frederick Barbarossa opted on the local Armenians' advice to follow a shortcut along the Saleph river, meanwhile the army started to traverse the mountain path. On June 10, 1190, he drowned near Silifke Castle in the Saleph river. There are several conflicting accounts of the event

28 The Hohenstaufen, also called Staufer, was a noble dynasty of unclear origin that rose to rule the Duchy of Swabia from 1079 and to royal rule in the Holy Roman Empire during the Middle Ages from 1138 until 1254. The most prominent kings Frederick I (1155), Henry VI (1191) and Frederick II (1220) ascended the imperial throne and also ruled Italy and Burgundy. The non-contemporary name is derived from a family castle on the Hohenstaufen mountain at the northern fringes of the Swabian Jura near the town of Göppingen. Under Hohenstaufen reign the Holy Roman Empire reached its greatest territorial extent from 1155 to 1268.

29 Pforta, or Schulpforta, is a school located in a former Cistercian monastery, Pforta monastery (1137–1540), near Naumburg on the Saale River in the German state of Saxony-Anhalt.

Since the 16th century the site has been a school. Notable past alumni include the philosopher Friedrich Nietzsche and the German chancellor Theobald von Bethmann-Hollweg. Today, it is a well-known public boarding school for academically gifted children, called Landesschule Pforta. It is coeducational and teaches around 300 high school students.

30 The Treaty of Hubertusburg was signed on February 15, 1763 at Hubertusburg Castle by Prussia, Austria and Saxony to end the Third Silesian War. Together with the Treaty of Paris, signed five days earlier, it marked the end of the Seven Years' War. The treaty ended the continental conflict

with no significant changes in prewar borders. Austria and Saxony renounced all claims to the Silesian territories ceded to Prussia in the 1742 Treaty of Berlin and the 1745 Treaty of Dresden. Prussia clearly stood among the ranks of the European great powers, while the treaty enhanced the rivalry with Austria.

31   The Seven Years' War was a global conflict that was fought between 1756 and 1763. It involved all five European great powers of the time — the Kingdoms of Great Britain, Prussia and France, the Habsburg Monarchy of Austria and the Russian Empire — plus many of Europe's middle powers and spanned five continents, affecting Europe, the Americas, West Africa, India, and the Philippines. The conflict split Europe into two coalitions: one was led by Great Britain (including the German state, the Electorate of Brunswick-Lüneburg ruled in personal union) and Prussia, supported by the Kingdom of Portugal and a few other small German states; while the other was led by France and included the Austrian-led Holy Roman Empire, including the Electorate of Saxony and most of the smaller German states, Russia (until 1762), the Kingdom of Spain, and Sweden. The Dutch Republic, Denmark–Norway, the Italian States, and the Ottoman Empire did not participate. Meanwhile, in India, some regional polities within the increasingly fragmented Mughal Empire, with the support of the French, failed to defeat a British attempt to conquer Bengal.

Although Anglo-French skirmishes over their American colonies had begun in 1754, with what became known in the United States as the French and Indian War, the large-scale conflict that drew in most of the European powers was centered on Austria's desire to recover Silesia from Prussia. Seeing the opportunity to curtail Britain's and Prussia's ever-growing might, France and Austria put aside their ancient rivalry to form a grand coalition of their own, bringing most of the other European powers to their side.

Faced with this sudden turn of events, Britain aligned itself with Prussia, in a series of political manoeuvres known as the Diplomatic Revolution. The Anglo-Prussian coalition prevailed, and Britain's rise among the world's predominant powers destroyed France's supremacy in Europe, and Prussia confirmed its status as a great power challenging Austria for dominance within Germany, thus altering the European balance of power.

32 Luther himself seems to have enjoyed the same wine. In a letter on the eve of his return to Wittenberg he writes from Schweinitz on Oculi Sunday, March 8, 1523, to his friend the Court Chaplain Spalatin, that he had come to Schweinitz, where the Elector's castle stood, in order to celebrate with the father the baptism of the son of a convert Jew named Bernard. "We drank good, pure wine from the Elector's cellar," he says, "we should indeed be grand Evangelicals if we feasted to the same extent on the Evangel.... Please excuse us to the Prince for having drunk so much of his **Grüneberger wine** ('quod tantum vini Gornbergici ligurierimus')".

(*In Luther (Complete)* by Hartmann Grisar)

33 Minnesang ("love song") was a tradition of lyric and song writing in Germany that flourished in the Middle High German period. This period of medieval German literature began in the 12th century and continued into the 14th. People who wrote and performed Minnesang were known as *Minnesänger* (minnesingers), and a single song was called a Minnelied.

The name derives from minne, the Middle High German word for love, as that was Minnesang's main subject. The *Minnesänger* were similar to the Provençal troubadours and northern French trouvères in that they wrote love poetry in the tradition of courtly love in the High Middle Ages.

34 Heinrich von Morungen or Henry of Morungen (died c. 1220 or 1222) was a German Minnesinger.

Almost nothing about his life can be deduced from Heinrich's songs. Possibly he is identical with the Hendricus de Morungen who is documented in Thuringia. This Hendricus belonged to the class of minor knights and presumably originated from the castle of Morungen near Sangerhausen. As a "retired knight" (*miles emeritus*) he received from his patron, Dietrich IV, Margrave of Meissen, a pension for his "high personal merits" (*alta suae vitae merita*). He transferred this in 1213 to the monastery of St Thomas in Leipzig, which he entered himself in 1217. According to 16th century sources, he died there in 1222 after a journey to India. In the Late Middle Ages, there was extant a "Ballad of the Noble Moringer", which transferred onto Heinrich von Morungen the stock theme of the return of a husband believed lost.

35 Hans Ernst Karl, Graf von Zieten (March 5, 1770–May 3, 1848) was an officer in the Prussian Army during the Napoleonic Wars.

36 Kurt Christoph, Graf von Schwerin (October 26, 1684–May 6, 1757) was a Prussian Generalfeldmarschall, one of the leading commanders under Frederick the Great.

He was born in Löwitz, Pomerania, and at an early age entered the Dutch army, with which he served at Schellenberg and at Blenheim.

In 1707 he became a lieutenant-colonel in the army of the duke of Mecklenburg-Schwerin, and was present at Ramillies and Malplaquet, and with the Swedish commander Stenbock at Gadebusch. In 1713 he was with Charles XII of Sweden in his captivity at Bender, and in 1718 was made major-general.

In 1719 he opposed the Hanoverian army which invaded Mecklenburg (in the course of which he fought a brilliant action at Walsmühlen on March 6, 1719) and in the following year entered the service of the King of Prussia. At first he was employed in diplomatic missions but in January

1722 – 1723 he received the command of an infantry regiment. In 1730, as a major-general, he was a member of the court martial which tried the crown prince Frederick for desertion and in 1733, at the head of a Prussian army, conducted with great skill the delicate and difficult task of settling the Mecklenburg question.

In the following year he became lieutenant-general and in 1739 general of infantry. During the life-time of King Frederick William, Schwerin was also employed in much administrative work. Frederick the Great, on his accession, promoted Schwerin to the rank of general field marshal and made him a count. Early in the First Silesian War, he justified his sovereign's choice by his brilliant leadership at the Battle of Mollwitz (April 10, 1741), which, when he had persuaded the king to leave the battlefield explaining that he may be captured as a defeat was likely, converted a doubtful battle into a victory which decided for the time being the fate of Silesia.

After the conclusion of the war he was governor of the important fortresses of Brieg and Neisse. In the Second Silesian War (1744–1745), Schwerin commanded the army which, marching from Glatz, met the kings army under the walls of Prague, and in the siege and capture of that place he played a distinguished part (September 10, 1744).

Some time afterwards, the King, being compelled to retreat from Bohemia, Schwerin again distinguished himself but resenting a real or fancied slight, retired to his estate, to which, and its inhabitants, he devoted his energies during the years of peace.

He reappeared on the field at the outbreak of the Third Silesian War (1756), and during the first campaign conducted the war on the Silesian side of Bohemia. In 1757, following the same route as in 1744, he again joined Frederick at Prague. On May 6 he followed the Battle of Prague, leading on a regiment of the left wing to the attack with its color in his hand, he shouted "Let all brave Prussians follow me!" after which he was struck and killed by a cannonball.

37 Hans Karl von Winterfeldt (April 4, 1707–September 8, 1757), a Prussian general, served in the War of the Polish Succession, the War of Austrian Succession, Frederick the Great's Silesian wars and the Seven Years' War. One of Frederick's trusted confidantes and advisors, he attracted enmity from other courtiers. Frederick entrusted him with considerable autonomy on the general staff, and Winterfeldt developed the first "modern" program of military intelligence gathering. He negotiated the Convention of Westminster and, for his efforts on Frederick's behalf, received the Order of the Black Eagle and the Order Pour le Mérite. He died from wounds received at Battle of Moys. His name is included on the Equestrian statue of Frederick the Great.

38 This fusilier regiment was raised in July 1741 for Ferdinand of Brunswick who had been appointed chef of the regiment on June 29, 1740. Its fusiliers came from regiment Sommerlatte, a unit in the Reich service who had served against the Turks in Hungary; and its grenadiers from the garrisons of Memel and Pillau.

The regiment had no recruiting canton in Prussia, its troops being recruited in the Duchy of Brunswick.

During the War of the Austrian Succession, the regiment was part of Frederick's army when he invaded Bohemia in 1744. In September, it was at the siege and capture of Prague where it then assumed garrison duty. At the end of the year, during its retreat towards Silesia, the regiment lost about half of its troops. In April 1745, it was sent to Upper Silesia. On May 22, it took part to the breakthrough from Jägerndorf to Neustadt.

(https://www.kronoskaf.com/syw/index.php?title=Jung_Braunschweig_Fusiliers)

From 1755, the regiment was designated as "Jung-Braunschweig" to differentiate it from Infanterie-Regiment Nr. 5 von Braunschweig. At this period, it garrisoned Königsberg in Neu Mark, Pyritz and Soldin.

39 Count Leopold Joseph von Daun (Leopold Joseph Maria, Reichsgraf von und zu Daun. September 24, 1705–February 5, 1766), later Prince of Thiano, was an Austrian field marshal of the Imperial Army in the War of the Austrian Succession and Seven Years' War.

During the interval of peace that preceded the Seven Years' War he was engaged in carrying out an elaborate scheme for the reorganization of the Austrian army and it was chiefly through his efforts that the Theresian Military Academy was established at Wiener-Neustadt in 1751. When a Third Silesian War broke out, he was not actively employed in the first campaigns of the war, but in 1757 he was placed at the head of the army which was raised to relieve Prague. On June 18, 1757 Daun decisively defeated Frederick for the first time in his career in the desperately fought Battle of Kolin. In commemoration of this brilliant exploit, the queen immediately instituted a military order bearing her name, and Daun was awarded the first Grand Cross of that order. The union of the relieving army with the forces of Prince Charles at Prague reduced Daun to the position of second in command and in that capacity he took part in the pursuit of the Prussians and the victory of Breslau.

Frederick now reappeared and won the most brilliant victory of the age at Leuthen. Daun was present on that field but was not held accountable for the disaster and when Prince Charles resigned his command, Daun was appointed in his place. With the campaign of 1758 began the war of manouevre in which Daun, though missing some opportunities to crush the Prussians through over-caution, at least maintained a steady and cool resistance to the fiery strategy of Frederick. In 1758 Major-General Laudon, acting under Daun's instructions, forced the king to raise the siege of Olmütz (Battle of Domstadt), and later in the same year Daun himself surprised Frederick at the Battle of Hochkirch and inflicted a severe defeat upon him (October 14). Despite the tactical success and capture of many munitions and supplies that Daun achieved at Hochkirch, his failure to pursue Frederick allowed the Prussians to block his path into Silesia, meaning that his victory counted for little. In the following year the war of manouevre continued, and on November 20 and 21 he surrounded the entire corps of General Finck at Maxen, forcing the Prussians to surrender. These successes were counterbalanced in the following year by the defeat of Laudon at Liegnitz, which was attributed partly to the dilatoriness of Daun, and Daun's own subsequent defeat by Zieten's bold attack in the great Battle of Torgau. In this engagement, Daun was so severely wounded that he had to return to Vienna to recuperate. However, Daun and his forces inflicted heavy casualties on the Prussians and were able to retreat in good order.

40 August Wilhelm, Duke of Brunswick-Bevern (October 10, 1715 in Braunschweig–August 2, 1781 in Stettin), Prussian soldier, son of Ernest Ferdinand, Duke of Brunswick-Lüneburg, was born in Braunschweig in 1715, and entered the Prussian army in 1731, becoming colonel of an infantry regiment in 1739. He won great distinction at the battle of Hohenfriedberg as a major-general, and was promoted lieutenant-general in 1750.

Bevern was one of the most experienced and exact soldiers in the army of Frederick the Great. He commanded a wing in the battle of Lobositz in 1756, and defeated the Austrians under Marshal Königsegg in a well-fought battle at Reichenberg on 21 April 1757. He took part in the battles of Prague and Kolin and the retreat to Görlitz, and subsequently commanded the Prussians left behind by Frederick in the autumn of 1757 when he marched against the French.

Bevern conducted a defensive campaign against overwhelming numbers with great skill but he soon lost the valuable assistance of General Winterfeldt, who was killed in a skirmish at Moys. He was eventually brought to battle and suffered a heavy defeat at the battle of Breslau on November 22. He fell into the hands of the Austrians on the following morning, and remained prisoner for a year. He was made general of infantry in 1759, and on August 11, 1762 inflicted a severe defeat at Reichenbach on an Austrian army endeavoring to relieve Schweidnitz. Bevern retired, after the peace of Hubertusburg, to his government of Stettin, where he died in peace in 1781.

41 Maurice of Anhalt-Dessau (October 31, 1712 in Dessau-April 11, 1760 in Dessau), was a German prince of the House of Ascania from the Anhalt-Dessau branch. He was also a Prussian soldier and General Field Marshall.

42 The Battle of Hohenfriedberg or Hohenfriedeberg, now Dobromierz, also known as the Battle of Striegau, now Strzegom, was one of Frederick the Great's most admired victories. Frederick's Prussian army decisively defeated an Austrian army under Prince Charles Alexander of Lorraine on June 4, 1745 during the Second Silesian War (part of the War of the Austrian Succession).

43 Kollin or Chotzenitz (June 18, 1757). Fought by the Austrians and Prussians. The King of Prussia's army was commanded by himself, and consisted of 32 battalions and 118 squadrons - in all, about 32,000 men, with 82 pieces of cannon.

The Austrian army, commanded by Count Daun, amounted to 42 battalions, 38 companies of grenadiers, and 103 squadrons, exclusive of 10,000 men under Nadasti and several thousand Croats. In the whole, not less than 60,000.

The loss nearly equal — about 16,000 killed and wounded.

The consequence of this battle, in which the Prussians were defeated, was the raising the siege of Prague, and the evacuation of Bohemia. (The Royal Naval and Military Calendar and National Record for 1821)

44 Georg Friedrich von Manstein (*1702 near Insterburg; †May 6, 1757 near Prague) was a colonel of Frederick the Great.

In 1714 Georg Friedrich left his parents' house and came via Königsberg in Prussia to Berlin, where he became a noble youth of the Prussian Queen, the mother of Friedrich II. In January 1716 Manstein joined the cadet corps, first in Magdeburg and one and a half years later in Berlin. In 1718 he joined the regiment "Anhalt" as an ensign in Dessau. In 1723 he was promoted to lieutenant, in 1729 to premier lieutenant, in 1736 to staff captain and in 1741 to colonel sergeant.

Manstein took part in the Second Silesian War. Because of his special bravery in the battle of Kesselsdorf he was promoted to lieutenant colonel on December 23, 1745. On 15 June 1747 Manstein received the Order of Pour le Mérite from the King. Manstein then headed several commissions of inquiry dealing with military offenses and was on secret missions for Frederick. In 1753 he was promoted to the rank of colonel.

During the Seven Years' War, Manstein took part in the Battle of Lobositz and after the victory he covered the withdrawal of the main army to Saxony. He was then appointed commander of Leipzig until his regiment returned to battle in March 1757.

In the Battle of Prague Manstein led the 1st battalion of his regiment. While trying to come to the aid of the heavily pressed 3rd Battalion, he was hit in the abdomen by three cartouche bullets around two in the afternoon and died of his injuries half an hour later.

45 Johann von Grant (1710–December 12, 1764) was a Royal Prussian Major General, Chief of Fusiliers Regiment No. 44 and Commander of Neisse Fortress.

46 The Heimkehle is a gypsum cave with a length of about 2000 meters, 750 meters of which are normally part of the guided tours. However, due to construction work at present (2008) only 600 metres are accessible. The largest cavern is 65 meters long, 65 meters wide and 22 meters high. As a result of the high solubility of gypsum there has been intensive karstification and a resulting formation of voluminous cave systems. Because it is close to the water table many of the room are or were filled with water. The cave receives an average of 20,000 visitors a year.

47 Michael Meyenburg, also Michel Meienburg, née Leyer or Liser (*around 1491 in Marktsteinach- †November 13, 1555 in Nordhausen), was a mayor of the free imperial city of Nordhausen who was close to the Reformation.

After studying law at the University of Erfurt in the years 1506-1509, Meyenburg became town clerk in Nordhausen and rose to the position of mayor. Early on he joined the ideas of Martin Luther and made friends with Justus Jonas and Philipp Melanchthon.

In his official capacity he also enjoyed the trust of representatives of the surrounding imperial cities of Mühlhausen and Goslar, whom he represented at district, imperial and city councils and in several trials before the Imperial Chamber Court. Having achieved financial wealth personally, he was able to make several financial loans, for example to the Counts of Stolberg.

Meyenburg was a partner in the Count-Mansfeldische Copper Works on the Steinach and had a share in this company, which was calculated at 27,880 gulden on his death.

He married Anna Reinicke, the daughter of the Mansfeld master smelter Hans Reinicke, and left his sons Caspar, Christoph, Hans and Michael. His daughter Ursula married Thomas Matthias. He died on November 13, 1555 and was buried in the Blasiikirche in Nordhausen.

48 The Erinyes also known as the Furies, were female chthonic deities of vengeance in ancient Greek religion and mythology.

49 Like Fischer and Gleim, Johann Heinrich Lucanus (1752-1828) was one of the co-founders of the Halberstadt "Literary Society" in 1785 and published "Gemeinnützige Unterhaltungen" (Charitable Conversations) in the Society's weekly journal. (with various titles 1785-1810), in continuations "Beyträge zur Geschichte des Fürstenthums Halberstadt" (Lectures on the History of the Principality of Halberstadt). Some books were also dedicated to the history of Halberstadt. Lucanus was government assistant councillor in Halberstadt and in 1797 he succeeded Gleim as secretary of the cathedral chapter. He spent the last years of his life in Silesia.
(https://st.museum-digital.de/index.php?t=objekt&oges=842 – translated)

50 The Friedrich d'or (French doré "goldener Friedrich (II.)") was a Prussian gold coin (pistole) nominally worth 5 silver Prussian Reichsthalers. It was used from 1741 to 1855 and since it was a silver standard regular issue coin and trade coin at this time, it had a different purpose to domestic silver coinage or Kurantgeld, the so-called window on the stock exchanges. It was normally traded at a small premium or discount to the face value of 5 thalers. In Prussian purchase contracts or bonds it was, due to its monetary usage, distinguished as the "preußisch Courant" or "Friedrich d'or".

51 Baumann's Cave (German: Baumannshöhle), located nearby Hermann's Cave, is a show cave in Rübeland in the district of Harz and is Germany's oldest show cave.

The grotto was formed in the Devonian limestone of the Elbingerode Complex at least since the Bode Valley was being shaped. The cave has been visited by man since the Stone Age and not first discovered in 1536 as many written accounts suggest. The year of discovery in 1536 in combination with the tale of the miner, Baumann, who is supposed to have discovered the cave, are part of a false story dating back to Nazi times when a politically suitable jubilee date was being sought.

The cave is frequently mentioned in the early scientific and travel literature as it has been open to the public with guided tours since 1649 when Valentin Wagner was installed as first cave guide. Baumann's Cave is probably the oldest regularly frequented and guided show cave, at least in Germany. Amongst its most famous visitors was Johann Wolfgang von Goethe. The cave's biggest chamber, the Goethesaal, is named after him and is fitted with seats and a stage for concerts and plays.

The cave was sealed off from an early date so that its rich display of stalactites and stalagmites has been largely preserved. The cave is particularly famous for, amongst other things, the numerous bones of cave bears that have been found there.

52 Grand Duke Alexei Petrovich of Russia (February 28, 1690–July 7, 1718) was a Russian Tsarevich. He was born in Moscow, the son of Tsar Peter I and his first wife, Eudoxia Lopukhina. Alexei despised his father and repeatedly thwarted Peter's plans to raise him as successor to the throne. His brief defection to Austria scandalized the Russian government, leading to harsh repressions against Alexei and his associates. Alexei died after interrogation under torture, and his son Peter Alexeyevich became the new heir apparent.

53 Regenstein, also Reinstein, was a Lower Saxon noble family, which was named after the eponymous Regenstein Castle near Blankenburg on the edge of the Harz Mountains of central Germany.

54 Johann Wilhelm Ludwig Gleim (*April 2, 1719 in Ermsleben; †February 18, 1803 in Halberstadt) was a poet,

patron of literature and collector of the German Enlightenment and an exponent of the culture of friendship of the Enlightenment. Called "German Anacreon" as an anacreonist, he was called a patriotic poet according to the fictionalization of his war poetry "Prussian Grenadier". As a promoter of literature and patriarch of German literature at the end of the 18th century, he was also known as "Father Gleim".

Gleim was the eighth of twelve children of a tax collector from the Altmark and his wife, a minister's daughter from the Cleve area. He grew up in Ermsleben, received a school education in Wernigerode and lost both parents at an early age. After studying law in Halle (1738-1741) and a longer stay with relatives, he went to Potsdam in 1743 and later to Berlin, where he became a tutor. In 1743/44 he became secretary of Margrave Friedrich Wilhelm von Brandenburg-Schwedt and accompanied him into the 2nd Silesian War. After the death of his employer, Gleim was secretary of Prince Leopold of Anhalt-Dessau for a short time, but he soon left his service, repulsed by his rudeness, hoping for an improvement of his situation.

In 1747 Gleim became cathedral secretary of the cathedral monastery in Halberstadt. In 1756 he acquired a canonry of the Walbeck Abbey near Halberstadt for further financial security. He exercised his activity at the cathedral for fifty years and died unmarried in Halberstadt, completely blind, as a wealthy citizen, well-known poet, influential collector, promoter and mediator. According to his wish he was buried in his garden on the Holtemme.

During his studies Gleim made poetic friends with Johann Peter Uz, Johann Nikolaus Götz and Paul Jacob Rudnik, with whom he formed the so-called "Second Hallesche Poetry School". Following important suggestions from the Hallesian aestheticians Alexander Gottlieb Baumgarten and Georg Friedrich Meier and with recourse to the ancient anacreonte, an attempt was made to bring a light tone to German poetry. Gleim's "Versuch in Scherzhaften Liedern" (1744/1745) — rhymeless poetry about the cheerful enjoyment of life — occupies a prominent position in this context. This volume of poetry stands at the beginning of the literary fashion of anacreontics, which was embodied by Gleim in particular as the 'German anacreon'.

Gleim attained a further peak of popularity during the Seven Years' War as the author of Prussian war songs based on the fiction that a grenadier was reporting on the events of the war. Gleim's poems were set to music by the Berlin lawyer and music lover Christian Gottfried Krause, but later also by Telemann and Schubart. In using the English Chevy Chase Trophes, Gleim found a catchy tone that Lessing particularly emphasized and which motivated him to publish the poems, which were initially printed sporadically in 1758, in a collected form and to add the laudatory preface that Gleim had met a new "Bardenton".

Gleim also found recognition as a fable writer. With his published letters he contributed to the development of a new "natural" style of writing. With his thorough awareness of the history of form, Gleim also dealt with the most diverse literary genres and often acted as a forerunner and precursor. His romances, the imitations and transmissions of the minstrels and the didactic poetry, which he mostly had published in private print, should be mentioned. Isolated within his work as well as within the literature of the Enlightenment is his great orientalizing poem "Halladat or The Red Book", which was inspired by the reading of the Koran. Published in 1774, the work was initially noticed and appreciated especially by intellectuals, was translated into Danish and Swedish and had several editions.

Supported by the socially oriented and virtuous idea of friendship of the middle 18th century, Gleim always tried to promote social and literary group formation. During his time in Berlin, he was in close personal contact with Karl Wilhelm Ramler, Johann Joachim Spalding, Ewald von Kleist and others. Later in Halberstadt, Gleim attracted intellectuals and poets to Halberstadt. Thus, at the beginning of the 1770s, the so-called "Halberstadt Poetry Circle" was formed with Johann Georg Jacobi, Wilhelm Heinse, Johann Benjamin Michaelis, Christoph August Tiedge, Klamer Eberhard Karl Schmidt, Leopold Friedrich Günther von Goeckingk. Gleim was also in close contact with Gotthold Ephraim Lessing, Johann Gottfried Herder, Friedrich Gottlieb Klopstock, Christoph Martin Wieland, Anna Louisa Karsch, Johann Heinrich Voß and others. The relationship with Johann Wolfgang von Goethe and Friedrich Schiller was ambivalent.

55 "The Anacreontic Song", also known by its incipit "To Anacreon in Heaven", was the official song of the Anacreontic Society, an 18th-century gentlemen's club of amateur musicians in London. Composed by John Stafford Smith, the tune was later used by several writers as a setting for their patriotic lyrics. These included two songs by Francis Scott Key, most famously his poem "Defence of Fort McHenry". The combination of Key's poem and Smith's composition became known as "The Star-Spangled Banner", which was adopted as the national anthem of the United States of America in 1931.

56 Gottlob Curt Heinrich Graf von Tottleben, Herr auf Tottleben, Zeippau und Hausdorf im Saganschen (also Tottleben, Todtleben Todleben (December 21, 1715–March 20, 1773) was a Saxon-born Russian Empire general known for his adventurism and contradictory military career during the Seven Years' War and, then, the Russo-Turkish War (1768–74) as a commander of the first Russian expeditionary force in Georgia.

Totleben was born in Tottleben, Thuringia, and served at the court of Augustus III, King of Poland and Elector of

Saxony. He fled Saxony after being accused of corruption. He then served for various periods at the courts of Saxe-Weissenfels, Bavaria, the Dutch Republic during the War of the Austrian Succession, and the Kingdom of Prussia. In 1747 he is mentioned as commander of a regiment of infantry of the Dutch Republic, but the regiment existed only on paper and was never realized. By then he already had a reputation as a scoundrel.

Count Totleben entered the Russian service during the Seven Years' War (1757–1763). He distinguished himself at the Battle of Kunersdorf (1759) and was promoted to General. Totleben gained particular fame for his brief occupation of the Prussian capital Berlin in 1760. Shortly, the advance of Frederick the Great's Prussian army forced him to retreat, however. In June 1761, he was accused of treachery and arrested in Pomerania. Sent in chains to St. Petersburg, he was sentenced to death via quartering, but Empress Catherine the Great pardoned him in 1763. Nevertheless, Totleben was deprived of all his titles and awards and sent into exile abroad (or to Siberia, according to one account).

57 A character in "Minna von Barnhelm oder das Soldatenglück" (Minna von Barnhelm or the Soldier's Happiness), a comedy in five acts by Gotthold Ephraim Lessing. The play was completed in 1767 but its composition began as early as 1763. Lessing officially gave the year 1763 as the date of creation on the title page, presumably to emphasize the proximity to the Seven Years' War, against whose background the play is set. Minna von Barnhelm is the best known comedy of the German Enlightenment and is one of the most important comedies in German-language literature.

58 Friedrich Bogislav von Tauentzien (April 18, 1710–March 21, 1791) was a Prussian general who served during the wars of King Frederick the Great.

Tauentzien hailed from the von Tauentzien family and was born in the village of Tauentzien near Lauenburg in Farther Pomerania. He participated throughout the Silesian Wars. Tauentzien fought alongside Frederick in many of the king's great battles, including Mollwitz, the capture of Prague, Hohenfriedberg, and Kolin. He distinguished himself during the defense of Breslau against Ernst Gideon Freiherr von Laudon in 1760 during the Seven Years' War.

Schiller, worked in Breslau (now Wrocław) From 1760 to 1765 as secretary to General Tauentzien during the Seven Years' War between Britain and France, which had effects in Europe. It was during this time that he wrote his famous Laocoön, or the Limitations of Poetry

59 The Literary Society was an association for the promotion of literature and culture in Halberstadt, the capital of the Halberstadt Principality of the same name during the Age of Enlightenment. It existed from 1785 to 1810.

The aim of the members of the Literary Society was to build up each other by sharing useful and pleasant knowledge in the spirit of the Enlightenment, to teach each other in a friendly manner and to work for the common good. Together they dedicated themselves to the promotion of literature and culture in Halberstadt and the surrounding area through instructive discussions.

From 1785 the Literary Society published the "Halberstädtische Gemeinnützige Blätter zum Besten der Armen" (Halberstadt Non-profit Papers for the Best of the Poor) on a weekly basis.

At the suggestion of the rector of Halberstadt Cathedral School, Gottlob Nathanael Fischer (1748-1800), the cathedral preacher Werner Streithorst (1746-1800), the Royal Prussian War Council Friedrich Wilhelm Eichholtz (1720-1800) and the Assistant Council Johann Heinrich Lucanus (1752-1828), about forty civil servants met on New Year's Eve 1784, Pastors, teachers, doctors, officers and some noblemen from the city and principality of Halberstadt to found a Literary Society on the first day of the new year 1785 in the spirit of the Enlightenment. It was agreed to meet every Wednesday for about three hours at different places in the city for joint discussions. Once a year a plenary assembly was to take place for all members in a restaurant with a large hall. In addition, efforts were made to establish contacts with other centres of the Enlightenment in the wider surroundings, such as in Halle and Magdeburg, in Dessau and in Berlin, as well as in Leipzig and in Braunschweig and in Wolfenbüttel.

The first director of the Society was the Halberstadt Cathedral Dean and hymnologist Georg Ludwig von Hardenberg (1720-1786), who died the following year.

The number of members rose relatively quickly in the first years to over 50 men, especially since Johann Wilhelm Ludwig Gleim (1719-1803) also became a member of the Society and therefore many members of his circle of poets joined the Society.

On May 7, 1788 the Literary Society organized a commemoration on the occasion of the hundredth anniversary of the death of the Brandenburg Elector Friedrich Wilhelm.

The Literary Society also built up its own library, whose catalogue was published in 1796.

After several well-known personalities of the Society had died at the beginning of the 19th century, not only the number of members decreased to about 20, but also the number of meetings and activities of the Society. After Halberstadt was defeated to the Kingdom of Westphalia and the town was occupied by the French, the activities of the Society were minimized until it was completely dissolved in 1810. After the destruction of the Kingdom of Westphalia the Society was not re-established.

60   Emilia Galotti is a play in five acts by Gotthold Ephraim Lessing (1729–1781), which premiered on March 8, 1772 in

Brunswick ("Braunschweig" in German). The work is a classic example of German bürgerliches Trauerspiel (bourgeois tragedy). Other works in this category include Schiller's Kabale und Liebe and Hebbel's Maria Magdalene. The story is based upon the Roman myth of Verginia.

Emilia Galotti is a drama of the Enlightenment, though it doesn't precisely follow the standard French model of the era. Although love is a central theme, in reality Emilia Galotti is primarily a political commentary. The arbitrary style of rule by the aristocracy is placed in stark contrast to the new and enlightened morality of the bourgeoisie. The more feudal ideas of love and marriage thus come into conflict with the growing tendency to marry for love, rather than family tradition and power. This combination results in a rather explosive situation. It was made into a film in 1958.

61 Johann Joachim Spalding (November 1, 1714–May 25, 1804) was a German Protestant theologian and philosopher of Scottish ancestry who was a native of Tribsees, Swedish Pomerania. He was the father of Georg Ludwig Spalding (1762–1811), a professor at Grauen Kloster in Berlin.

He grew up as a son of the parish priest in Tribsees and studied himself philosophy and theology at the Universities of Rostock and Greifswald, afterwards working as an auxiliary preacher in his hometown of Tribsees. In 1755 he became a pastor in Lassan, then two years later served as a minister in the town of Barth.

In 1764 he received the titles of provost and *Oberkonsistorialrat*, and gained recognition for his sermons at St. Nicolai-Kirche and at Marienkirche in Berlin. He was a highly influential minister who had as friends, renowned personalities that included Ewald Christian von Kleist and Johann Wilhelm Ludwig Gleim. As a protest against the Wöllnersche Religionsedikt (Wöllner Edict of July 9, 1788), he resigned from his official duties.

Spalding was an important figure of the German Enlightenment. In 1748 he released Betrachtungen über die Bestimmung des Menschen (Reflections on the Destination of Man), a publication that is considered to be a manifesto of German Enlightenment theology. In this work he rejected dogmatic authoritarianism and confessional orthodoxy, while promoting a common sense philosophy that explained an individual's path from sensuality to spirituality ultimately leading to immortality.

62   Nathan the Wise Act IV.

63   The House of Welf (also Guelf or Guelph) is a European dynasty that has included many German and British monarchs from the 11th to 20th century and Emperor Ivan VI of Russia in the 18th century.

64   Donar's Oak (also Thor's Oak or, via *interpretatio romana*, Jove's Oak) was a sacred tree of the Germanic pagans located in an unclear location around what is now the region of Hesse, Germany. According to the 8th century *Vita Bonifatii auctore Willibaldi*, the Anglo-Saxon missionary Saint Boniface and his retinue cut down the tree earlier the same century. Wood from the oak was then reportedly used to build a church at the site dedicated to Saint Peter. Sacred trees and sacred groves were widely venerated by the Germanic peoples.

Sacred groves and sacred trees were venerated throughout the history of the Germanic peoples and were targeted for destruction by Christian missionaries during the Christianization of the Germanic peoples. Ken Dowden notes that behind this great oak dedicated to Donar, the Irminsul (also felled by Christian missionaries in the 8th century), and the Sacred tree at Uppsala (described by Adam of Bremen in the 11th century), stands a mythic prototype of an immense world tree, described in Norse mythology as Yggdrasil.

65   Wotan is the Old High German name of the Germanic god Odin.

Odin is a widely revered god in Germanic mythology. Norse mythology, the source of most surviving information about him, associates Odin with wisdom, healing, death, royalty, the gallows, knowledge, war, battle, victory, sorcery, poetry, frenzy, and the runic alphabet, and portrays him as the husband of the goddess Frigg. In wider Germanic mythology and paganism, the god was known in Old English and Old Saxon as Wōden, in Old Dutch as Wuodan and in Old High German as Wuotan.

66 The Krkonoše—Riesengebirge (German), Riesageberge (Silesian German) or Giant Mountains, are a mountain range located in the north of the Czech Republic and the south-west of Poland, part of the Sudetes mountain system (part of the Bohemian Massif). The Czech-Polish border, which divides the historic regions of Bohemia and Silesia, runs along the main ridge. The highest peak, Sněžka—German: Schneekoppe), is the Czech Republic's highest point with an elevation of 1,603 meters (5,259 ft).

On both sides of the border, large areas of the mountains are designated national parks (the Krkonoše National Park in the Czech Republic and the Karkonosze National Park in Poland) and these together constitute a cross-border biosphere reserve under the UNESCO Man and the Biosphere Programme. The source of the River Elbe is within the Krkonoše. The range has a number of major ski resorts, and is a popular destination for tourists engaging in downhill and cross-country skiing, hiking, cycling and other activities.

67 Idistaviso is the name of a plain (Latin *campus*) where, according to Tacitus Germanicus met a Germanic combat unit under Arminius in a first open field battle in 16 AD. The battle is considered the largest of the Germanicus campaigns (14 to 16 AD) and the Augustan Germanic wars. The location of the battle is suspected by researchers to be at Evesen, a district of Bückeburg in Lower Saxony, or more

abstractly on the right bank of the Weser before and after Porta Westfalica.

68 Charlemagne was engaged in almost constant warfare throughout his reign, often at the head of his elite scara bodyguard squadrons. In the Saxon Wars, spanning thirty years and eighteen battles, he conquered Saxonia and proceeded to convert it to Christianity.

The Germanic Saxons were divided into four subgroups in four regions. Nearest to Austrasia was Westphalia and furthest away was Eastphalia. Between them was Engria and north of these three, at the base of the Jutland peninsula, was Nordalbingia.

In his first campaign, in 773, Charlemagne forced the Engrians to submit and cut down an Irminsul pillar near Paderborn. The campaign was cut short by his first expedition to Italy. He returned in 775, marching through Westphalia and conquering the Saxon fort at Sigiburg. He then crossed Engria, where he defeated the Saxons again. Finally, in Eastphalia, he defeated a Saxon force, and its leader Hessi converted to Christianity. Charlemagne returned through Westphalia, leaving encampments at Sigiburg and Eresburg, which had been important Saxon bastions. He then controlled Saxony with the exception of Nordalbingia, but Saxon resistance had not ended.

Following his subjugation of the Dukes of Friuli and Spoleto, Charlemagne returned rapidly to Saxony in 776, where a rebellion had destroyed his fortress at Eresburg. The Saxons were once again defeated, but their main leader, Widukind, escaped to Denmark, his wife's home. Charlemagne built a new camp at Karlstadt. In 777, he called a national diet at Paderborn to integrate Saxony fully into the Frankish kingdom. Many Saxons were baptized as Christians.

In the summer of 779, he again invaded Saxony and reconquered Eastphalia, Engria and Westphalia. At a diet near

Lippe, he divided the land into missionary districts and himself assisted in several mass baptisms (780). He then returned to Italy and, for the first time, the Saxons did not immediately revolt. Saxony was peaceful from 780 to 782.

He returned to Saxony in 782 and instituted a code of law and appointed counts, both Saxon and Frank. The laws were draconian on religious issues; for example, the *Capitulatio de partibus Saxoniae* prescribed death to Saxon pagans who refused to convert to Christianity. This led to renewed conflict. That year, in autumn, Widukind returned and led a new revolt. In response, at Verden in Lower Saxony, Charlemagne is recorded as having ordered the execution of 4,500 Saxon prisoners by beheading, known as the Massacre of Verden ("Verdener Blutgericht"). The killings triggered three years of renewed bloody warfare. During this war, the East Frisians between the Lauwers and the Weser joined the Saxons in revolt and were finally subdued. The war ended with Widukind accepting baptism. The Frisians afterwards asked for missionaries to be sent to them and a bishop of their own nation, Ludger, was sent. Charlemagne also promulgated a law code, the Lex Frisonum, as he did for most subject peoples.

Thereafter, the Saxons maintained the peace for seven years, but in 792 Westphalia again rebelled. The Eastphalians and Nordalbingians joined them in 793, but the insurrection was unpopular and was put down by 794. An Engrian rebellion followed in 796, but the presence of Charlemagne, Christian Saxons and Slavs quickly crushed it. The last insurrection occurred in 804, more than thirty years after Charlemagne's first campaign against them, but also failed. According to Einhard:

The war that had lasted so many years was at length ended by their acceding to the terms offered by the King; which were renunciation of their national religious customs and the worship of devils, acceptance of the sacraments of the

Christian faith and religion, and union with the Franks to form one people.

69 The city of Minden goes back to an old Saxon fishing and ford settlement called "Minda" in 798 on the western bank of the Weser, where important traffic routes had been converging since prehistoric and early historical times. During the Saxon Wars, whose goal was the Christianization and integration of the Saxons into the Frankish Empire, Charlemagne founded the diocese of Minden around 800. A prerequisite for this was the existence of a church and a "civitas", because according to canon law a bishop was only allowed to reside in one city. Since there were no cities in the mission area on the right bank of the Rhine, the emperor elevated existing settlements to cities in the canonical sense. The first bishop of Minden, Ercanbert, had the cathedral and the fortified cathedral castle (Domburg) built on a small hill south of the fishing town.

70 Friedrich Ludwig Wilhelm Philipp Freiherr von Vincke (* December 23, 1774 in Minden; † December 2, 1844 in Münster) was a Prussian reformer who, among other things, enforced the municipal self-administration of the cities and advocated a new trade code.

Ludwig von Vincke came from the old noble family von Vincke. His parents were Ernst Idel Jobst von Vincke (21 January 1738-21 August 1813), hereditary lord of Ostenwalde and cathedral dean in Minden, and his wife Luise Sophie von Buttlar (5 September 1739-18 May 1806).

Ludwig von Vincke received his school education from 1784 in the boys' boarding school in Hanover run by Pastor Joachim Friedrich Lehzen. From 1789 to 1792 he attended the Royal Pedagogy College in Halle. Contrary to family tradition, he then decided not to pursue a military career but an administrative career in the Prussian civil service. From 1792 he was enrolled at the University of Marburg and studied political science with Johann Heinrich Jung-

Stilling for three semesters. In Erlangen, he founded the "Kränzchen der Erlanger Westfalen" ("Wreath of the Erlangen Westphalians") on May 24, 1794. After his studies, he received a position in the Prussian civil service as a trainee at the Kurmark Military and Domain Chamber in Berlin on June 23, 1795. Already on November 28, 1795, he received a simultaneous employment at the Manufacturing and Commerce Institute in Berlin. Then, on August 2, 1797, he received the appointment as assessor at the Kurmark Military and Domain Chamber. On August 8, 1798 he was appointed District Administrator of the Eastern District in the Principality of Minden. He then rose to the position of President of the Military and Domain Chamber in Aurich/East Frisia on October 8, 1803 but was appointed President of the Military and Domain Chamber in Münster and Hamm as early as November 10, 1804, as their President Baron vom Stein was appointed Minister in Berlin, leaving the presidential chair of the Chambers of Münster and Hamm vacant. Vincke succeeded Baron vom Stein and held this office until 1806.

71 Large congregations maintained themselves in Gladbach and Kleve; the former died out in the 17th century, and the latter in the 19th, although there have always been several Mennonite families living in Kleve. Mennonites expelled from adjacent territories and towns gathered in Krefeld in the 17th century. They laid the foundation for the velvet and silk industry there, which soon acquired a leading position in Germany.

(Hege, Christian. "Düsseldorf (Nordrhein-Westfalen, Germany)." Global Anabaptist Mennonite Encyclopedia Online. 1956. Web. June 24, 2020.

https://gameo.org/index.php?title=D%C3%BCsseldorf_(Nordrhein-Westfalen,_Germany)&oldid=120215)

72 Christoph Wilhelm Heinrich Sethe (*April 25, 1767 in Kleve; †April 30, 1855 in Berlin) was a German lawyer.

Sethe was born as the eldest son of eight children of the Royal Prussian Court Councillor Caspar Henrich Sethe (1732-1806) and his wife Christine Marie Grolman (1733-1819) in the Prussian Duchy of Kleve into a Rhineland family of lawyers. One of his siblings was the lawyer Christian Diedrich Heinrich Sethe (1778-1864). He spent his childhood in Kleve, where he attended the Kleve Latin School in 1774. At the age of sixteen he began to study law at the University of Duisburg, where he enrolled on 15 October 1783. From April 30, 1785 he studied at the Friedrichs-Universität in Halle on the Saale and later also at the Georg-August-Universität in Göttingen. In Halle in 1789 he joined the Corps Guestphalia Halle which was founded in the same year. He completed his legal clerkship in 1790 with the examination in Berlin. In 1791 he began his legal career as an assessor in the Cleves government. In 1796 he married Henriette Philippine Helene Sack.

During the French period, which brought with it the introduction of French law in the French occupied or influenced areas on the Rhine, he continued his career successfully. In 1812 he became Procurator General at the Court of Appeal in Düsseldorf and State Councillor in the Grand Duchy of Berg. After the uprising of the Russian youth rebels in 1813, Sethe rejected the prosecution of those responsible, as demanded by Napoleon. He was therefore summoned to Paris and received as "Advocat du Rhin" by Napoléon Bonaparte.

Under the Prussian government Sethe was appointed to the Court Council, Royal Privy Councillor and in 1819 to Chief President of the Rhineland Court of Appeal and Cassation. He headed the Rheinische Immediat-Justiz-Kommission, which in 1816 was to compare Prussian and French law with regard to territorial legislation for the Rhineland. He successfully defended the principles of freedom, which the French Code civil in particular had also brought to the area on the right bank of the Rhine.

Elevation to nobility (ennoblement) was accompanied by the award of the Order of the Black Eagle in 1850. Sethe declined this because of his bourgeois sensibilities. Due to the firm connection between the bestowal and the elevation, he was nevertheless officially attributed to the nobility.

73 Johann Heinrich Schütte (June 11, 1694 in Soest–January 20, 1774 in Kleve) was a German physician and natural scientist.

Johann Heinrich Schütte studied medicine at the University of Altdorf and with Georg Wolfgang Wedel at the University of Jena. After his doctorate in 1719 at the University of Utrecht, he first became City Physician in Vianen. After a stopover in Soest he moved to Kleve in 1725 and became a doctor of the "Schwelmischen Gesundbrunnen" (Schwelm Health Spa) in 1731. In 1732 he became garrison doctor in Hamm for a short time. Later he worked as country physician of the duchy of Kleve and the county of Mark.

During his time in Jena he published the *Flora Jenensis* of his fellow student Heinrich Bernhard Rupp in 1718. As a medical student, he had been forbidden to give lectures on botany in Jena, which were much better than those of the then Professor Johann Adrian Slevogt. When Slevogt tried to get hold of the manuscript in order to prevent its publication, Schütte bought the manuscript of *Flora Jenensis* from Rupp in 1717 and had it printed in 1718. This important work would probably never have been printed without Schütte's intervention.

In 1720 he published the *Oryktographia Jenensis*, which is one of the oldest writings on the geology of Thuringia. After describing some "plays of nature" he also deals with nautilids, ammonites, snails and a number of shells from shell limestone. He gives the exact locations where he or his assistants have seen or collected the discussed objects.

In 1741 he recognized the usability of a mineral-rich spring in Kleve, which had been discovered a little earlier, and founded the spa resort (1742-1914) of Bad Kleve. In 1748, he anonymously published an advertising brochure describing the journey of a fictitious health spring tourists from Amsterdam, emphasizing Kleves' advantages in detail.

74 Johann Moritz (John Maurice) Prince von Nassau-Siegen, called: "The Brazilian", (* June 17, or June 18, 1604 in Dillenburg; † December 20, 1679 in Berg und Tal in the district Hau of the municipality Bedburg-Hau) was a Dutch field marshal. Born as son of Count Johann VII of Nassau-Dillenburg, he came from the widely ramified Nassau dynasty of princes, from which the House of Orange also emerged. In 1652 he was elevated to the status of a prince of the Reich.

Moritz entered the service of the Republic of the United Netherlands in 1621 and, under the leadership of Prince Frederick Henry of Orange, distinguished himself during the siege of Groenlo in 1626 and before Maastricht in 1632.

In 1636 he was appointed Governor General of the possessions of the Dutch West Indies Company in Brazil (Dutch Brazil). Although he had only a small force at his disposal, he conquered a large part of the country and administered it so excellently that it flourished. His extensive collection of natural history and ethnography, gathered in Brazil, changed the image of the New World through its dissemination to the European courts.

In 1637 he sent an expedition of nine ships and about 800 soldiers to the African coast that conquered the Portuguese fortress and most important trading post on the coast of Guinea, São Jorge da Mina, for the Dutch. In the spring of 1638 he advanced south along the Brazilian coast, but besieged Bahia in vain.

After the Portuguese and Spanish fleets had been almost completely destroyed by the Dutch off Itamaracá (January

12-17, 1640), the war in Brazil began anew and was fought with great cruelty. To keep the large number of adventurers under his banner, he undertook an expedition to Chile (1643).

In Brazil, two places he founded were named after him, the Moritz Castle at the mouth of the Rio São Francisco and the town of Mauritsstad (Moritzstadt, today Recife).

Returning to Holland in 1644, he was appointed governor of Wesel and general of the cavalry. His friendship with the Brandenburg Elector Friedrich Wilhelm, whom he had met in 1635, was strengthened when the latter married Louise Henriette, the eldest daughter of the Dutch governor Friedrich Heinrich von Oranien, in 1646. In 1649 the elector appointed him as his governor in Kleve and Mark, from 1658 also of Minden. As Dutch commander of the fortresses on the right bank of the Rhine and as governor of Brandenburg, Johann Moritz thus had a dual function, which made him a guarantor of the stability of the western territories of Brandenburg.

His experience, negotiating skills and good contacts predestined him for high-ranking diplomatic missions in the service of Brandenburg. In 1652 Emperor Ferdinand III elevated him to the rank of Imperial Prince. On this occasion, Johann Moritz presented "his" city of Siegen with the famous coronet on the Nikolai Church in 1658. Also in 1652, at the request of the Great Elector, he was appointed Lord Master of the Order of St. John of the Bailiwick (jurisdiction of a bailiff) of Brandenburg and was previously hastily knoghted as a Knight of the order of St. John by the Order's Senior Georg von Winterfeld. Johann Moritz also held this office with great success. He succeeded in developing the Order's economic and cultural life in the area devastated by the Thirty Years' War. This also included the new construction of the Johanniter Castle in Sonnenburg (Neumark).

In 1658 he was Brandenburg's envoy in the election of Emperor Leopold I in Frankfurt, concluded the defensive treaty between England and Brandenburg in 1661, received the command of the Dutch troops against Münster in 1665, became the first field marshal of the Netherlands in 1671, commanded the Dutch in the war against Louis XIV (1672-74) and took an outstanding part in the Battle of Senef on 11 August 1674.

In 1674 he became governor of Utrecht and retired in 1676. He died on 20 December 1679 in Berg und Tal near Kleve.

75 The Schwanenburg Castle (English: Swan Castle), in North Rhine-Westphalia, where the dukes of Kleve resided, was founded on a steep hill. It is located at the northern terminus of the Kermisdahl where it joins with the Spoykanal, which was previously an important transportation link to the Rhine.

It is already conceivable that in Roman times there was a military base at this point, high above the Rhine, halfway between Xanten and Nijmegen.

The Swan castle was first mentioned in 1020 in the monastery annals. The swan tower, collapsed on October 7, 1439. "300 years before God's birth Caesar has built this". This can be read on an inscription above the entrance of the Swan Tower, which was installed by Adolph I, Duke of Cleves after the tower was rebuilt.

The knight's hall, built around 1170, stood where today the car park surrounded by lime trees is located in the outer courtyard. Remains of the richly decorated hall have been dug up in the courtyard of the castle and can be seen today.

76 A lindworm's appearance varies across countries and the stories in which they appear. The most common depiction of lindworm is a wingless creature with a serpentine body, a dragon-like head, scaled or reptilian skin and two clawed arms in the upper body. The most common depiction of them implies that such lindworms do not walk on their two

limbs like a wyvern, but move like a mole lizard: they slither like a snake but they also use their arms to move themselves.

The head of the 16th century lindworm statue at Lindwurm Fountain in Klagenfurt is modeled on the skull of a woolly rhinoceros found in a nearby quarry in 1335. It has been cited as the earliest reconstruction of an extinct animal.

77 Betty Jacobi (1743-1784) Elisabeth Nicolai, nicknamed Betty, née von Clermont was the wife of Friedrich Heinrich Jacobi.

The house of the Jacobi family in Pempelfort was the literary meeting place for philosophers (Gotthold Ephraim Lessing), writers (Johann Wolfgang von Goethe) and (Alexander von Humboldt).

Goethe held Betty Jacoby in high esteem and corresponded regularly with her and her husband. Betty also maintained a lively correspondence with Sophie von La Roche, one of the first editors of a German women's magazine (1783–84).

78 The Lucanus Library is part of the Augustinian Collection. The main focus of the Augustinian collection was on documents and records on the history of the city and principality of Halberstadt.

79 Simon Heinrich Lucanus, "Government Secretary and Archivist", was been in charge of the royal archive at the Petershof in Halberstadt for 52 years and died on October 6, 1737 and was Philipp's maternal grandfather. Philipp's brother, Simon Heinrich Sack, was named after him.

80 The Sorrows of Young Werther (German: Die Leiden des jungen Werthers) is a loosely autobiographical epistolary novel by Johann Wolfgang von Goethe. First published in 1774, it reappeared as a revised edition in 1787. It was one of the most important novels in the Sturm und Drang period in German literature, and influenced the later Romantic movement. Goethe, aged 24 at the time, finished

Werther in five-and-a-half weeks of intensive writing in January—March 1774. The book's publication instantly placed the author among the foremost international literary celebrities, and was among the best known of his works.

81 Goethe's attitude to women and Betty Jacobi in particular:

At Frankfurt Cornelia was visited by some friends who played a part in her brother's life. They were Frau Betty Jacobi, the wife of Fritz Jacobi, and Johanna Fahlmer, a younger sister of Fritz Jacobi's mother, with her niece, Fritz Jacobi's half-sister Lolo. Fraulein Fahlmer was a daughter of her father's second wife and considerably younger than her nephews. Being Jacobi's aunt she was called "Auntie" (Tantchen) even as a young girl, and in Goethe's letters she always figured as Auntie Fahlmer. These three young women contributed not a little to cement a friendship between Goethe and Fritz Jacobi which in spite of profound difference of religious conviction lasted to the end of their lives. The maiden name of Helene Elisabeth Jacobi (called Betty) was von Clermont. She was born October 5, 1743, and died prematurely on February 9, 1784. She was of Dutch nationality and was married in 1764 to Fritz Jacobi. Her visit to Frankfurt falls in the year 1773. Goethe was very fond of her and describes her in "Truth and Fiction" as genuinely Dutch in her appearance, "without a trace of sentimentality in her feeling, true, cheerful in speech, a splendid Dutch woman, who without any trace of sensuality reminds one of the plump type of Rubens's women." Auntie Fahlmer was born June 16, 1744, in Düsseldorf and died October 31, 1821, in her native city. She visited Frankfurt during the summer of 1772 and the spring of 1774. She was a friend of both Wolfgang and Cornelia Goethe and became more and more attached to the latter after her marriage and during the years 1773-1777 she carried on a lively correspondence with Goethe. Somewhat more than a year after Cornelia's death, June 8, 1777, she became the wife of the widower Johann Georg Schlosser. The only procurable picture of her is a portrait made at an advanced age.

(Carus, Paul (1912) "Goethe's Relation to Women (Illustrated).,"*The Open Court*: Vol. 1912 : Iss. 1 , Article 3. Available at: https://opensiuc.lib.siu.edu/ocj/vol1912/iss1/3)

82 Johann Heinrich Jung (September 12, 1740–April 2, 1817, in Karlsruhe), better known by his assumed name Heinrich Stilling, was a German author.

He was born in the village of Grund (now part of Hilchenbach) in Westphalia. His father, Wilhelm Jung, a schoolmaster and tailor, was the son of Eberhard Jung, charcoal burner, and his mother was Johanna Dorothea née Fischer, the daughter of Moritz Fischer, a poor clergyman and alchemist. Jung became at his father's wish a schoolmaster and tailor.

After various teaching appointments he went in 1768 to study medicine at the University of Strasbourg. There he met Goethe, who introduced him to Herder. In the second volume of his autobiography Dichtung und Wahrheit. Aus meinem Leben, Goethe discusses Jung.

In 1772 Jung settled at Elberfeld as physician and oculist, and soon became celebrated for cataract operations. He performed over 3,000 cataract operations during his lifetime. In 1778 he accepted an appointment as lecturer on agriculture, technology, commerce and veterinary medicine in the newly established College of Cameralism (Hohe Kameral-Schule) at Kaiserslautern, a post which he continued to hold when the school was absorbed into the University of Heidelberg in 1784.

In 1787, he was appointed professor of economic, financial and statistical studies at the University of Marburg. In 1803, he resigned his professorship and returned to Heidelberg, where he remained until 1806, when he was granted a pension by Charles Frederick, Grand Duke of Baden, and moved to Karlsruhe, where he resided until his death in

1817.

He was married three times, and fathered thirteen children. His granddaughter Elise von Jung-Stilling was painter and founder of private painting school in Riga.

83   The Rhenish Kirmes festival with sideshows and funfair was always considered a special highlight in the course of the church year, especially since it was a local holiday that strengthened the bond with the homeland.

84   The Treaties of Peace of Nijmegen (*Traités de Paix de Nimègue*; German: *Friede von Nimwegen*) were a series of treaties signed in the Dutch city of Nijmegen between August 1678 and October 1679. The treaties ended various interconnected wars among France, the Dutch Republic, Spain, Brandenburg, Sweden, Denmark, the Prince-Bishopric of Münster, and the Holy Roman Empire. The most significant of the treaties was the first, which established peace between France and the Dutch Republic and placed the northern border of France very near its modern position.

85   In the Battle of Mookerheyde, Spanish forces defeated Dutch forces composed of German mercenaries on April 14, 1574 during the Eighty Years' War near the village Mook and the river Meuse not far from Nijmegen in Gelderland. Two leaders of the Dutch forces, brothers of William the Silent, were killed: Louis of Nassau (born 1538) and Henry of Nassau-Dillenburg (born 1550).

During the winter of 1573/74, Louis and Henry of Nassau raised a mercenary army in Germany of 6500 infantry and 3000 cavalry. They proceeded towards Maastricht to rendezvous with their elder brother William the Silent, Prince of Orange, who led 6000 Dutchmen. They planned to march their combined forces toward Leiden, which was under siege by a large Spanish force since October 1573.

The strength of Count Louis' forces diminished en route. More than a thousand men deserted and seven hundred were killed by the Spanish in a night attack. The remaining troops were mutinous because the Dutch had been unable to pay them. Louis crossed the Meuse with only 5,500 infantry and 2,600 cavalry. Before Louis could join forces with William, Luis de Requesens temporarily lifted the Siege of Leiden so that 5,000 infantry and 800 cavalry could counter Louis' advance. The Spanish army was led by Sancho d'Avila and Bernardino de Mendoza. The armies met near the village of Mook. Well timed attacks by the Spanish lancers destroyed the Dutch cavalry and the Spanish proved victorious.

The Dutch suffered a disastrous defeat, losing at least 3,000 men. The Dutch army of mercenaries, still not paid, soon dispersed. William long hoped that his brothers had been captured, but Louis and Henry were apparently killed and their bodies were never recovered.

The Spanish then resumed the siege of Leiden, which failed when Dutch forces relieved the city in October.

In the course of the battle, Spanish forces seized the command baton that William the Silent had given his brother Louis. The baton, long forgotten, was discovered at the Jesuit residence in San Cugat in Catalonia. In 2017, the General Superior of the Jesuits, Arturo Sosa, returned the baton to King Willem-Alexander of the Netherlands in a ceremony at the Vatican. The transfer was symbolic, in that ownership of the baton is retained by Catalonia as part of its cultural and historic patrimony. The baton had passed to the Jesuits as part of the estate of Luis de Requesens, Governor General of the Spanish Netherlands in 1574. The Dutch plan to display it at the National Military Museum.

86 Christoph Martin Wieland (September 5, 1733–January 20, 1813) was a German poet and writer. He is best-remembered for having written the first Bildungsroman (*Geschichte des Agathon*), as well as the epic *Oberon*, which formed the basis for Carl Maria von Weber's opera of the

same name. His thought was representative of the cosmopolitanism of the German Enlightenment, exemplified in his remark: "Only a true cosmopolitan can be a good citizen."

87 Susanne Katharina Seiffart von Klettenberg (December 19, 1723 – December 16, 1774) was a German abbess and writer. She was a friend of Katharina Elisabeth Goethe, the mother of writer Johann Wolfgang von Goethe. Klettenberg corresponded with Goethe and he shaped a character, "Beautiful Soul," after her in his novel "Wilhelm Meister's Apprenticeship". She was also a friend of Friedrich Christoph Steinhofer (1706–1761), a former co-episcopus of the Moravian Church.

88 The first version is called "Stella. A play for lovers in five acts". Goethe finished the transcription in April 1775. The play was premiered in Hamburg on February 8, 1776 and printed in the same year.

The first version differs from the second in the finale. Although Stella and Fernando do not die a joint love-death in the tragedy of 1806, they commit suicide – each for himself – with poison or with a handgun. The story ended completely differently in 1775. The young Goethe allowed himself a polygamous version, which may not have pleased the more morally strict citizens among the audience: When the curtain falls, Stella, Cäcilie and Fernando want to stay together with Lucie, according to the motto "one apartment, one bed and one grave".

89 Charlotte Buff (January 11, 1753, Wetzlar–January 16, 1828, Hanover) was a youthful acquaintance of the poet Goethe, who fell in love with her. She rejected him and instead married Johann Christian Kestner, vice-archivist and privy councillor to the Hanoverian court. The character of Lotte, in Goethe's novel "The Sorrows of Young Werther", is partly based on her. Their relationship was characterized by heartiness and lack of constraint. Goethe bought the

wedding rings for her and Kestner, in Frankfurt am Main. Charlotte and Kestner had four daughters and eight sons, among them August Kestner.

90 Gnadenthal Castle is a classicistic castle complex in the Donsbrüggen district of Kleve, about three kilometers northwest of the city centre of Kleve. Located in the nature and landscape conservation area of the Düffel, the castle complex is a listed building.

On the site of the present castle there was a manor house in the Middle Ages, which was used as a monastery by Augustinian canons in the 15th and 16th centuries and destroyed in the Eighty Years' War. At the beginning of the 18th century, Johann Moritz von Blaspiel had a baroque castle with gardens built on the former monastery grounds, which was modified in the style of classicism by the von Hoevell von Westerflier family at the beginning of the 19th century. During the accompanying redesign of the palace garden, the sculptures in it were removed because they no longer corresponded to contemporary taste. Six of these valuable sculptures were rediscovered by chance in a pit in the 1950s.

91 Poem in "Hof Gedachten" (Old age, country life, and garden thoughts at Sorgvliet) by Jacob Cats (November 10, 1577–September 12, 1660) a Dutch poet, humorist, jurist and politician. He is most famous for his emblem books.

92 Van Spaen (also: Van Spaen la Lecq) was a family whose members have belonged to the nobility of the United Kingdom of the Netherlands since 1814 and which died out in 1888.

93 Frederick I (July 11, 1657 in Königsberg-February 25, 1713 in Berlin) from the House of Hohenzollern had been Elector of Brandenburg and Duke in Prussia since 1688 and crowned himself as Frederick III in 1701 as the first king in Prussia.

After assuming power on May 9, 1688, Frederick, popularly known as Crooked Fritz because of his bent spine, continued the domestic and foreign policy of his father Frederick William. In the same year he supported William III of Orange in his landing in England. In the Palatinate War of Succession he took part in the siege of Bonn in 1689, but rarely commanded his troops. As an admirer of Louis XIV of France, Frederick strove for the elevation to kingdom status. However, he only obtained the approval of Emperor Leopold I when he needed his troops in the threatening war against France. On January 18, 1701, Frederick crowned himself king of Prussia in Königsberg Palace. In the War of Spanish Succession he supported Emperor Leopold I as agreed with the Prussian army, which distinguished itself in the Second Battle of Höchstädt in 1704.

Under Frederick's reign, the country experienced a financial decline due to the extravagant court and the corrupt Three Counts Cabinet on the one hand, but also a cultural rise due to the inclusion of persecuted Huguenots, the founding of the later Prussian Academy of Sciences and the expansion of Berlin into a Baroque royal residence. With the elevation to a kingdom, Frederick laid the foundation for Prussia's development into a major European power.

94 Jan Steven van Calcar (c. 1499–1546) was a German-born Italian painter.

Calcar was born in the Duchy of Cleves sometime between 1499 and 1510. Vasari refers to him several times, mainly with respect to his having been a pupil of Titian. Calcar entered Titian's school in 1536 and was accepted to his faculty for his extraordinarily accurate copies of the works of that master. Calcar appears to have worked first at Dordrecht, but the greater part of his life was spent at Naples, and there, as Vasari tells us, "the fairest hopes had been conceived respecting his future progress".

95 The County of Mark (German: Grafschaft Mark, French: Comté de La Marck colloquially known as Die Mark) was a county and state of the Holy Roman Empire in the Lower Rhenish—Westphalian Circle. It lay on both sides of the Ruhr river along the Volme and Lenne rivers.

The Counts of the Mark were among the most powerful and influential Westphalian lords in the Holy Roman Empire. The name Mark is recalled in the present-day Märkischer Kreis district in lands south of the Ruhr in North Rhine-Westphalia, Germany. The northern portion (north of the Lippe river) is still called Hohe Mark ("Higher Mark"), while the former "Lower Mark" (between the Ruhr and Lippe Rivers) is—for the most part—merged in the present Ruhr area.

96 Initially, businessmen who mockingly belonged to the Hanseatic League were called *Pfeffersäcke* (pepper sacks) as were also Nuremberg merchants or the merchants of the *Vereenigde Oostindische Compagnie* (East India Company). The word can be traced (for example as Dutch *peperzak*) first sporadically from the 13th century and then later, especially since the 16th century, was generally used as a scornful term for a rich merchant or wholesaler. This name came into being because the prosperity of some of them was based on the trade in spices from overseas, for which the term "pepper" stood for in the Middle Ages. To this day, "pepper sack" is sometimes used derogatorily for rich people who are ruthlessly concerned only with money and power, and to this day it is disparagingly used to refer in particular to Hamburg's upper class.

97 "Consolatrix Afflictorum" is the Latin name of the Keve miraculous image. Translated it means "Comforter of the afflicted". The picture measures 7.5 by 11 centimetres and shows Our Lady in front of the silhouette of Luxembourg.

Since Hendrick Busman placed the image in the wayside shrine in 1642, it has remained in its place unchanged. Over the centuries, an entire pilgrimage city has developed around the wayside shrine. This is why the wayside shrine with the picture of grace is no longer located along the wayside, but in the middle of downtown Kevelaer.

Millions of people have come to see the picture of Our Lady since 1642. They pray, seek comfort and show their gratitude. Many have brought gifts and offerings for the "Comforter of the afflicted" as a sign of their devotion. Some can be admired with the picture behind glass. One of them is a rosary from Pope John Paul II, who visited the pilgrimage city of Kevelaer during his 1987 trip to Germany. (https://www.kevelaer.de/tourismus/inhalt/gnadenbild/ – https://de.wikipedia.org/wiki/Gnadenbild — translated.)

98 The Beguines and the Beghards were Christian lay religious orders that were active in Northern Europe, particularly in the Low Countries, in the 13th–16th centuries. Their members lived in semi-monastic communities but did not take formal religious vows. In the archives of North Rhine Westphalia we find the following record: "Sale of properties of the former Beguine monastery 'Zum Berge Zion' in Kleve (Augustinian nuns) to the citizens of Kleve, Ludwig Köhler and Christian Mertens: disputes between the two buyers 1803-1807." (https://www.archive.nrw.de/LAV_NRW/jsp/findbuch.jsp?ArchivNr=185&tektId=995&id=0346&klassId=50 - translated)

99 Philipp Wilhelm writes the story in more detail in his booklet *Geburt meiner Kinder und Kindeskinder* (Birth of my Children and Children's Children), which he wrote in his own hand:

"In 1775, March 10, Maria Jakobs of Emmerich in the Duchy of Cleves, a Mennonite, gave birth to *my* daughter, whom I took to myself after her mother had died and through the preacher Baumann of Holzhausen, who is here in the royal estate of Rothenhof, through the sacrament of Holy Baptism, she was incorporated into the community of our highly praised Saviour Jesus Christ and received the name Philippina Antoinetta. I represented the godparents together with my dear wife, née Ottilie Baumann. This dear daughter of mine has been legitimized by His Royal Majesty of Prussia, Our Most Gracious Sire, upon my most humble request by a legitimation patent of April 16, 1787. God Almighty wants to restore grace and mercy to this child and to rule and guide her through His Holy and Good Spirit, in all virtues and righteousness for the sake of His dear Son, Our Lord and Saviour, Jesus Christ. Amen.

Rothenhof, March 30, 1795 — Philipp Wilhelm Sack"

It is not clear why Gertha von Dieckmann adapted this story to make the daughter an adopted child of the mother, graciously taken into Philipp's care. It is obvious that the child was born out of wedlock, yet, as our authoress is keen to point out, being a Mennonite, formal marriage was not an issue anyway. Philippine was born on March 10, 1775. Philipp's marriage to Ottilie took place probably in 1774 according to the Sack Foundation records. If these dates are at all correct, it would be an apparently strange overlapping of events. This is especially so because of Ottilie's extremely congenial acceptance of the child of this other relationship of Philipp. As the story earlier dwells on the relationship between the Jacobi couple, it would be open to all sorts of speculation.

Of course, if the child was really three years old when adopted by Philipp, then perhaps the date of his marriage to Ottilie actually took place in 1778 or later. This theory would seem to be substantiated by the fact that the birth of the first child of the couple took place in 1780. It was not novel in the family for a man to adopt their own child – the same happened with his brother Simon Heinrich, still a subject of speculation to this day.

Gertha probably chose her version of events as more suitable to the current morals at the time of writing or so as not to offend other members of the family. In any case, she managed to leave a number of clues behind for us.

100 The Lordship of Myllendonk (sometimes spelled "Millendonk") was an estate of the Holy Roman Empire, located in western North Rhine-Westphalia, Germany. It was bordered by the Duchy of Jülich to the west and north, the Lordship of Dyck to the south, and the Archbishopric of Cologne to the east and southeast. The lordship contained Grevenbroich and the Castle of Myllendonk. From 1700 Myllendonk was an Imperial Estate with a vote in the Bench of Counts of Westphalia.

The Lords of Myllendonk are first mentioned in 1166 as belonging to one of the most important lines in the Lower Rhine. The Dukes of Guelders gained overlordship of the territory in 1268, and overlordship passed to the Archbishopric of Cologne in 1279. The line was annexed to the Pesch Myllendonk family in 1263, and in c. 1350 passed to the House of Mirlaer which renamed itself to Myllendonk-Mirlaer. Myllendonk was eventually inherited by Johann Jakob, Count of Bronckhorst and Anholt, the Dukes of Croÿ in 1682, the Countess of Berlepsch in 1694, and through the female inheritance to the Counts of Ostein in 1700. Myllendonk was also raised to the Bench of Counts of Westphalia in 1700 as an immediate Imperial Estate.

The Counts of Ostein ruled Myllendonk until 1794 when the French conquered the German territory on the western side of the Rhine River. The Counts of Ostein were compensated with the secularised Abbacy of Buchau in 1803. Myllendonk itself remained French until the Congress of Vienna awarded the territory to Prussia in 1814. The following year the Lordship was abolished at the territory was annexed into the newly created Province of Rhineland.

101 In the Catholic Church, the Angelus is the morning, noon and evening ringing of the church bells during which the Angelus prayer is prayed. The morning and evening ringing can also indicate the time when the church is opened and closed.

102 When Napoleon Bonaparte came into power in 1799, he made the Tuileries the official residence of the First Consul and, later, the imperial palace. In 1808, Napoleon began constructing the northern gallery which also connected to the Louvre, enclosing a vast square (place). (wikipedia.org)

The French Revolution, on the other hand, broke out without any reason given by the King, who, on the contrary, willingly gave up privileges he had long possessed; "the nation was reckless, immoral and irreligious; the heads of the parties sought to transform the monarchy into a vain aerial entity; it was persecuted by an ignorant, innovative spirit, without any protection of rights or feelings of their fellow citizens the wicked end by even more wicked means, by sedition, plunder, murder and seduction. They were replaced by more daring ambitious people who based their rule on corpses, robbery and denial of God. These, too, fell under the sway of their companions, replacing a directorial government that vacillated between tyranny and legal pretense, disparaged itself by immorality and greed and was finally replaced by a bold commander and chased away with scorn and without resistance, who created a perfect autocracy." (Source: Freiherr vom Stein, Bd. 3, Berlin 1932 / Internet-Portal "Westfälische Geschichte" URL: http://www.westfaelische-geschichte.lwl.org – translated).

103 Otto von Arnim (* August 13, 1785 in Minden; † April 29, 1820 in Meissen near Minden) was a German government official.

From 1817 to 1820 he was district administrator of the Prussian district of Minden in Westphalia.

Otto von Arnim was born in Minden in 1785 as son of the von Arnim family from Uradel in Brandenburg. In 1804 he passed the high school certificate at the Joachimsthaler Gymnasium in Berlin and then studied law and administration at the university in Halle (Saale) for four semesters. In 1809 he became an assessor of the French tribunal in Minden. From 1811 to 1814 he was a notary public in Haus Heyde near Herford, in 1814 a justice of the peace in Bünde and in 1815 an assessor of the district and city court in Minden. In 1816 he became government assessor at the district government in Minden. On April 8, 1817 he was appointed, subject to the aptitude test, to the position of District Administrator of the district of Minden; he held this office until his death in 1820.

104 Interesting to note here: Widukind or Wittekind became a hero for German nationalists in the early 20th century. German neo-pagans saw him as an heroic defender of Germany's traditional beliefs and their gods, resisting the Middle Eastern religion of Christianity. Christian nationalists also lauded him, linking Charlemagne with the humiliation of French domination after World War I, especially the occupation of the Rhineland, portraying Charlemagne as a "French" invader. (wikipedia.org). Perhaps our authoress is also being influenced here.

105 The Schalksburg is an abandoned hilltop castle near Hausberge, a district of Porta Westfalica, in the district of Minden-Lübbecke in North Rhine-Westphalia. The castle was located on the right bank of the Weser in the valley of the Porta Westfalica breakthrough below the Jakobsberg in a position dominating the valley.

It was first mentioned in records around 1018 as Schalarborg or Scalaborg but the founders and founding period are unknown.

The owner, Duke Bernhard II. (Saxony), got into a dispute with Emperor Heinrich II. around 1020 and blocked his way to Bremen. After the siege, Bernhard surrendered and probably lost Schalksburg Castle. It is possible that the castle then fell to the Herren vom Berge, whose dynasty in turn died out at the end of the 14th century. In 1398, the castle then came into the possession of the Principality of Minden and became a state castle. In the course of the office administration the seat of the office Hausberge was established here.

The castle thus became the starting point for the settlement of today's Hausberge, which was granted market rights in 1618.

In 1679 the Schalksburg was plundered by the French. After it became increasingly dilapidated in the following years, it was demolished between 1707 and 1723.

Of the once extensive complex, which was demolished from 1708 onwards, only small structural remnants remain, including the former gatehouse. The single-storey quarry stone building above a half-deepened basement was probably built before 1562. The roof was extensively renovated in 1663. The directly adjoining coachman's apartment was built in 1708 as a two-storey plastered solid structure, the upper floor of which was partly timber-framed. Major alterations were carried out in 1813. The old interior layout was largely destroyed in the course of the renovation work carried out in the early 1990s. These measures resulted in a far-reaching loss of the original substance. The immediate surroundings of the monument have now been devalued by "historicising" new buildings which occupy the former castle grounds.

106 See the book "The Making of Prussia" by the same authors from this publisher.

107 That the couple, dressed and sitting in the honeysuckle bower, putting their hands one on top of the other's, corresponded to the customs of the time.

This ist best illustrated in "The Honeysuckle Bower" (about 1609), a self-portrait of Peter Paul Rubens and his first wife Isabella Brant. The painting is a full-length double portrait of the couple seated in a bower of honeysuckle, surrounded by love and marriage symbolism. The honeysuckle and garden are both traditional symbols of love and the holding of right hands represents union through marriage.

108 The Peace of Basel of 1795 consists of three peace treaties involving France during the French Revolution (represented by François de Barthélemy).

The first was with Prussia (represented by Karl August von Hardenberg) on April 5.

The second was with Spain (represented by Domingo d'Yriarte) on July 22, ending the War of the Pyrenees.

The third was with the Landgraviate of Hesse-Kassel (represented by Friedrich Sigismund Waitz von Eschen) on August 28, concluding the stage of the French Revolutionary Wars against the First Coalition.

109 At this point Gertha von Dieckmann's narrative ends. It seems that she either never finished the last concluding chapter or it has been lost from the manuscript. In this edition, we have tried to bring the book to a conclusion and have added information about how the offspring of Philipp Wilhelm became the movers and shakers in the world. Fortunately, Gertha had been the editor of the so-called "Silver Book" of the Sack Family Foundation and in the 1926 second edition had written extensive articles about our subjects children and their families. In this way it has been possible to construct a final chapter for this book which demonstrates the amazing influence Philipp and Ottilie had on their descendants.

110 The 13 Cuirassier regiments of Old Prussia (Kavallerieregimenter der altpreußischen Armee) were formed in the mid-17th to mid-18th centuries, and formed the basis of Frederick the Great's vaunted cavalry.

The cavalry regiments were the largest organization units of the old Prussian mounted troops. Between 1644 and 1806, 35 cavalry regiments were gradually formed. Initially called Regiments of Horse (Regiment zu Pferde), eventually these regiments were also differentiated according to different types of troops: Cuirassier Regiment, Dragoon Regiment, Hussar Regiment. The first mounted (horse) troops were simply called cavalry, then the dragoons (mounted infantry), and the hussars only midway through the 18th century. The size of the regiments varied between the types of troops. In the course of time, the regiments also changed within a cavalry type. At the time of Frederick the Great, Cuirassier and Dragoon regiments usually consisted of five squadrons, hussar regiments of ten squadrons. In the early-modern period (up to about 1800), units bore the name of their colonels, also called the Proprietor (Inhaber). If the regiment belonged to the king or one of the princes, he had colonels who commanded the regiments for him, and the regiment bore the name of the king. After the Prussian military reorganization in 1806, the units were given numbers.

Cuirassier Regiment No 6 was the "Horse Regiment" formed 1794 by Karl Wilhelm von Byern,

111 Julius Wolff (September 16, 1834 in Quedlinburg–June 3, 1910 in Charlottenburg) was a German poet and writer.

He was the son of the cloth manufacturer Wolff. He was born in today's Haus Markt 8–9 in Quedlinburg and attended grammar school in his native town and then the University of Berlin, where he studied philosophy and economics. After study trips he returned to Quedlinburg, where he took over his father's cloth factory, which he had to sell in 1869. Wolff founded the Quedlinburg Harz newspaper, took part in the Franco-Prussian War of 1870–71 as a land army officer and after his return in 1872 he settled in Berlin as a freelance writer. He was a member of the Quedlinburg freemason lodge "Zur goldenen Waage".

112 Thomas Immanuel Heyn (May 1, 1859 in Kantreck-August 18, 1918 in Greifswald) was a Protestant clergyman and member of the German Reichstag.

Heyn attended high school in Pyritz and the universities of Greifswald and Bonn. In 1883 he was appointed assistant preacher in Brietzig, in 1885 deacon in Pyritz-Altstadt, in 1890 pastor at St. Jacobi in Greifswald, in 1902 pastor at the Petrikirche in Berlin but not confirmed, in 1911 pastor at the Kaiser-Wilhelm-Gedächtniskirche in Berlin and confirmed in mid-February 1912. He published numerous religious and political essays.

From 1912 to 1918 he was a member of the German Reichstag for the electoral district government district of Stralsund 1 Landkreis Rügen, Stralsund, Landkreis Franzburg and the Progressive People's Party.

113 Buschiri bin Salim, probably actually Abushiri ibn Salim al-Harthi (December 15, 1889, executed), was one of the leaders of the uprising of the coastal population of the Zanzibar mainland (in today's Tanzania) against the assumption of power by the German East African Society in 1888.

Buschiri was a plantation owner near the old port city of Pangani (on the Indian Ocean between Dar es Salaam and Tanga). He was counted among the group of coastal Arabs. His father was Arab of Omani descent and his mother was African.

German colonial propaganda later often called him a "slave trader". This finds no basis in contemporary reports, such as those of the *Koloniallexikon* or Wissmann's report to the German government.

In August 1888, Buschiri took part in the uprising that broke out in Pangani against the German East African Society. He quickly became the leader of the movement in the northern coastal strip between the British territory and Dar es Salaam. The movement was successful at first and eventually led to the collapse of the colonial society's rule. This caused the German government to intervene. The deployment of German government troops, including a cruiser squadron under Rear Admiral Deinhard on the cruiser frigate SMS Leipzig, then gradually led to the defeat of the uprising.

The German commanders, Rear Admiral Deinhard and Reich Commissioner Wissmann, concluded ceasefire agreements with Buschiri, which, however, did not last. Buschiri himself captured Europeans several times and released them after negotiations and ransom payments. The most prominent prisoners in 1888 were the renowned German Africa explorer Hans Meyer (who was the first to conquer Kilimanjaro the following year) and his companion Oskar Baumann.

After Buschiri, already beaten militarily, was captured by African opponents on the way to Mombasa and handed over to the German military, he was briefly tried by a court martial and publicly hanged on December 15, 1889.

114 The Röder family is first mentioned in the 14th century with estates in Harzgerode, where they had a saddle farm and a house on the market to fiefdom from the princes of Anhalt. The members of the family were often in the service of the princes of Anhalt and held functions at court, especially during the times of the collateral line Anhalt-Bernburg-Harzgerode. In 1654 the family acquired additional estates in the Anhalt town of Hoym. From the extinction of the collateral line in 1709 until the extinction of the Bernburg line in 1863, both towns belonged to the Principality or Duchy of Anhalt-Bernburg, then to the Duchy or Free State/State of Anhalt.

Famous members of the family were the lawyer Karl von Röder and the entomologist and local historian Viktor von Röder. (http://recherche.landesarchiv.sachsen-anhalt.de/Query/detail.aspx?ID=195752 – June 2020 translated).

For more details about the von Röder dynasty (and about descendants of the Rothenhof family), please refer to the two volumes of *These are the Generations* by Flora von Roeder by the same publisher.

115 Robert Justus Kleberg (September 10, 1803 — October 30, 1888), christened Johan Christian Justus Robert Kleberg, was a German Texan from Herstelle, Westphalia, then part of the Kingdom of Prussia. He was a veteran of the Battle of San Jacinto and the brother of Louis Kleberg. He arrived in Texas in 1836 with his wife Philippine Sophie Rosalie "Rosa" von Roeder, who was a child of the at one-time aristocratic von Roeder family, which was allied with the wealthy and aristocratic Sack family of Nordrhein Westphalia. Robert and Rosa had eleven children, seven of whom lived to adulthood; Clara, Johanna, Caroline, Rudolph, Marcellus, and Robert, Jr.

He is the namesake of Kleberg County, Texas. His sons also achieved success. Rudolph Kleberg (1847-1924) became a United States congressman, Marcellus Kleberg (1849-1913) studied law and served as city attorney for Galveston, Texas, and the youngest Kleberg son, Robert Justus Kleberg, Jr. (1853-1932) managed the King Ranch and later married Alice Gertrudis King, the youngest daughter of cattle baron, Captain Richard King.

116 Rudolph Kleberg (June 26, 1847–December 28, 1924) was a U.S. Representative from Texas, great uncle of Robert C. Eckhardt and uncle of Richard M. Kleberg, Sr.

Born in Cat Spring, Texas, Kleberg was instructed by private tutors and graduated from Concrete College, De Witt County, in 1868. He enlisted in Tom Green's brigade of Cavalry in the Confederate States Army in the spring of 1864 and served until the close of the Civil War.

After the war, Kleberg studied law in San Antonio. He was admitted to the bar in 1872.

Kleberg commenced practice in Cuero, Texas. The next year, he founded the Cuero Star in 1873. After a few years of practice, Kleberg was appointed as prosecuting attorney of De Witt County 1876-1890.

Entering electoral politics, he served as a member of the State senate 1882-1886. In 1885, he was appointed as United States attorney for the western district of Texas.

Kleberg was elected as a Democrat to the Fifty-fourth Congress to fill the vacancy caused by the death of William H. Crain. He was reelected to the Fifty-fifth, Fifty-sixth, and Fifty-seventh Congresses and served from April 7, 1896, to March 3, 1903.

He was not a candidate for renomination in 1902. Resuming the practice of law, he moved with his family to Austin, Texas, in 1905. There he was appointed as the official reporter for the court of criminal appeals February 24, 1905.

He served until his death in Austin on December 28, 1924. He was interred in Oakwood Cemetery.

117 Wesley Newcomb Hohfeld (August 9, 1879, Oakland, California–October 21, 1918, Alameda, California) was an American jurist. He was the author of the seminal Fundamental Legal Conceptions as Applied in Judicial Reasoning and Other Legal Essays (1919).

During his life he published only a handful of law journal articles. After his death the material forming the basis of Fundamental Legal Conceptions was derived from two articles in the Yale Law Journal (1913) and (1917) that had been partially revised with a view to publication. Editorial work was undertaken to complete the revisions and the book was published with the inclusion of the manuscript notes that Hohfeld had left, plus seven other essays.

The work remains a powerful contribution to modern understanding of the nature of rights and the implications of liberty. To reflect Hohfeld's continuing importance, a chair at Yale University is named after him. The chair is currently occupied by Gideon Yaffe as of 2019 and was last held by Jules Coleman, who retired in 2012.

118 In the meantime it is known that he returned to Germany and died in Höxter Westphalia August 15, 1846. In fact he had seven children with his wife Johanne Antoinette Luise von Beesten.

119 "Pastor of Holzhausen am Limberge (Regional District of Minden) born Aug. 31, 1760, died on Aug. 17, 1834.

The immortalized man saw the light of day at Herford, where his father was cantor, sexton and organist. He received his education at the same grammar school and studied theology in Halle in the years 1783-86. After being a tutor for several years, he became second preacher in his hometown in 1795 and married a native of Lemgo, Stockmeier. In 1797 he became first preacher and in 1820 he was transferred to Holzhausen under Limberge. He always handled his ministry with the greatest loyalty to his profession and visited the sick almost daily. This loyalty became the cause of his death. He, who had never been ill, caught a cold during a distant visit to the sick in winter and had to suffer from it for a long time until his passing away. He was very much loved by his congregation and he was very diligent in his preaching, and he was very hospitable. If one of the teachers failed to keep school, he took over the lessons with the greatest willingness. He took the most intimate interest in all new liturgical apparitions, although he never wrote anything himself, except for some poems on special occasions, e.g. the inauguration of the "new school etc. - His only son, who studied theology, carelessly shot himself while hunting. - Arendt." (Neuer Nekrolog der Deutschen 1834, Volume 12, 225 – translated.)

120 The Joachimsthalsches Gymnasium (also: Joachimsthal Gymnasium) was a secondary school (Fürstenschule: princely school) for gifted boys, founded in 1607 in

Joachimsthal, Brandenburg, which was located in Berlin from 1636 and from 1912 in Templin.

121 Wilhelm Anton Ficker (October 28, 1768 in Paderborn–March 8, 1824) was a German physician.

He was the youngest son of Ferdinand Wilhelm Ficker († 1768), pulpitist and secretary at the prince-bishop's court chamber and his wife Anna Katharina Orbans († 1784). He attended the grammar school in Paderborn and the grammar school in Osnabrück and then began to study medicine at the University of Münster and continued this at the University of Göttingen. In Göttingen in 1791 he received a prize donated by the medical faculty for his treatise *De temperamentis quatenus ex fabrica corporis et structura pendent*. In 1792 he received the title of Dr. med. at the medical faculty of the University of Erfurt for his dissertation *De tracheotomia et oesophagotomia*.

In order to prepare for his future task as a senior surgeon and head of surgery, he undertook several journeys to Vienna in Austria, to Würzburg and served as a field doctor in various Prussian field hospitals after his studies from 1792 to 1794. In May 1794 he returned to Paderborn and took over the post of senior country surgeon and obstetrician appointed by his then sovereign, Prince Bishop Franz Egon von Fürstenberg. In 1796 he was awarded the title of professor of surgery with a salary supplement and was promoted to midwife teacher.

With the voluntary financial support of the estates and the population he was able to establish and operate a hospital for the impoverished in 1797, which was continually expanded through his efforts and in 1824 King Frederick William IV granted him a certain property. This institution, which at that time treated 4,659 sick people and in which various wound doctors were trained, he presided over free of charge as director and doctor until his death. He was also a member of the city council for the care of the poor in

Paderborn.

He also campaigned for the spread of the smallpox vaccination and instructed the vaccinators on this. In addition, he trained and taught midwives, who he also trained until his death.

From 1809 he worked as a spa physician in Driburg.

Because he did not want to leave the works he had started, he refused various recruitments, for example he was offered the position of the first doctor in the hospital in Kassel. In 1810 he refused the appointment as professor of surgery and the surgical clinic in Halle and in 1816 he could have become a personal physician in Detmold or government and medical councillor in Minden.

Wilhelm Anton Ficker was married and had six children. His son, Ludwig Wilhelm Ficker, continued his work, but died already on 21 October 1828. His grandson (son of Ludwig Wilhelm Ficker) was the historian Julius von Ficker.

In 1792 he published his inaugural dissertation Tracheotomie und Laryngotomie (Tracheotomy and Laryngotomy), published in Latin, which was also published in German in 1793.

In Würzburg, during his stay after his studies, he was a staff member of the Würzburg-based advertising department and the Oberdeutsche Literaturzeitung. In 1796 he first published the instruction for midwives, which was issued as a special edition for the Archdiocese of Salzburg, the Paderborn Monastery and the Principality of Anhalt-Dessau and was later reprinted three times. Also in this year he published his first volume *Beiträge zur Arzneiwissenschaft, Wundarznei- und Entbindungskunst* ("Contributions to the science of medicine, wound healing and childbirth"), which was followed by the second volume in 1802. In 1804, he published his first volume of essays and observations, each of which dealt with the theory of excitation; in 1806, he edited the second volume.

He continued to work at the Medizinisch-Chirurgische Zeitung and the Hallische Literaturzeitung, delivered many articles for the journals of Justus Christian Loder, Christoph Wilhelm Hufeland, Christian Friedrich Harleß, Karl von Graefe, Johann Bartholomäus von Siebold's collection of rare and exquisite surgical observations and experiences of German doctors and wound specialists, for the Medical Annals and for Johann Heinrich Fenner von Fennebergs *Taschenbuch für Gesundbrunnen und Bäder zum Gebräche für Ärzte und Nichtärzte* (Pocketbook of Healthy Springs and Baths for Doctors and Non-doctors).

He published his experiences as a spa physician in Driburg in two annual reports in the *Driburger Taschenbuch* 1811 and in the *Driburger Taschenbuch* 1816, which was published in Paderborn.

122 Johann Gottlieb Fichte (May 19, 1762–January 29, 1814) was a German philosopher who became a founding figure of the philosophical movement known as German idealism, which developed from the theoretical and ethical writings of Immanuel Kant. Recently, philosophers and scholars have begun to appreciate Fichte as an important philosopher in his own right due to his original insights into the nature of self-consciousness or self-awareness. Fichte was also the originator of thesis – antithesis – synthesis, an idea that is often erroneously attributed to Hegel. Like Descartes and Kant before him, Fichte was motivated by the problem of subjectivity and consciousness. Fichte also wrote works of political philosophy and has a reputation as one of the fathers of German nationalism.

123 Since the 18th century, the term Corps of Engineers or "Genie-Korps" (Corps of Geniuses) has been used to refer to military units engaged in construction. Originally, engineering corps developed during the fortress war in the Republican Netherlands. They were decisively developed in the Kingdom of France and expanded in other European

early modern states. Corps of Engineers were forerunners of the modern pioneer corps.

124 Gebhard Leberecht von Blücher, Fürst von Wahlstatt (December 16, 1742–September 12, 1819), Graf (count), later elevated to Fürst (sovereign prince) von Wahlstatt, was a Prussian Generalfeldmarschall (field marshal). He earned his greatest recognition after leading his army against Napoleon I at the Battle of the Nations at Leipzig in 1813 and the Battle of Waterloo in 1815.

www.ingramcontent.com/pod-product-compliance
Lightning Source LLC
LaVergne TN
LVHW032203070526
838202LV00008B/305